Crossroads of the
Natural World

EXPLORING

NORTH CAROLINA

WITH

Tom Earnhardt

Foreword by William G. Ross Jr.

Crossroads of the

UNIVERSITY OF NORTH CAROLINA PRESS : : : CHAPEL HILL

Natural World

THIS BOOK WAS PUBLISHED

with the assistance of the Blythe Family Fund of the University of North Carolina Press.

Designed by Kimberly Bryant and set in Utopia and Aller types by Rebecca Evans.
Manufactured in China

The paper in this book meets the guidelines for permanence and durability of the Committee on Production Guidelines for Book Longevity of the Council on Library Resources. The University of North Carolina Press has been a member of the Green Press Initiative since 2003.

Library of Congress Cataloging-in-Publication Data
Earnhardt, Tom.
Crossroads of the natural world : exploring North Carolina with Tom
Earnhardt / Tom Earnhardt ; foreword by William G. Ross Jr.
page cm
Includes bibliographical references and index.
ISBN 978-1-4696-0699-6 (hardback)
1. Biodiversity—North Carolina. 2. Natural history—North Carolina. I. Title.
QH105.N8E27 2013
577.09756—dc23   2012035432

17 16 15 14 13   5 4 3 2 1

Photos that appear in this book without captions are by the author except where noted: p. i, wild mushrooms in Umstead State Park; pp. ii–iii, western view from Hanging Rock; pp. vi–vii, Prickly Pear Cactus at Fort Bragg; pp. x–xi, sunset over North River; p. xii, Chipmunk in author's Wake County yard; pp. 10–11, 200-million-year-old leg bone found in Triassic basin south of Durham; p. 12, metamorphosed stone from quarry near Black Mountain; pp. 82–83, caterpillar on branch; p. 84, Yellow Lady's Slipper (photo by Mike Dunn); pp. 156–57, Grandfather Mountain; p. 158, Black Bears in Asheville watershed near Black Mountain; pp. 212–13, Terns at Baldhead Island; p. 214, woody buffer along North Fork of Swannanoa River; p. 282, Black Walnut tree.

This book is dedicated to my wife, Dana—
my North Star at home and partner on all projects in the wild.

And to Izaak and Rachel—
children who grew to become the best teachers of my life,
and whose curiosity and desire to protect the natural world
were the inspirations for this book.

Contents

Foreword WILLIAM G. ROSS JR.

I have the privilege of introducing you to Tom Earnhardt and his book, *Crossroads of the Natural World*. If you know anything about Tom, you know about his passion for nature, especially nature in North Carolina, and about his belief in the power of story. So I cannot resist the temptation to introduce this book with a story of how Tom used both his knowledge of nature and his storytelling ability to make a difference in the lives of the people of North Carolina.

In midsummer 2007, the North Carolina legislature was rushing to adjourn its session. At that moment, the Nature Research Center (NRC), the proposed new wing of the N.C. Museum of Natural Sciences, was hanging by a political thread. The NRC was a central part of a larger project called Green Square. If the project was going to become reality, Green Square had to have startup funding. The price tag was $25 million.

The project had support in one chamber of the legislature, but the most powerful person in the legislature, the leader of the state senate, had yet to weigh in. Supporters of the innovative project, including me, had been unable to secure the senate leader's support. Without it, the project was dead in the water.

For Tom—then the president elect of the Friends of the N.C. Museum of Natural Sciences—the situation was a call to action. He camped out at the senate leader's office. When the senator returned, Tom was there. The senator offered Tom two minutes to make his case. Tom stepped into his office and told the story of the Nature Research Center—how it would connect citizens to science, set a new standard in our state for innovative and green design in public buildings, and build partnerships with the state's universities and natural-resource agencies.

Tom's story had power. The conversation stretched toward an hour. It expanded into a discussion of energy-efficient lighting, water conservation, and butterfly gardens. In the end, the senator gave Tom what he sought. Soon I received a call from Tom with the happy news: "We have the senator's commitment to the funding we need!"

Thanks to Tom's action, the Green Square project had life. Five years later, on April 20, 2012, the Nature Research Center opened its doors to the public; six months after that, 850,000 people from North Carolina and the world had visited the innovative new museum.

The American poet Muriel Rukeyser once wrote, "The universe is made of stories, not of atoms." In this book, Tom presents a North Carolina that is, like the universe in Rukeyser's description, made of stories. Tom can tell these stories because they come from his life, from his passion for the nature of his native state, and from his experiences in North Carolina and around the world. Tom's knowledge, accomplishments, enthusiasm, and wisdom shine through these stories, all enhanced by his unassuming manner.

Tom paints two pictures in this book. One is of North Carolina *as a crossroads*—a crossroads of the natural world. The other is of North Carolina and its people as being *at a crossroads*—a crossroads from which our choice of way forward will make all the difference.

Crossroads of the Natural World is an invitation to action. Tom Earnhardt—lawyer, leader, teacher, naturalist, but most of all, storyteller—invites us to understand and appreciate the natural legacy that we have inherited in North Carolina, and he calls us to apply that understanding and appreciation to the choices we make going forward. Every North Carolinian should read Tom's book, savor his insights and stories, and heed his call to action. Our story, and the future of our state's natural resources, depends on it.

Crossroads of the Natural World

PROLOGUE

Just as I was completing the first draft of the manuscript for this book, my life careened into the emergency room at Duke University Hospital. Within twenty-four hours, I was in surgery for an unknown infection, followed by days in the intensive care unit and even more time at Duke Hospital. After being discharged, I remained on antibiotics and endured physical therapy for several months. I am convinced that I received the best available treatment throughout the ordeal, but a mystery remained. In spite of the efforts of many specialists, including infectious disease experts, the culprit—the pathogen causing the infection—was never identified.

In the days preceding hospitalization, I had been on the Outer Banks in the surf, in a maritime forest, and in salt marshes filming an episode of the UNC-TV series *Exploring North Carolina*. Could the infectious bug have come from one of my favorite wild places and entered my system through a tick, a meal, a sneeze, my place of lodging, or a handshake? Could my body have attacked itself with a violent, but fleeting, autoimmune disorder? All of these possibilities, and many more, were examined, but there was still no answer. Once I quit asking why and began to celebrate my recovery, I had time over several months to rethink and question much of what I had written. Was my praise of North Carolina's biodiversity and unique combination of geology and climate deserved? Is our fauna and flora any more special than that found in other temperate regions of equal size? Or is my opinion of North Carolina just regional, provincial pride in the place I call home?

Pride in "king and country" is nothing new. No matter where I have traveled—in nations large and small, rich or poor—I have noticed cultural, regional, and natural symbols around which people rally. Appreciation of such symbolism is frequently celebrated in large cities. I remembered observing this pride of identity with a particular location on a trip to New York City in the early 1990s. While visiting Times Square one evening, with its bright lights and city sounds, I heard someone proclaim, "We are standing at the crossroads of the world."

I was reminded that, while traveling in previous years, I had also stood in three other great squares of the world: Tiananmen Square in Beijing, Red Square in Moscow, and Trafalgar Square in London. At each location, I had also been assured by locals that "their square" was a crossroads of commerce, culture, and history, or of the world's great "isms" of the time, capitalism and communism. As I walked through New York's Times Square that night, I remember a powerful, epiphanic feeling that I was both fortunate and proud to live in one of the great crossroads of the natural world: North Carolina.

So what is it about this slice of land, measuring roughly 500 miles east to west and 180 miles north to south at its widest point, that makes it so exciting? Depending on your perspective, the Tar Heel State can be viewed as a "natural" epicenter or a land where several natural boundaries converge. Either way, we live at one of nature's unique crossroads. Quite simply, there are very few relatively small geographic areas on Earth that can compare with North Carolina in geologic, climatic, and ecological diversity. During my recuperation, assisted by pain medication and antibiotics, I grew keenly aware of my strong bias toward the Tar Heel State, having lived over six decades in this corner of the world; but there is much evidence and many examples to support this state's status as a crossroads of the natural world.

Geologically, North Carolina has long been at the edge of change. Every 500 to 700 million years, the tectonic plates of Earth shift slowly to create supercontinents where the planet's land masses come together, the last being Pangaea that formed some 300 million years ago. The landscape of the Carolinas has been at the cusp of several continental collisions, when parts of the earth's crust that would become North America, Africa, and other modern landforms slammed together. Great change and upheaval occurred during these collisions and violent separations, giving us the Appalachians, the Uwharrie Mountains of the Piedmont, and the Triassic basin where the Research Triangle Park is located. Other East Coast states share features that grew out of changing land masses, but few are as dramatic as those in the terrain of North Carolina.

Over the last 2 million years, a series of events, which were both climatic and geologic, made North Carolina a boundary line for another reason. This was the time commonly known as the Ice Ages, a period during which a series of enormous ice sheets formed and melted (retreated) across much of the Northern Hemisphere. These mantles of ice and snow, some of which were over a mile deep, scraped the landscape clean as they plowed south through present-day New York, Pennsylvania, and the Ohio River valley. Geologists tell us that during the Ice Ages, as many as twenty alternating cycles of cooling (glacial periods) and warming (interglacial periods) occurred. None of the great ice sheets of these glacial periods—which essentially bulldozed the landscape of the northern and central United States and Canada—ever reached North Carolina, allowing ecosystems to thrive and evolve. Being just south of the glacial boundary, the plants, fungi, fish, insects, reptiles, and mammals of North Carolina remained relatively untouched and available to repopulate the landscapes of an eastern America left barren by the great ice sheets as they retreated to the north. During the Ice Ages, North Carolina was a cooler place, with spruce-fir forests dominating many areas, but much of today's familiar fauna and flora was also present.

Even today, North Carolina remains an ecological boundary where plants and animals from northern and southern ecosystems come together. We are simultaneously subtropical, subarctic, and temperate. How can this be? Because of our latitude and proximity to the Gulf Stream as it passes near our shores, the southeastern corner of our state holds plants and animals commonly found in Florida. Here, we can mark the East Coast northern reach of the Cabbage Palm, trees native to subtropical zones (from Baldhead Island south). Eastern North Carolina is also the northern range of the American Alligator and the Diamondback Rattlesnake.

The boreal forests of spruce and fir that define New England and Canada reach south into North Carolina's high mountains, which include forty-three mountains over 6,000 feet in altitude (and arguably more than fifty if you include those with twin peaks), with Mount Mitchell topping the list at 6,684 feet. These altitudes are remarkable considering that the highest mountains in South Carolina (3,547 feet), Georgia (4,695 feet), and Virginia (5,722 feet) aren't even close. Tennessee claims ten peaks over 6,000 feet, but *nine* of these are "shared peaks" on the border with North Carolina. For all states east of the Dakotas, the Tar Heel State is unquestionably the land of the tall.

Altitude makes a difference in determining which ecosystems can thrive. One commonly cited climate calculation used by the North Carolina Museum of Natural Sciences holds that every 1,000 feet in altitude is the equivalent of traveling 300 miles to our north (other sources use 200 miles). Even using the smaller number, for our many peaks over 6,000 feet in height, the temperatures and ecosystems found at the top are roughly the equivalent of traveling 1,200 miles (200 × 6) to the north, or well into Canada. This is why North Carolina's "islands in the sky" host numerous cold-weather plants and animals commonly found far to our north. We are the effective end of the southern habitat range for such northern species as the Appalachian Brook Trout, the Common Raven, and the Northern Red Squirrel. Our climate and topography make us a "border nursery" for many plants and animals. Adjoining states—Virginia, South Carolina, Georgia, and Tennessee—may quibble that they, too, hold some end-range species and ecosystems, but North Carolina is undeniably an epicenter of north-south diversity for resident species. Our neighbors, which harbor enviable biodiversity, lack the altitude and converging ocean currents to produce climates and ecosystems as varied as those of the Tar Heel State.

In addition to our resident species of fauna and flora, North Carolina serves as a southern or northern destination—sort of an international airport—for many species of birds. Migratory waterfowl, including Tundra Swans, Snow Geese, and numerous ducks, from Alaska, Canada, and other points north use North Carolina as their East Coast wintering grounds. Neotropical songbirds, including almost three dozen species of warblers, the Purple Martin, and the Ruby-Throated Hummingbird, take winter vacations in Central and South America but live and raise their young during the spring and summer in our varied ecosystems.

Two other important dividing lines occur here. Any angler worth his or her salt knows that the North Carolina coast is the meeting place for finfish and shellfish from cold- and warm-water ecosystems. Our unique mix of northern fish, such as Striped Bass and Tautog, and southern species, including Tarpon and Redfish, occur because the waters of the cold Labrador Current and the warm Gulf Stream meet off the Outer Banks. Look at any book about seashells and you'll see the same thing—numerous southern mollusks extending north to Cape Lookout, Cape Hatteras, or Cape Fear and northern shellfish for which North Carolina's capes are at the end of their southern range.

The last boundary line I'll mention is barely noticeable, but it can be followed: the Eastern Continental Divide. It runs along ridge lines, across mountaintops, and between mountain gaps. The line begins in Pennsylvania just south of the state border with New York. From there, it follows the spine of the Appalachians through Maryland, West Virginia, Virginia, and North Carolina; moves along the western border of South Carolina and into Georgia; and bisects the flatlands of Florida. Rain falling on the west side of this imperceptible line flows into the Gulf of Mexico, and rain falling on the east side flows toward the Atlantic Ocean. The Eastern Continental Divide not only separates rainwaters into two great basins, but it also is the line separating many species of freshwater creatures and even plants. Thus, as strange as it may seem, once you get west of Asheville, you will encounter finfish, mollusks (bivalves and snails), and crayfish that do not occur naturally just a few miles to the east—because of this invisible dividing line.

Taken together, these examples of overlapping ecosystems and geologic/climatic boundaries should convince you that North Carolina is truly a crossroads, an epicenter of nature, and a land of many borders. Even now, however, some of my friends are not completely convinced. While recuperating from the mystery malady, I became acutely aware that my enthusiasm for North Carolina's natural treasures raised questions of objectivity. Several good friends, and even my daughter, Rachel, asked me how I can honestly compare North Carolina to the natural diversity of an immense state like California, or to regions with tropical rain forests and extreme biological diversity such as are found in the Amazon basin of South America and in equatorial Africa.

California does have more diversity of life forms, climate, and topography than North Carolina, especially when you consider its dramatic altitude range from Mount Whitney at 14,500 feet to Death Valley at minus 250 feet. You must remember, however, that the distance from its southern border with Mexico to its northern border with Oregon is approximately 650 miles. That is about the same distance that separates Charlotte and Toronto if you head north and Charlotte and Miami if you head south. Over such long north-to-south distances, significant diversity in climate and life forms occurs. Remember, however, that North Carolina is only 180 miles from top to bottom at its widest point, making it a compact area with uncommon diversity.

There is also no debate that tropical rain forests hold the greatest diversity of life on the planet. Only a few acres of these warm, moist places can host several times more plants, insects, mammals, and birds than are found in all of Europe or North America combined. Again, remember that when I asked you to consider North Carolina as a natural epicenter, as a boundary or crossroads of the natural world, I was not referring only to biological diversity but to a unique coalescence of several factors. I do not retreat from the truth of my earlier statements: for a temperate geographic area of modest size, North Carolina has as much geologic, climatic, and ecological diversity as any place on the planet.

This book was written to help you understand and explore the boundaries, ecosystems, and seldom-taught natural history of our state. Perhaps the time will come when you are standing in one of the world's great squares or in front of a famous landmark and someone will proclaim it to be at the "crossroads of the world." If I have done my job well, at that moment you, too, will feel fortunate and proud to live in North Carolina, one of the great crossroads of the natural world.

After you have read this book, I hope that you will be inspired by the myriad living things around us and learn from natural events from our past that may yet affect our future. I am a realist, however, and understand that knowledge of North Carolina during the Ice Ages, information about our distant "dinosaurian" past, and the ability to identify the invasive species of plants and animals will not pay your bills. I am convinced that a great many of us, new North Carolinians and natives alike, do not have sufficient knowledge or appreciation of this land to develop what many writers before me have called a "sense of place." Knowing more about the natural world around us cultivates a sense of awe in each of us, as well as the desire to be good stewards of this remarkable state. More important, knowledge of where we live and what makes our state unique helps us to be better teachers, more effective leaders in all levels of government, smarter business owners, and, above all, better parents.

As a fan of North Carolina's wild places and things, I have long believed that our natural history, landscapes, and ecosystems have not always gotten the attention they deserve. As we attempt to solve problems and confront a variety of challenges facing our state—the effects of climate change, sustainable food and fiber production, efficient energy use, the providing of educational opportunities, job creation, and the alleviation of poverty—we must be open to the possibility that there are lessons to learn and connections to be made from the study of natural history and science. I believe passionately that the condition of our natural resources, the quality of life that we enjoy, and our economic future are all inextricably bound. Unfortunately, I am afraid that much of the natural world of North Carolina, which has long entertained and sustained us, is also at a crossroads and threatened by our own actions and inaction.

In writing this book, I have made every effort to ensure that the facts and information proffered are scientifically sound and intellectually honest. Some chapters have a strong historical flavor, intended to guide the reader through the evolution of North Carolina's physical landscape, changes in fauna and flora, and even the arrival of modern humans over 12,000 years ago. Other essays deal with timely issues, such as sea-level rise, loss of habitat, and the need for more contact with nature by our children.

This book was not written to be a field guide to the state's insects, birds, geology, native trees, or invasive plants. You will find that virtually every subject in these areas is well covered in one of many specialty books prepared by talented scientists, illustrators, and writers. (See the suggested readings list at the end of the book for guidebooks and references relating to North Carolina and the Southeast.) These essays have a primary goal of challenging the reader to examine individual and institutional attitudes relating to natural resources. Some essays will make you feel good about yourself and this state, while others may make you feel uncomfortable—like an unexpected question from a child or a Sunday-morning sermon that challenges your daily routine and core beliefs. I know this because, while writing this book, I experienced discomfort in a number of instances—often in the form of questions from my daughter—as I confronted my own inaction regarding our natural treasures. By design, there is a sequence, or flow, to the organization of this book, but each chapter can also be viewed as a stand-alone essay. Feel free to move around and cherry-pick the topics that interest you most; this is a naturalist's prerogative. In the end, however, I hope that you will read every chapter. These essays, like parts of the natural world that appear to stand alone, are in fact interconnected.

I first learned about natural resources from a father, a mother, and friends who did not burden me with Latin species names and scientific jargon. I have carried this tradition forward in my own family and in these essays. Where they are critical for understanding, I included scientific names in the text. However, because I am fully aware that the use of common or local names for plants and animals can be imprecise and lead to confusion, I have included a "Glossary of Common to Scientific Names" at the end of the book. In some places, I will list more than one common name; for example, North Carolina's Official State Saltwater Fish is the Channel Bass, which is also known as Red Drum or Redfish. In the glossary, you will find that they are all the same fish: *Sciaenops ocellatus*. By providing such information, I have sought to make each essay more readable and enjoyable while achieving a greater degree of clarity.

I have also taken the liberty of capitalizing each common name of a particular species—plants, insects, birds, fish, mammals, and fungi. A wildflower (Purple Coneflower), bird (Osprey), tree (Chestnut Oak), or fish (Appalachian Brook Trout) stands out when capitalized, and I believe this to be important for readers new to this material. I know that blanket capitalization of common names may fly in the face of tradition in some scientific communities and style manuals. Taking advantage of the author's prerogative was done not to tweak or challenge existing norms but for the sake of consistency and to make the material more approachable and reader friendly.

As you have already seen in this prologue, I will from time to time use numbers to describe the extent, age, or size of North Carolina resources, such as the number of mountains rising over 6,000 feet. I'll also try to convey the number of turtles, birds, salamanders, and freshwater shellfish found within our borders. There are estimates for the number of woody trees and shrubs, wildflowers, fungi, and moths. There are also numbers for the generations of American Indians who have lived on this land and the ages assigned to geologic regions of our state. As I wrote the manuscript and talked with many experts, it was clear that numbers and estimates sometimes varied from source to source, but invariably they were always close. For the purposes of this book, it makes no difference whether North Carolina's inland waters hold 265 or 269 species of freshwater fish; both numbers are impressive.

There should be room for honest differences between scientists and experts as new information becomes available. For example, in little more than a decade, over 7,000 species (new to science or new to the region) have been discovered in the Great Smoky Mountains National Park during the "All Taxa Biodiversity Inventory." Unfortunately, we may have also lost some species forever during the last decade, including some types of ants, amphibians, spiders, moths, wildflowers, fungi, or shellfish. Although I will strive to give you the most up-to-date numbers or estimates, do not let exact numbers hinder your understanding of the big picture: North Carolina is a unique location on this planet and home to impressive numbers in the natural world.

Some of these essays contain references to time spans, eras, periods, and the like. For the sake of clarity, I have tried to stick to three abbreviations: B.P., B.C.E., and C.E. When referring to geological or archaeological dates of the distant past, I will often give a year followed by the abbreviation "B.P." (Before Present), as in: "Paleo-Indians began to settle across much of what is now North Carolina and the southeastern United States around 12,500 B.P." When referring to widely recognized historical dates, B.C.E. (Before Common Era) and C.E. (Common Era) will be used in place of the more traditional B.C. or A.D. Historical events occurring *before* the year 1 C.E. will be followed by B.C.E., as in: "The Parthenon in Athens, Greece, was finished around 440 B.C.E." Events *after* the year 1 C.E. will be followed by C.E. For example: "Construction on the Town Creek Indian Mound in North Carolina's southern Piedmont began around 1100 C.E."

Finally, in the acknowledgments you will find a listing of people—mentors, writers, family members, and friends—who have shaped my view of the natural world and given me time to explore it. One important association needs to be emphasized, however. This book would not have been possible without my long collaboration with and numerous friendships at the North Carolina Museum of Natural Sciences in Raleigh. There is no better state, or regional, natural history museum in the United States today. It was at the museum where much of what I have learned has been tested, where many of these essays took form, and where I was ultimately convinced that North Carolina is a major crossroads of the natural world.

■ My recovery from the effects of the unknown pathogen is now complete. I was the beneficiary of the best medicine that science has to offer, but I came away knowing that medical science cannot answer every question. The same is true about our knowledge of the natural world. It is only through exploration and observation—and sometimes through sheer luck—that discoveries are made. No matter where you live in North Carolina or which parts of the state you visit, there is an outdoor laboratory nearby. It is my great hope that the essays in this book will stir your imagination and inspire you to seek your own answers in places wild and wonderful.

PART I.
A TAR HEEL TIME LINE
The Early Years

Left fibula

Left tibia

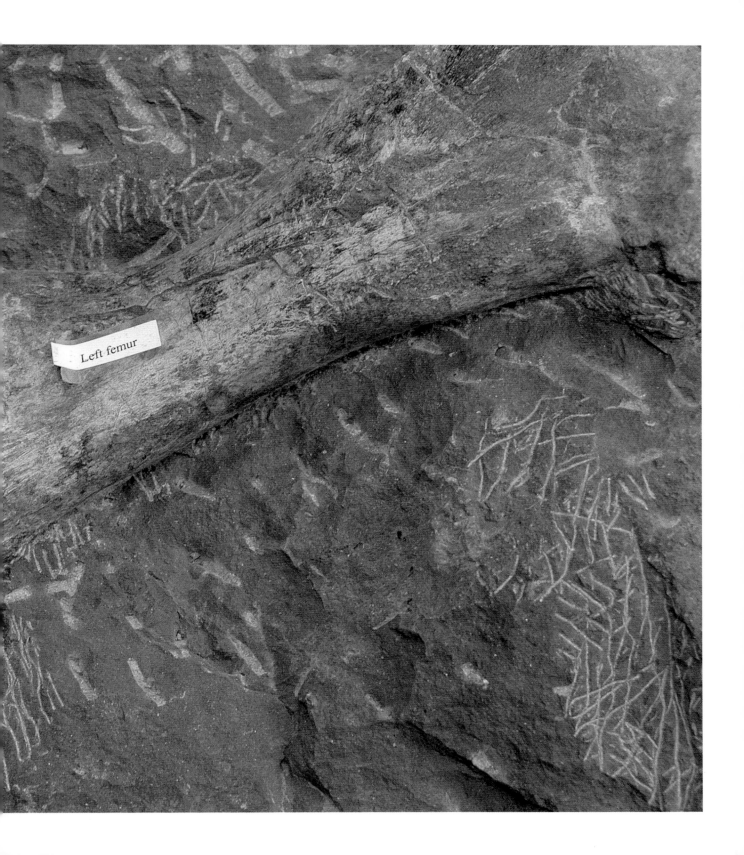

■ Forty feet below ground in one of North Carolina's largest cities is a secure, supermarket-sized facility that holds few books yet houses the most complete library on North Carolina ever written. Stories—mysteries, thrillers, histories, and survival dramas—are written in stone, bone, wood, and feathers. Three longtime residents of the facility, known as Level B, are elephants that called North Carolina home as recently as 11,000 years ago.

1

THREE ELEPHANTS IN THE BASEMENT

You have to know the secret elevator code to access Level B, and then you must have the keypad-lock numbers to open the heavy double door with reinforced hinges. Once you enter this secure basement facility, forty feet underground, you leave the twenty-first century and enter a nondescript cement warehouse the size of a supermarket. The unfinished gray concrete ceilings are sixteen feet high and supported every forty feet by massive concrete pillars. The floor space is separated into poorly lighted corridors by countless shelves and several hundred locked, morgue-style wooden and metal cabinets. Level B is rarely visited by politicians, theologians, or captains of industry. To my knowledge it is also not seen by military experts, climatologists, or state planners. Yet, perhaps more than any one place I know, Level B holds secrets—keys to our past and future—that affect us all.

On the long, gray aisles are thousands of specimens imaginable only to witches and sorcerers, including mushrooms, beetles, bats, wasps, pollen, seeds, and teeth of dragons (actually dinosaurs). From Tar Heel skies you'll find eagles, owls, vultures, warblers, swans, ravens, and hummingbirds. On the walls and shelves staring down at visitors are Red Squirrels, Eastern Gray Squirrels, tiny Northern Flying Squirrels, and Fox Squirrels the size of cats. There are large animals that we call "big game"—White-Tailed Deer and Black Bear. Leaning against some of the walls like wagon wheels are cross sections of enormous trees—Bald Cypress, American Chestnut,

(top) Level B at the North Carolina Museum of Natural Sciences is a supermarket of the past containing important secrets and keys to our past and future. If it ever grew, swam, crawled, or flew in North Carolina, chances are it can be found among the 3 million specimens of the museum's research collection.

(bottom) Ferns that lived in the Triassic basin more than 200 million years ago were found on sedimentary rock just south of Durham. They closely resemble the Christmas Fern found in North Carolina today.

White Oak, Eastern Hemlock, and Fraser Fir—cut from enchanted virgin forests of the nineteenth century. Nearby, resembling stacks of cordwood, are the bleached bones of whales, which are marked with tags giving species name, location, and date found. Some residents in this warehouse of natural history are recently extinct (Passenger Pigeon), have been extirpated (Mountain Lion), or are endangered (Leatherback Turtle). If it ever lived, crawled, or flew in North Carolina, chances are it now resides in this depot of the past.

Equally impressive are mineral treasures that should pique the interest—or greed—of any pirate, collector, or rock hound. Lying on some aisle floors are clear quartz crystals the size of tree stumps and large clusters of purple amethyst. In pull-out drawers are crystals of red garnet, golden topaz, green hiddenite, and blue-green aquamarine. Chunks of fool's gold (iron pyrite), copper, and lead are spread randomly on cabinet tops. Out of view, locked in the cabinets, are uncut precious stones—emeralds, sapphires, rubies, and, yes, even small North Carolina diamonds. In the same secure storage, you will also find what Spanish and English explorers sought but never found: gold nuggets from the Piedmont that never need polishing.

Perhaps most daunting to me is the southeast corner of Level B, which is devoted to the geology and paleontology collections. I am one of many Americans who find the numbers used in geologic time challenging; here, specimens are so old, or were formed so long ago, that the numbers are almost unfathomable. Most begin with a quite substantial number followed by a comma and *six* zeros. For example, some of the "young" rocks of reddish sandstone or mudstone from the Triassic basin around Durham and Research Triangle Park (see chapter 3) are over 200 million (200,000,000) years old. Nearby are specimens from Stanley County's Uwharrie Mountains that are about 540 million years old. Some beautifully metamorphosed rocks (transformed under intense heat and pressure deep within the earth), with folds and twists like saltwater taffy, are from the Black Mountain area and tip the scales of time at 700 million B.P. The senior citizens of the geology collection on Level B, however, are more than 1 *billion* years old—the number 1 followed by *nine* zeros—and come from ancient stone formations near Blowing Rock.

Although inanimate, the rocks and minerals on Level B tell the story of continents crashing together and pulling apart. Only a small portion of the state's landscape (largely in the northwestern counties) is considered part of "original North America." Most of our mountains and much of the Piedmont are considered "suspect terrain," meaning that they may not have been part of North America but rocky debris left during one of the collisions. Another swath of the Piedmont is called "exotic terrain," land that *definitely* came from somewhere else on the globe and got stuck here during one of the continental train wrecks in which most of world's continents collided to form supercontinents. In the final analysis, the present land mass we know as North Carolina varies widely in age, with most Piedmont and Mountain terrain ranging from 200 million to over 1 billion years old. On this old geologic tableau, a staggering diversity of life has evolved.

Inanimate rocks and minerals are not the only items in this subbasement of time that are profoundly old. These corridors also house indisputable fossil evidence of multicellular life stretching back 545 million years. On slabs of gray slate from the southern Piedmont in Stanley County are the tracks of worms that lived a half billion years ago. Ferns the size and shape of those in your garden are forever imprinted in reddish sedimentary rock, but these ferns lived over 200 million years ago. Resting on the floor, too heavy for the cabinets, are large chunks of petrified wood and plaster casts surrounding stone from which teeth, vertebrae, or ribs protrude. Most of this stone and bone comes from the periods of the Geological Time Scale we call the Triassic, Jurassic, or Cretaceous—windows of the past between 250 and 65 million years ago. Again, these numbers represent time spans of life on this land so outrageous that they defy comprehension for many of us.

If you haven't guessed already, Level B is the research collection seldom

Elephant teeth in North Carolina? The drawers of Level B contain pachyderm teeth, dating to the Ice Ages, that were found in such familiar locations as Wayne and Onslow Counties.

seen by the general public, the "dry storage" of the North Carolina Museum of Natural Sciences in Raleigh. Almost all of the specimens were found inside Tar Heel borders. This subterranean library of biology and geology is located directly across West Jones Street from the North Carolina General Assembly. In another museum building less than two miles away is an equally impressive "wet collection" of reptiles, fish, amphibians, and shellfish in various liquid preservatives. Together, they comprise the Museum Research Collections containing more than 3 million items, one of most comprehensive collections of its kind in the United States. Like the Smithsonian in Washington, D.C., and the American Museum of Natural History in New York, North Carolina's ever-expanding collection provides research opportunities for scientists from many disciplines. Equally important, the collections will provide a baseline for future researchers seeking answers to three basic scientific questions: What was here, when were they here, and how many were there?

Three Elephants: The Showstopper

In this storehouse of the past is an area that is, for me, the showstopper. Lining a corridor in the southeast corner of Level B is a series of locked wooden cabinets with six-foot-wide pullout shelves. There you will find the remains of three elephants that once made North Carolina and the southeastern United States their home. There are whole and partial tusks of ancient ivory six feet in length, femurs (upper leg bones) so heavy that I can barely lift them, and dozens of yellowish-brown grinding teeth the size of a bread loaf. Unlike the bones of dinosaurs and ancient reptiles still imbedded in stone, many of these pachyderm bones, teeth, and tusks look as fresh as the piles of modern whale bones on the far side of the room.

For me, it was an important "ah-ha!" moment when I realized that North Carolina had been home to three elephants, and that they *still lived here* after the last Ice Age, one of a number of global cooling cycles during the Pleistocene Epoch. I am not talking about parts of three individual elephants, but the teeth, tusks, and bones from *three species of elephants*, the ancestors of which roamed North America, Europe, and Asia for almost 4 million years and were still here as late as 11,000 B.P. (even later in Siberia and Alaska). I can comprehend such a number—there are only *three* zeros after the comma—in a place that I can envision, North Carolina. These were land animals as large as, or larger than, any found in Africa or India today, and they lived here with mountains, rivers, plants, birds, and small

Tusks from a Columbian Mammoth that "recently" roamed the Southeastern United States are on display at the Nature Research Center of the museum. More giant tusks can be found in the drawers of Level B.

animals that each of us would recognize instantly. In geologic time, twelve millennia is nothing.

Perhaps in your yard, and most certainly in your town, walked the eleven-foot-tall long-haired Wooly Mammoth (perhaps the most recognizable Ice Age animal) and the Columbian Mammoth, a twelve-foot, ten-ton giant that looked much like today's African or Indian elephants, only with much larger tusks. The third, and probably most common, species was a smaller forest dweller, the Mastodon, which was also elephant-like but with smaller tusks. All of these extinct "elephants" were part of a large group of giant mammals called proboscideans, distinguished by tusks and muscular trunks.

I was first introduced to Tar Heel elephants by Dr. Dale Russell at the North Carolina Museum of Natural Sciences. Fit and trim in his seventh decade, he was armed with boundless energy, an elegant vocabulary, and precise diction. Russell had traveled to the remote corners of the world to search for dinosaurs of the Jurassic and Cretaceous periods and the reptiles and early dinosaurs of the Triassic period. Dale was one of the keepers of the elevator code and secret keypad numbers to the doors on Level B.

The day that Dale Russell introduced me to the three elephants in the basement, I began to appreciate a more exciting, and sobering, history of our state and region than I had previously encountered in high school or college. To be sure, the museum—along with its Nature Research Center, rising five stories and fronting two blocks of West Jones Street—features natural history exhibits and dioramas telling of North Carolina's past and present. The story of the three elephants is there for all to see, but until the moment of my three-elephant epiphany in the aisles of Level B, I had believed that most of the significant stories told in natural history museums unfold slowly over millions of years of geologic time. My close encounter with the three elephants in the basement underscored for me that dramatic change can occur rapidly. The disappearance of three species of proboscideans, and many other species of large mammals, not so very long ago is a cautionary tale for all of us.

Natural History as a Stepchild

For most of us, the core of our American history is Eurocentric. We now know that Norsemen, or Vikings, explored and even colonized Greenland, eastern Canada, and perhaps New England as far back as 1,000 years ago. A couple of hundred years later, the Portuguese may have established fishing outposts in the same areas. At least one English writer has even speculated that early Chinese explorers in giant teak sailing vessels may have visited the East Coast of North America in 1421. For most of us, however, American history began when adventurers came in great numbers following Columbus's landfall in the Caribbean in 1492, concentrating most of their efforts in Central and South America. The English failed at Roanoke Island (the Lost Colony) in the 1580s but established a shaky foothold at Jamestown, Virginia in 1607, and at Plymouth Rock, Massachusetts, in 1620. The Dutch planted their flag near the mouth of the Hudson River (present-day New York) in 1609. The rest, as they say, is history.

From a technical standpoint, history is the story of the past derived from written records—books, maps, scrolls, and stone tablets. Everything before written records is considered prehistory, or prehistoric. Real history, as recorded in deciphered alphabets, reaches back a little over 2,500 years in Europe to the Greek and Roman civilizations and a couple of thousand years earlier in Egypt, the Middle East (modern Syria, Iraq, and Iran), India, and China. Central and South America also have a written history going back 2,000 years thanks to the discovery and partial deciphering of hieroglyphs from the Inca, Aztec, and Mayan peoples. In North America and in the Carolinas, however, most of the time before the arrival of the European explorers and colonists (around 1500) is considered prehistoric due to the lack of written records. And let's face it: the term "prehistoric" for most of us connotes a less reliable and less authentic history. I have long believed the differentiation between historic and prehistoric to be misleading and inaccurate (see chapter 2). The same can also be said about our views of natural history.

Despite the absence of a written record from American Indians and other explorers (those arriving before Columbus) describing ancient forests and long-forgotten birds, fish, and mammals, the collections on Level B and in other natural history museums give us a detailed history lesson in stone and bone. Level B is a library of the land, and it reveals, in its own way, as precise a history of North Carolina as do the books, maps, and other important documents held by the North Carolina Collection in Chapel Hill and the North Carolina State Archives in Raleigh. This brings me back to the three elephants and the extraordinary slice of history they represent.

Somewhere along the line, a great deal of important natural history of America, including that of North Carolina, was relegated to the tepid, less-relevant pool of "prehistory." By learning "real history," we are told we are better prepared to avoid the mistakes of the past. Don't get me wrong: knowledge of humanity's past actions, mistakes, wars, and triumphs is critical. The historic record matters. We should pay attention to experts on economic history, civil rights, equal rights, and foreign policy even though they do not always agree in their analysis of past events. Knowledge of natural history—the history of creatures, climate, and geology—of our country and state is just as important for our future survival and prosperity as knowledge of kings and queens, wars, treaties, and past economic problems. "Natural history" is regarded by too many policy makers and leaders as a stepchild of history, and thus it has never been fully embraced. The fact that evolution is still openly questioned by some elected officials, that the overwhelming consensus of the scientific community on global warming is mocked by a chorus of "deniers," and that planners at all levels don't want to deal seriously with sea-level rise are indications that the study of natural history and science has minimal appeal. For all serious students of history, including natural history, William Shakespeare said it best in *The Tempest*: "What's past is prologue." Our state's elephants lived in the recent past, a time of change that should be of extraordinary relevance to each of us.

From a geologic standpoint, North Carolina and the Southeast are not much different today than the same landscape of 12,000 B.P. The mountains and gorges of western North Carolina have eroded very little in this short span of time and would be instantly recognizable. In mountain years, 12,000 years is barely a short nap. Mount Mitchell, Grandfather Mountain, Pilot Mountain, and other landmarks have changed little over the last few thousand years except for the mantel of vegetation covering them. North Carolina's seventeen river basins would look much the same, except for the many man-made lakes prevalent along the Catawba, Little Tennessee, Yadkin-Pee Dee, Roanoke, Cape Fear, and Neuse basins.

Twelve thousand years ago, the Coastal Plain of Virginia and the Carolinas was different and wider because sea level was approximately 125 feet lower than present levels. Much of the planet's freshwater was still captured in the retreating glacial ice. Fortunately for North Carolina, none of the ice sheets gouged our landscape in the way they bulldozed the terrain of states as little as 350 miles to our north. Twelve millennia ago, when elephants grazed along present-day I-40 and I-95, there was no Pamlico Sound, and the present location of today's Outer Banks would have been high and dry with the coastline several miles to the east. Under the waters of the Atlantic covering our continental shelf, we can still see the evidence of ancient shorelines and find stumps of conifer forests that provide us with accurate dates through radiocarbon dating (see chapter 2).

In addition to a definitive fossil record of elephants in North Carolina, Level B also holds a fantastical array of megafauna as diverse as the largest land animals found today in Africa and North America combined. Enormous ancient bison, known as *Bison antiquus* (also now extinct), with bones and horns much larger than the American Bison found in Yellowstone National Park today, inhabited much of North America between 20,000 and 10,000 years ago. The ancestor of today's bison, they too disappeared along with the elephants. Other megafauna grazed and browsed Piedmont prairies and Longleaf Pine savannas. After the last Ice Age, there were horses (more like the zebra's of Africa today), musk ox, and camels (resembling the llamas of South America). In the forests and wetlands, there were giant beavers weighing 300 to 500 pounds. With beavers so large, can you imagine the trees?

Another true giant of the Southeast was the Giant Ground Sloth. As large as the American elephants, these megafauna, with long claws to pull down tree limbs, were also herbivores. An almost compete skeleton found near Wilmington now stands twelve feet tall in a diorama of the North Carolina Museum of Natural Sciences. More bones of these strange, slow-moving creatures can be found—you guessed it—on Level B.

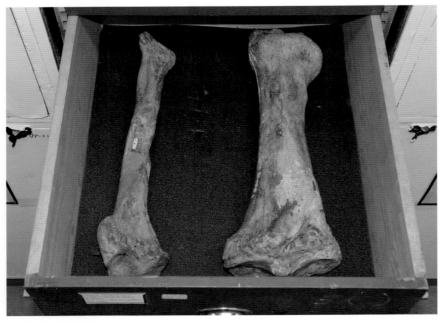

This twelve-foot-tall skeleton of a Giant Ground Sloth (top) was discovered during excavation for a park in Wilmington. Other enormous bones (bottom) of these former residents of North Carolina can be found on Level B.

With all of these herbivores, there were plenty of carnivores to feed on them. There was an American Lion larger than those of Africa today. There were other great cats, including several saber-toothed cats with long canine teeth and powerful shoulders. With such fearsome felines, you can be sure there were also big dogs in the Pleistocene. North Carolina was home to the Dire Wolf, a large canine similar to the Gray Wolf still found today in the northern United States and Canada.

I used the adjective "fantastical" to describe these animals for good reason. In addition to being very large, they were also strange. Two more animals that fit into this category are giant land tortoises (several species) and the Glyptodont. We have all seen pictures of the giant tortoises of the Galapagos, which weigh up to 500 pounds. Several species of similar tortoises were part of the Pleistocene megafauna that once roamed your favorite park or golf course in Charlotte and Wilmington. But I've saved the strangest for last. As late as 11,000 years ago, the Glyptodont, an enormous, plant-eating mammal with heavy, segmented bony plates, roamed much of the present-day United States, including North Carolina. A relative of the much smaller Armadillo found in the South and Southwest today, it was about the same size and shape as a Volkswagen Beetle. Glyptodonts were equipped with an armored body, head, and tail and could weigh well over 1,000 pounds. This was surely among the strangest animals to live among the other extinct creatures now inhabiting Level B. Can you imagine *any landscape* with three kinds of elephants, bison, several species of saber-toothed cats, giant sloths, bears, wolves, horses, camels, bear-sized beavers, tortoises weighing several hundred pounds, and VW Beetle–sized armored mammals?

I stated earlier that Level B tells a cautionary tale. In the blink of an eye in geologic time, virtually all of the giants became extinct. Some species, including the elephants, had roamed the Americas during most of the Pleistocene Epoch lasting 2 million years. During this time, great ice caps formed and then melted every 100,000 years or so. Sea levels rose and fell, often by several hundred feet over a few thousand years. But it wasn't until the blip in time between 10,000 and 13,000 years ago that most of the megafauna vanished. Just because some European adventurer didn't write it down at the time doesn't make this extinction event any less true or less-relevant history.

The New Animal

Extinction is nothing new and is very much a part of the natural order of things, but so many animals disappearing all at once begs for an explanation. For many scientists, the answer to the mass-extinction riddle begins with the arrival of a new mammal of relatively small stature in the time frame during which the great megafauna were making their exit. The one creature whose scientific name we all know, *Homo sapiens* (modern humans), became part of the American fauna.

Level B contains no artifacts of North Carolina's early human inhabitants—no spear points or stone-cutting tools from the Late Pleistocene. If you want to see such tools and explore North Carolina's human history, you have to go the North Carolina Archaeological Research Center (Department of Cultural Resources) or the Research Laboratories of Archaeology at the University of North Carolina at Chapel Hill. At both places, you will find the indisputable evidence of men and women who arrived in the Southeast at least 12,000 years ago (see chapter 2) and lived among the giants. The collections on Lane Street and in Chapel Hill contain numerous stone, clay, shell, and even wooden artifacts—including projectile points, knives, and scrapers—from across North Carolina and ranging in age from a few hundred years to more than twelve millennia.

Just as Dale Russell allowed me to cradle the bones and tusks on Level B, I have also been allowed to hold on Lane Street and in Chapel Hill (only while wearing white cotton gloves) the ancient tools of hunter-gatherers we know as Paleo-Indians. They are not an ancient "lost people" but the direct ancestors of the American Indians living here today. Long established evidence says they arrived in North America *at least* 13,500 years ago, while newer data from carbon dating on the West Coast appears to have pushed back the arrival horizon to more than 15,000 years. It is believed that many Paleo-Indians came via a land bridge across the Bering Strait connecting Russia and Alaska. Remember, at that time, melting glaciers still held huge quantities of the Earth's freshwater, and sea levels were much lower than today, in the range of 150 feet or more.

Other theories relating to the arrival of humans in North America have been proposed. One suggests that because sea levels were much lower, numerous islands were exposed, making island hopping along today's Russian, Alaskan, and Canadian coastlines a likely route into the Americas. Some archaeologists even suggest that some of the early arrivals may have been accidental tourists who were blown, or drifted, across the Pacific in small boats to western shores of the Americas. Other researchers have hedged their bets by suggesting that there were multiple waves of early immigrants arriving by various means over several thousand years. Archaeological evidence has been uncovered in both North and South America in recent years that will most certainly move back the arrival of humans in the Americas by several thousand years; just how many more millennia earlier is still an open question.

Regardless of exactly how these humans got here or when they arrived, we can say with certainty that the three elephants and other mega-animals shared the landscape of the Late Pleistocene with them. The skills and habits of Paleo-Indians are revealed by their tools, fire pits, and even ancient quarries. The tools alone—their shape, size, materials, and craftsmanship—tell a compelling story of intelligent, resourceful people. For more about these extraordinary people—the men and women who lived in your North Carolina neighborhood—see the next chapter, "Human Antiquity." Here, however, I tell the story of early North Carolinians only as it relates to the demise of the three elephants and other megafauna.

We know that man and mammoth overlapped because of dating techniques used by archaeologists, paleontologists, and geologists. Perhaps the best known in this category is radiocarbon dating, in which the decay rate of the radioisotope carbon 14 (naturally occurring in organic compounds) is measured to provide a precise date or age of *organic* materials—wood particles, animal bone, or food waste—found at a historic site. Using radiocarbon dating and other radiometric dating techniques, scientists are able to arrive at extremely accurate actual, or absolute, measurements. Once actual dates are established in soil stratigraphy (layers), relative dates or ages of animal bones or human artifacts can also be assigned to specimens found above or below those with an actual date. When both relative and absolute dating techniques are used to determine the age of fossils or relics relating to early Americans or Ice Age megafauna, the results can be astonishingly accurate. (For more about "actual" and "relative" dating, see the sidebar titled "Actual and Relative Age" in chapter 2.)

Because it is certain that the ancestors of modern humans and extinct Ice Age mammals shared the land, it is not surprising that some scientists, both archaeologists and paleontologists, argue that humans are directly responsible for the elimination of the three great elephants and other animals. Such a conclusion seems almost too obvious. We know that the stone tools of man and the bones of megafauna, including Ancient Bison and the Woolly Mammoth, have been found together in North America. Mammoth bones have been found exhibiting cuts and scrape marks made by stone tools. It has long been clear that the sharp, beautifully made projectile points used by Paleo-Indians were capable of killing the largest animals. Does such evidence prove that modern humans hunted the great animals to extinction and that man is the main culprit in the extinction mystery?

I prefer another variation of the man-is-guilty scenario. Human intervention, it is argued by some scientists, could have *inadvertently* caused ecosystems to collapse with the killing of slow-reproducing key species, such as elephants (which have a gestation period of twenty-two months). Even the loss of a few elephants in an area would have had an impact. These jumbo grazing mammals were critical links in maintaining plant ecosystems. Think of it this way: when herds of cows are removed permanently from pastureland, bushes and trees will quickly spring up in place of the former pasture if the land is not mowed or maintained. Thus, when key grazing animals disappear—elephants or cows—grasslands (such as "Piedmont prairies") and grazing areas will quickly diminish in size. Smaller grasslands would have also caused a decline in other, smaller grass-eating herbivores. With steep declines in the populations of plant eaters, the demise of the great cats and dire wolves would have followed shortly. These are plausible theories, but we still do not know for certain whether man and his stone tools directly or inadvertently brought about the extinction of the great megafauna.

Still other scientists speculate that man may have *indirectly* brought about the demise of megafauna. They argue that the culprit wasn't stone tools but unseen microbes, or pathogens, carried by humans or their domesticated dogs. Although there is no smoking gun to support the microbe theory, such a scenario is plausible in the same way that common diseases introduced by European settlers—measles, mumps, and smallpox—almost decimated American Indian populations in the fifteenth and sixteenth centuries. Without more proof, we are left with several possibilities to ponder: humans are either *directly*, *inadvertently*, or *indirectly* responsible for the mass extinction in the Late Pleistocene.

Other theories, however, exonerate humankind from any responsibility. Some argue that warming temperatures and droughts occurred after the continent-sized glaciers of the last Ice Age disappeared; therefore, climate change may have been the villain that caused ecosystems to crash. This theory holds that the largest animals—including elephants, ancient bison, and the ground sloth—required a huge forage base and could not adapt to dwindling food supplies caused by rising temperatures; consequently, their numbers plummeted. A marked decline in herbivore numbers would have meant that megacarnivores—especially the big cats, requiring many pounds of meat protein each day—also found themselves in an ecological dead end with fewer grazers on which to prey. A final theory relating to climate change is the Younger Dryas impact hypothesis, which states that an impact in the Northern Hemisphere from a comet caused an abnormally cold period (causing animal populations to crash) around 13,000 years ago. This hypothesis has largely been discounted by research climatologists, who can find little supporting evidence for the impact event. The earlier mentioned climate-warming theory, as a cause for mass extinction, also has its detractors. Much of the megafauna, including the elephants, had been in North America and Eurasia for at least a couple of million years and had survived many warming and cooling cycles. Why was the climate change following the last Ice Age, which reached its glacial maximum just 18,000 years ago, so different from other glaciations that it simply erased the largest land mammals to walk the Earth?

Familiar Issues

Do some of the issues facing the almost forgotten creatures of the last Ice Age sound familiar? Isn't modern man, with sophisticated weaponry and forest-clearing tools—in place of stone-tipped spears and stone axes—directly responsible for the extinction of the Passenger Pigeon and the Ivory-Billed Woodpecker? And except for a little luck and some timely intervention, didn't we almost wipe out the American Buffalo, the California Condor, and several species of whale?

Has human activity, causing an increase in greenhouse gasses since the beginning of the Industrial Revolution, turned up the thermostat on our planet? Or is climate change, or the less politically correct term "global warming," part of a natural cycle of warming and cooling that has occurred many times since the beginning of the Ice Ages? Are the predictions of melting ice at the polar ice caps and sea-level rise—voiced by scientists working at major universities in many countries—overblown and unnecessarily depressing the prices of beachfront homes? And finally, if temperatures go up a few degrees and sea level rises three feet or more by the end of this century, is it really a big deal? (See chapter 14 for more on that question.)

Personally, I have concluded that it is a very big deal, and that is why the three elephants in the basement, and the other extinct megamammals that now reside with them, have so captured my imagination. I'm certain that the men and women living in North Carolina twelve millennia ago—who were very intelligent people—never dreamed that the elephants in their neighborhoods would disappear. To those early inhabitants, the thick-shelled giant tortoises and the armored Glyptodont must have looked eternal. The earliest Tar Heels must have also thought that no human or force of nature could ever challenge, much less eliminate, the huge cats with dagger-length teeth.

And let's not forget that humans have always liked to live near the water, both for the view and for the fish. Remember that 12,000 years ago, sea level was much lower than it is today. The earliest beach dwellers camped on a shoreline up to twenty miles to the *east* of today's beaches, with present-day Manteo, Morehead City, and Wilmington many miles inland. Do you suppose that Paleo-Indians argued about whether sea level was rising as one generation after another had to move westward and landward to escape the rising waters? Did their elders, or leaders, order the building of shell and sand seawalls in a futile effort to hold back the ocean to save their hides (literally) and their settlements?

The North Carolina history that affects us the most, and which is directly applicable to the conditions that we face today, is not found only on the printed page in great libraries. Rather, it is the story told by stone, bone, and radiocarbon signatures of an incredible array of creatures that flourished only a comma followed by *three* zeros ago. Remember that the story of man and mammoth in the Carolinas is a cautionary tale containing the twin plotlines of extinction and adaptation: why and how did the largest and strongest land mammals to evolve on this planet vanish forever in an instant? Their story, part of our natural history, should not be relegated to a less-relevant "prehistoric bin" of evidence. With this tweaked version of North Carolina history serving as impetus, it is my hope that politicians, theologians, generals, and captains of industry will ask for the secret code and spend time getting to know the three elephants on Level B, while also remembering the words of William Shakespeare: "What's past is prologue."

■ If you think you have to travel to Europe, Africa, the Middle East, or China to find people with long histories and impressive cultures, you would be wrong. Across North Carolina and the Southeast, there are families with roots stretching back at least 600 generations. Their ancestors opened quarry operations, established trade routes, and plied the waters of eastern North Carolina in forty-foot boats—all before the Great Pyramids of Egypt sprang up by the Nile.

2

HUMAN ANTIQUITY

At the upper end of Hickory Nut Gorge east of Asheville, along Old U.S. 74 (now a scenic highway), is the tiny village of Gerton. In the 1950s, the most prominent landmarks in Gerton were the post office, Bearwallow Baptist Church, and Rhodes's Amoco station. Because proprietors Chester and Mary Lee Rhodes provided all automotive needs, the Asheville newspaper, groceries, and burgers from their grill, most days in Gerton began and ended at the Amoco station. It was also the place to get news of the gorge and instant information on any other topic—where to borrow an unusual tool, how to eliminate wasp nests, when to stake tomatoes, or how to find out the age of an antique. Such community gathering places served as the Google of earlier generations, and it was at Rhodes's Amoco that I frequently sought advice.

In early June 1956, I found a nearly perfect arrowhead (the name given to every stone point) on the edge of a field near my family's summer cabin, and I went to Rhodes's to show it off. Each of the men who made up the afternoon soda-and-cigarette clientele examined my arrowhead and told me stories about stone points they had found as boys. Chester Rhodes interjected that one of the most reliable places to find more arrowheads was a newly planted field across from the Gerton post office. He and others drew me a map to the special field. By the next morning, I had recruited two friends for an arrowhead hunt at the less-than-secret place about a mile from our cabin. For my mom and dad, and for other parents of the time, a two-mile round trip by three scruffy ten-year-olds was hardly worthy of concern—as long as we were back by lunch.

When we arrived home triumphantly almost five hours later with pockets bulging, I was a changed ten-year-old. Walking between rows of newly emerging corn, I had picked up more than a dozen stone points in several shapes and sizes—some broken, some complete. My friends had been equally successful. The real prizes of the morning included a perfect "spearhead" almost five inches long and two-thirds of a beautifully grooved stone ax, which was a tomahawk to my friends and me. Each of us had left in the field many stone flakes and some partially completed, or broken, stone tools. As I walked through our cabin's front door, I had a hundred questions, and I knew that even the collective wisdom at Rhodes's Amoco couldn't answer all of them. Who had made the arrowheads? How old were they? Were all the points from the same time period? How did the makers of these stone tools notch and chip them into such exquisite shapes? Most important, where had the American Indian people of Hickory Nut Gorge—the original North Carolinians—gone?

It has been over fifty years since that magical day in Gerton. I have since learned that a large percentage of children from my generation, especially those from small towns and rural areas, also found arrowheads. We grew up in different quadrants of this state, and each had his or her own magical field, forest path, or stream bank that yielded stone treasures from the past. I have also discovered that for most of us, discovery occurred quite by accident. My best find happened while I was standing next to an eroded red-clay ditch near Huntersville (north of Charlotte). I picked up a long slender rock that had obviously been shaped. Many years later, archaeologists identified it as a tool, a polished stone celt over fifteen inches in length. A celt is an elongated polished stone tool usually with a flat or rounded end and a sharpened edge used for cutting. Celts were used primarily as woodworking tools. Each artifact, whether intact or broken, was a reminder that long before my ancestors or any other Europeans arrived, the same land had provided sustenance for countless American Indian families.

It is not as easy for today's kids to find points and broken pieces of pottery, known as shards. Many of the places open to me and others in years past have changed. Corn and tobacco fields near small towns have become shopping centers, golf courses, and subdivisions, and some of the winding dirt roads of the 1950s have now morphed into interstates. Even small farms, once the backbone of the Tar Heel economy, have been replaced by more efficient megafarms. If you look closely, however, along roadside ditches next to less-traveled two-lane roads or along a creek bank during a dry spell, lithic treasures are still to be found. Better yet, in late April or early May—before the crops come up—politely ask a farmer if you and your children can search the edges of a freshly plowed field. Whether you search the sandy fields of the Coastal Plain, the clay soils of the Piedmont, or a steep mountain hillside, you can be assured that American Indians walked or lived on the same terrain.

Please keep in mind that most of the stone artifacts that I and others picked up were random pieces that had been exposed by a plow or erosion and were not found as part of any site excavation. Also remember that *it is never acceptable to trespass* on another person's land in search of points without first seeking permission. It is also illegal to take any projectile points or relics from state parks and federal lands. Even the stone flakes commonly found on the ground at Morrow Mountain State Park and other parks must be left alone; these, too, are artifacts left by early quarrymen and toolmakers. Also, *never dig or excavate* any site in search of artifacts. Because the context in which they are found can provide important clues to their age and origin, only professional archaeologists and anthropologists should supervise excavations. With these caveats in mind, I can assure you that nothing will connect your children to the original stewards of this land, the American Indian, like a stone point found in the soil near your home.

On the bookcase across from my desk, still around to jog my memory, are many of the same stone tools found in the Gerton field fifty years ago, the stone celt from Mecklenburg County, and several dozen other items that I found over the years. In recent decades, I have shown my small collection to professional archaeologists, and each has estimated that some of the points—made of different types of stone in varied shapes and sizes—are up to 9,000 years old (7000 B.C.E.), while others were made as recently as 1,000 years ago (1000 C.E.). Several have placed the age of the fifteen-inch celt at about 2,500 years. When I hold any stone implements in my hands, I cannot help but wonder who made them and what there lives were like. Suffice it to say, there were hardworking men and women occupying the land now called North Carolina long before the pyramids of Egypt were built.

When my own children were in their preteen years—their "age of discovery"—I took them back to the same field near the Gerton post office

For many generations, children across North Carolina have had "arrowhead" collections—treasures picked up along creek banks and in plowed fields. These stone tools (the largest being a fifteen-inch stone celt) were found by the author in the 1950s. They represent a range of shapes, sizes, and materials and span several thousand years of American Indian history.

hoping to find stone treasures between the corn rows of early summer. My own experience was not to be repeated. In place of the gently sloping cornfield were several vacation homes with shade trees and grassy yards. As luck would have it, however, my daughter, Rachel, found one complete point made of white quartz in the ditch beside the road. I wondered aloud if the new residents of the old field had any inkling that their houses were built where American Indians had hunted, harvested edible plants, raised families, and crafted stone tools over many millennia. The same question can be asked about families living on farms, in subdivisions, and in towns almost anywhere in the Carolinas. The simple fact is that most of us know little, or nothing, about the hundreds of generations of Native people who lived in every corner of this region.

A New Perspective on Ancestry

I have observed over the years that the oldest North Carolina families—those of European ancestry—often point with pride to a family history reaching back eight or nine generations. Families with roots predating the American Revolution are certainly worthy of note, and I even know a few North Carolinians who can trace their family origins to the late 1600s near the Virginia border in today's Currituck and Camden Counties. Such long family histories are impressive—until you compare them to the ancestry of *any* American Indian. By my calculation, the unbroken family tree of North Carolina's Native people stretches back 600 generations.

Usually defined as the time between a mother's first offspring and the first child of that offspring, generations are frequently calculated at twenty years apart, or more recently at twenty-five years. That's four or five generations per century. Generations can vary in length, however, depending on the region of the world and the time in history. These is little dispute among my archaeologist friends that the first humans to inhabit the southeastern United States, Paleo-Indians, arrived here at least 12,000 years ago. Although a growing number of experts, especially in Virginia and South Carolina, insist that the first humans appeared in the Southeast thousands of years earlier, for many scientists, the jury is still out (see chapter 1). The discovery of ancient fluted Clovis points in a number of locations in North Carolina and the excavation of several Paleo-Indian sites—including the Hardaway Site on the Yadkin River by famed UNC–Chapel Hill professor Joffre Coe in the 1940s and 1950s—leave little doubt that the forebearers of today's American Indians have enjoyed the Tar Heel climate and landscape for twelve millennia or more.

It must be emphasized that these very early people are not an ancient or lost people. Regardless of contemporary tribal names—Meherrin, Cherokee, Catawba, or Haliwa-Saponi—the American Indians living in Virginia and the Carolinas today are the direct descendants of Paleo-Indians. Thus, when you divide 12,000 years of occupation and use by generations of twenty years each, you get 600 generations of American Indians with ties to North Carolina soil. The actual number of generations is probably larger because, for most early people around our planet, childbearing occurred at a younger age.

I include these estimates of generational numbers not to diminish in the slightest the connection any North Carolinian has to this land. All Tar Heels have reason to be proud no matter where their forbearers hailed from—northern Europe, Africa, the British Isles, South America, or the Middle East. Rather, by showing the connection of American Indians to this soil over many millennia, I hope to underscore the importance of including more history and culture of the first North Carolinians in school curricula and our personal knowledge of the land.

Today, we categorize early Native populations by their lifestyles. During the Paleo-Indian period, nomadic people, primarily hunter-gatherers traveling in small family units, hunted and collected edible plants across the entire southeastern landscape between 12,500 and 10,000 B.P. Their calling cards are very distinctive stone points: the fluted Clovis and the Hardaway. Following the disappearance of much of the Ice Age megafauna (see chapter 1), and as the climate warmed, the first people of North Carolina entered the Archaic period, often broken into three phases—the Early, Middle, and Late Archaic—spanning the years between 10,000 and 3000 B.P. This 7,000-year-long period of American Indian history also had a number of distinctive point shapes that bear different names in different states and regions. In North Carolina, projectile points from the Archaic period bear such names as Palmer, Kirk, Morrow Mountain, Guilford, and Savanna River. During this time in southeastern Indian history, settlement patterns began to evolve from seasonal to permanent. Along with hunting small animals, trapping fish, and gathering acorns and nuts, Native peoples in the Archaic period planted and harvested the first crops of gourds, the fruit from the Pawpaw Tree, and maypops, the fruit of the Passion Flower vine. In the Late Archaic, about 3,500 years ago, the first pottery vessels for cooking and storage began to appear in the clay-rich land of North Carolina.

We can also be certain that regional travel and barter were well established in the Archaic period. Early human populations quickly identified the best stone for making points, knives, and scrapers. Large pieces of stone would have been too heavy to carry long distances, but unfinished "blanks" known as quarry blades could be carried in large numbers for trade or personal use. They were the right size for the end user to shape into the point or cutting tool desired. Quarry blades—made from hard, easily shaped volca-

Distinctive Clovis (top) and Hardaway (bottom) points used by Paleo-Indians date to a time at the end of the last Ice Age when the megafauna of North Carolina—elephants, big cats, and giant bison—still roamed, but would soon disappear. (Artifacts from the Research Laboratories of Archaeology at UNC–Chapel Hill)

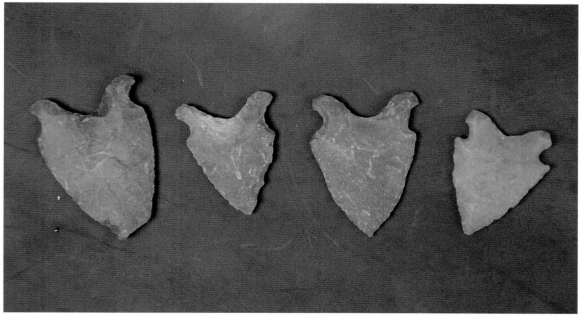

nic rhyolite from Morrow Mountain—have been found in caches, numbering in the dozens to hundreds, in states north and south of the Carolinas. From this evidence, archaeologists have concluded that Morrow Mountain (now protected as Morrow Mountain State Park) and other sites in the Uwharrie Mountains had active quarries as early as 10,000 years ago.

The Archaic period was followed by the Woodland period—from 1000 B.C.E. to 1550 C.E.—a time when settlements and larger villages became permanent. This was also the time that modern "tribes" evolved and agriculture flourished. It was during this period that the bow and arrow was introduced (around 300 B.C.E.), trade evolved, and agriculture saw the introduction of corn and beans. With the high-tech bow and arrow—which largely replaced the atlatl tool used to increase the velocity and distance of spears—new styles of smaller, triangular-shaped stone points quickly evolved, such as the Yadkin and Uwharrie style points. In addition to the Woodland period Indians, another culture, the Mississippian, appeared in south-central North Carolina around 750 C.E. and lasted until 1550 C.E. The Mississippian culture was characterized by larger towns and ceremonial mounds. You will note that both the Woodland and Mississippian cultures have an end date around 1550 C.E.—the time when the Spanish, French, and English arrived and changed forever the human history of North America.

Much later stone tools, such as these Savannah River–style points from the Archaic period (between 3,000 and 1,000 B.C.E.), were also distinctive in their shape and design, which often remained unchanged for hundreds of years until a new style evolved. (Artifacts from the Research Laboratories of Archaeology at UNC–Chapel Hill)

The end of the Archaic period (around 1500 B.C.E.) saw the beginning of agriculture in North Carolina. One of the first crops may have been maypops, the fruit of the Passion Flower vine.

The projectile points in this collection represent almost 12,000 years of human occupation in North Carolina, ranging from the Clovis tool on the top row (left to right: Clovis, Hardaway, Kirk, Palmer, and Guilford) to the much younger Uwharrie point on the bottom row (left to right: Savannah River, Yadkin, and Uwharrie). It is believed that North Carolina's Clovis points date to approximately 10,500 B.C.E. (over 12,000 years ago), while the Uwharrie points were a preferred point as late as 1300 C.E. (800 years ago). (Artifacts from the Research Laboratories of Archaeology at UNC–Chapel Hill)

The Emergence of Modern Humans

It is now widely accepted in scientific communities that early man sprang from Africa and migrated to Asia and Europe. Between 80,000 and 100,000 years ago, there were modern humans, *Homo sapiens*, in Africa, Europe, and Asia. There were other branches on the human tree (the *Homo* genus), including Neanderthal (*Homo neanderthalensis*), but all except *Homo sapiens* became extinct in Asia and Europe by approximately 30,000 B.P.

As mentioned in the previous chapter, bands of modern humans, now referred to as Paleo-Indians, migrated to North America from Asia between 13,500 and 15,000 years ago (and remember that a growing number of scientists are presenting evidence that some migrations occurred even earlier). It is believed that many of these early immigrants crossed a land bridge between Asia and North America (the site of today's Bering Strait) just as the great ice sheets of the last Ice Age began to retreat. Sea level was much lower, more than 150 feet below today's levels, meaning that the land bridge was actually the exposed seafloor between today's Russia and Alaska. Within several centuries of their arrival, modern man could be found across North America. Let me emphasize again that these first people, whether they reached today's southeastern United States 12,500 years ago or earlier, are the direct forebearers of today's American Indians.

Perhaps it is because of the content of the courses we took in high school or college, but few among us whose ancestors came from Europe, Africa, or Asia have studied or appreciated the long history of modern humans in the Americas. We often know far more about the people of the past from other parts of the world—the ancient Egyptians, Greeks, Romans, Babylonians, Chinese, and even the Celts—than those who once walked, lived, and hunted on the very lands on which our homes, businesses, and highways are built. We are all impressed by the Romans, who ruled and left distinctive buildings across the known world 2,000 years ago, and by the Greeks, who built the Parthenon beginning in 447 B.C.E. We know about the Great Wall of China, built in phases starting around 500 B.C.E. with additions and changes for the next 1,200 years. Starting about 4500 B.P., the Babylonian Empire flourished next to the Tigris and Euphrates Rivers in the country we now know as Iraq. The ancient Egyptians built most of the Pyramids between 5000 and 4000 B.P. Finally, one of the best-known English landmarks, Stonehenge, the handiwork of the ancient Celts, was constructed in phases beginning about 5100 B.P. Although there are no Great Walls or Pyramids in North Carolina, archaeological digs across this state have yielded stone tools and artifacts that tell a story of consistent or continuous human use predating much of the European-African-Asian antiquity with which we are so familiar. Part of the problem, I believe, is that we equate American Indians with "Stone Age" people who did not leave a written record and whose history, therefore, is somehow less important.

Reevaluating the Stone Age

Over the years, I have had the opportunity to visit several of the world's great museums in the Americas, Europe, and Asia. On occasion, I have been startled by artifacts in collections that seemed out of place. For example, at the Benaki Museum in Athens, which holds relics from every period of Greek civilization, and in the venerable British Museum in London, I was puzzled by displays of stone projectiles and other stone tools. What were these points that looked eerily similar to many I have found in the red-clay fields of North Carolina doing in the same museums that held bronze and marble statuary and other cultural treasures of Greece, Italy, and early England?

The simple fact is that in all areas where humans have lived and thrived through time, there has been a Stone Age. In Spain, Greece, Italy, France, the British Isles, Egypt, India, and China, stone tools—knives, scrapers, points, celts, farm implements, and pounding tools—were used until cultures utilizing copper, bronze, and iron evolved over time. For many of us, however, the phrase "back to the Stone Age" is derogatory and used to describe people who are backward or, at best, have minimum technological skills. Stone Age people are unsophisticated and primitive, right? But is that how you would categorize the early Athenians, Celts, Romans, Egyptians, and Chinese, who also used flint knives, stone-tipped arrows, and clay pots? Every great culture had its own Stone Age.

The people at the end of the Stone Age, before the various ages of metal, are categorized as Neolithic people (literally meaning "new stone age"). The Neolithic era is not a fixed time period but a sliding scale in different regions and among different cultures. During the Neolithic, people around the world transitioned from a hunter-gatherer existence to a more sedentary existence in established settlements with agriculture providing most of the food. This was also the time when many plants became domesticated and clay pottery, tempered by fire, came into existence. As more food was being produced, clay vessels became necessary to cook, store, and transport it. During this era, stone implements in many cultures were slowly replaced by tools made of copper, bronze, and, later, iron. Across Europe and in much of the Middle East, including the Fertile Crescent of Egypt, Syria, and modern-day Iraq, the Neolithic period was in full swing about 5000 B.C.E. The Bronze Age (one of the first metals used to make tools and weapons) spread across most of the region between 2500 and 750 B.C.E.

In Central and South America, the Neolithic period, with its settlement and agrarian revolution, arrived about 3500 B.C.E. and was established in eastern North America by 2500 B.C.E. In North Carolina, we can date our earliest clay pots to about 1500 B.C.E., about the same time that agriculture and plant domestication began to increase. At the time the first explorers arrived—whether you believe the Vikings, Chinese, Portuguese, or Spanish were the first to discover the New World—all people of North and South America were still Neolithic cultures, that is, still in the New Stone Age.

Stone axes, projectile points, agricultural tools, and weaponry were still in use on both continents in the Western Hemisphere. It should not be forgotten that it has not been long since all of Europe, Africa, and Asia depended on flint, rhyolite, and obsidian for most of their tool needs—just look at the stone tools on display in the world's great museums.

The Native peoples of the Southeast, whether they lived 500 or 12,000 years ago, were extraordinarily talented. The skills needed for simple survival would challenge each of us today. Each band of Native people, and later tribes, had to identify and locate edible plants, determine the location of the best varieties of stone for toolmaking, develop fishing and hunting skills, and learn how to preserve food and hides. They had to learn which plants and fungi had dietary and medicinal value. Just to survive, the earliest North Carolinians had to know the natural food cycles, such as the annual migration routes of large animals, including elk and bison. Many were skilled fishers who knew the spawning runs of Atlantic Sturgeon, Striped Bass, and White Shad on the Roanoke, Cape Fear, Neuse, and Tar Rivers. They learned when and where chestnuts, acorns, and walnuts were most plentiful, and when migratory birds such as the Passenger Pigeon would darken the skies and fill the limbs of trees to the breaking point.

Other skills were well advanced among American Indians in the Southeast. Along with developing skills as stone workers, potters, and weavers, they were early boat builders. Between 4,000 and 4,500 years ago, at about the same time that Egypt's Great Pyramids were being built, commerce was already taking place on North Carolina waterways.

Mike Dunn of the North Carolina Museum of Natural Sciences made a significant discovery in the winter of 1986–87. Dunn, then a district naturalist for the North Carolina state parks, was working with winter bird populations on Phelps Lake in Pettigrew State Park during a period of low water. He noticed some carved, elongated pieces of wood protruding from the sediment of the lake. What Dunn had found were dugout canoes made from the trunks of giant cypress trees. Fortunately, they were extremely well preserved by the acidic waters and sediments of the lake. To date, over thirty partial and complete boats, the largest being almost forty feet long, have been found, ranging in age from 700 to 4,600 years old. To put this in perspective, the youngest log canoe, aged with radiocarbon dating, was plying the waters of Phelps Lake about 100 years before Columbus arrived in the West Indies, while the oldest canoe is approximately the same age as the Great Pyramid of Giza. The waters of the lake and the surrounding shoreline have yielded a number of stone artifacts and pieces of pottery corresponding to ages of the canoes. It does not seem logical that Phelps Lake is the only lake in the Coastal Plain of North Carolina (where most of our natural lakes are located) holding ancient canoes. It should come as no surprise when the sediments of other lakes yield additional ancient watercraft in the years to come.

Grand Structures

I am often asked whether American Indians in this state left behind something other than canoes, pottery, and stone artifacts, perhaps some kind of large building or structure. In south-central North Carolina (Montgomery County), Town Creek Indian Mound (a re-creation), built about 1100 C.E., is our best surviving example of mound building from the Mississippian period. In Jackson County, Judaculla Rock, about fourteen feet across and covered with petroglyphs (picture writing) thought to be 2,000 to 3,000 years old, was left by the ancestors of the Cherokee. On Harkers Island and other coastal islands, there are early twentieth-century photographs and even some faint remnants of large middens, or shell mounds, left by early inhabitants. Across our state, however, are even larger Native American projects and creations that North Carolinians pass by every day without taking notice.

Tom Magnuson, president of the Trading Path Association in Hillsborough, has perhaps more than any one person helped identify significant pathways first used by American Indians and early settlers alike. With old maps and a great eye for terrain, Magnuson has marked the locations of fords (stream crossings) and heavily used trails across North Carolina. Many of these routes appear on the earliest maps of North Carolina's interior. For example, if you live in Charlotte and go through the heart of the city at the intersection of Tryon and Trade Streets, you are at an ancient crossroads of two Native American pathways. Today, Interstate 85—from the South Carolina border through Charlotte, Salisbury, and Hillsborough and into Virginia—closely follows the Trading Path.

It was not the Europeans who found the shallow, hard-bottomed locations, or fords, across the Catawba, Yadkin, and Cape Fear Rivers, nor was it the settlers pushing westward who found the "gaps" in the Appalachians, like the Swannanoa Gap on I-40 between Black Mountain and Old Fort. Shallow Ford over the Yadkin River west of Winston-Salem and Cowen's and Tuckaseegee Fords over the Catawba River were an integral part of the

ACTUAL AND RELATIVE AGE

Before the advent of radiocarbon dating techniques, more commonly known as "carbon dating," around 1950, the ages of archaeological sites and artifacts were often difficult to pin down. It had long been a basic rule in archaeology that the layers of soil on top were younger than the layers, or the stratigraphy, below. It was discovered that when carbon dating was used to determine the age of organic material—wood, bone, charcoal, seed pits, or other formally living material—very accurate measurements could be made and an *actual* age could be assigned.

All living organisms take in carbon 14 while they are alive but stop absorbing it once they die. After death, carbon 14 begins to break down at a fixed rate through radioactive decay, and the amount of carbon 14 diminishes over time. By comparing the quantity of carbon 14 remaining in formally living organic material to carbon 14 found in the atmosphere, an actual age can be obtained from samples. Therefore, when stone points or pottery chards are found with organic material in "context"—in the same layer of soil in which the organic material is found—we can assign the same actual age to the artifacts. Although carbon dating has been used on objects up to 50,000 years old, the accuracy of actual dates is greater if the ages of organic materials, or objects to be dated, are 25,000 years old or less.

In North Carolina, charcoal and bone from ancient cooking pits and even woven cane mats have been found and dated using carbon 14 radiometric dating. It was through measuring carbon 14 in the cypress wood canoes from Lake Phelps that very accurate ages could be obtained for canoes ranging from 700 to 4,600 years old. The measurement of carbon 14 in organic material is just one of several radiometric dating techniques that provide actual dates.

By knowing the actual age of objects found in layers of soil through radiometric dating, it is possible to assign *relative* dates, younger or older, to the nonorganic artifacts found in the stratigraphy above and below. Relative ages assigned to objects found in stratigraphy in close proximity to items of a known age can be very accurate.

Finally, it was observed that stone points and tools found in layers where actual dates could be assigned frequently had telltale, distinctive shapes. Points from the same stratigraphy, of the same age, and of a similar shape were given names to differentiate them from other equally distinctive shapes and ages. Thus you will often hear archaeologists categorize points as Clovis, Hardaway, Kirk, Guilford, or Savannah River. These designations by shape and age allow for another kind of relative dating. Points with distinctive shapes of a known age have become "horizon markers" or "index artifacts." Hardaway and Palmer points are totally different in shape from the much younger, equally distinctive Savannah River points. When Hardaway, Kirk, or Savannah River points are found many miles apart, an archaeologist can assign an age range based on the known ages of similarly shaped index artifacts. Thus, even the "arrowheads" I found fifty years ago in the Gerton cornfield can be given a name and an approximate age based on their shape.

region's transportation infrastructure long before the first Spanish, English, or German travelers arrived. Significant pathways, gaps, and fords are remnants of American Indian history, no less than the Roman roads that tell historians about Rome's footprint in Europe and the Near East.

Near some fords are other large relics in the form of stone *V*'s and *W*'s in North Carolina rivers. These are the fish weirs, often called fish dams, used by Indians to trap fish on their migratory runs. Although many have been destroyed during modern road construction and covered by man-made reservoirs across the Piedmont, there are still a number of Indian weirs, which are themselves large stone artifacts. Some are believed to date to the end of the Archaic period or the beginning of the Woodland period—some 3,000 years ago. Few are in better condition or have a more perfect *V* than the weirs on the Mayo River, a tributary of the Dan River, north of Winston-Salem near the Virginia border. Some of the "arms" of the fish weirs, made of large, carefully laid stone boulders, measure more than 100 feet in length.

Stone "fish weirs" were used by American Indians to harvest fish in rivers in the Piedmont and mountains. This large stone weir, with a near perfect *V*, is located in the Mayo River near Eden, North Carolina.

On the Mayo and on other rivers, Indians would funnel migratory fishes into traps—including such fish as Striped Bass, Hickory Shad, American Shad, Blue-Back Herring, and even sturgeon (two species). Even when the Native American population had largely disappeared from their ancestral areas, European settlers continued to use their stone fish traps. Although these structures are enormous, they are often difficult to see at river level. Some can be seen from the air and even in satellite images.

Tool Makers vs. the Mouse Users

Dr. Randy Daniels of East Carolina University has documented the presence of fluted Clovis points—the signature tool of the earliest Paleo-Indians—in two-thirds of North Carolina's 100 counties. It is virtually impossible to take your dog for a walk anywhere in North Carolina and not stand in the footprints of men and women who lived at least 5,000 years before the Pyramids began rising along the banks of the Nile.

Perhaps the day will come 5,000 years from now when an archaeologist of the time excavates a southeastern landfill from our time, the twenty-first century. In the middle of the landfill, she will find a hand-sized chunk of scratched, weathered plastic with a short piece of plastic-coated copper wire hanging from it. Records will show that it is an ancient "computer mouse" used by men and women who sat too much in one place and were frequently overweight. Near the mouse, the archaeologist will also find numerous plastic bottles of the same actual age in the same strata of debris. The find will demonstrate to her that the people of the "mouse era" had been wasteful and unwilling, or unable, to perfect and produce degradable compounds.

In the soil a few feet *beneath* the old landfill, the archaeologist will also find a perfectly preserved stone point, side notched at the top. Because of its distinctive, iconic shape, she will know that she has found a Hardaway point, not quite as old as the Clovis but with a relative age of about 15,000 years at the time it is found—10,000 years older than the plastic mouse. She will know that the maker of the point was a skilled hunter and craftsman and a person who left a very light carbon footprint, a sign of good land stewardship. Examination will show that the Hardaway point is made of rhyolite, a very hard, fine-grained volcanic rock from the Uwharrie Mountains. After the dig, the archaeologist and her colleagues will discuss the day's finds and wonder out loud: "Which people were the most advanced—the mouse users or the stone-tool makers?"

■ What do the potters of the Sanford/Seagrove area, many of the world's foremost research enterprises, the Raleigh-Durham International Airport, and some of the most fearsome creatures ever to roam the planet have in common? They all reside in close proximity to each other because of a geological event that occurred some 220 million years ago when the Earth parted and a gaping basin was formed.

3

TRIASSIC TRILOGY

IBM, Potters, and Phytosaurs

North Carolina's Research Triangle Park, the potters of the Sanford/Seagrove area, and some of the most important fossil beds in the eastern United States all owe their existence to a geological event. Across the United States, much of what has shaped our nation's fortunes and character was also predetermined by geology—the oil in Texas and Oklahoma, the deepwater port of New York, the iron mines of Michigan's Upper Peninsula, and the coal deposits underlying West Virginia and Pennsylvania. Fortunately—or unfortunately, depending on your perspective—North Carolina was not endowed with oil, mountains of iron ore, enormous coal reserves, or a protected deepwater port; we were blessed, or cursed, with lots of sticky, gooey clay.

My father was born on a farm near Charlotte in 1906, and like many Tar Heels who lived and survived the Great Depression, he was impressed when individuals did well, especially when the fates had dealt them a bad hand. Conversations with Dad were often peppered with colloquialisms from his rural past. One of the highest compliments he could bestow on anyone was that he or she had "turned a sow's ear into a silk purse." This meant that a person had made something grand, or valuable, out of something seemingly worthless or ordinary. In the early 1970s, Dad applied the sow's-ear-to-silk-purse metaphor to an economic miracle performed by former governor Luther Hodges and his friends. He was referring to the real estate between Raleigh, Durham, and Chapel Hill, which, beginning in the late 1950s, was transformed into Research Triangle Park (RTP).

What many people don't realize or have forgotten is that the parcels of the land on which RTP was built had long been considered among the sorriest, most worthless tracts of real estate in this region. Much of the soil at the surface, and for many feet down, was too "poor" to farm and not at all suitable for major housing developments because it wouldn't pass the perk test (short for percolation). Mixtures of clay and other soils found in other parts of our state make for good farmland, but when it's *all* clay, or when there are too many fine clay particles, water cannot move through the dense soil, making it incompatible for farming and home septic systems. During a summer clerkship in a Durham law firm in 1970, I once heard a senior attorney in the office tell a client that the soil near the airport (now Raleigh-Durham International) "wouldn't grow pine or kudzu."

It is for these reasons that stretches of the real estate southeast of Durham, except for the airport, were largely undeveloped and relatively cheap. In my father's vernacular, the sow's ear was the inhospitable land unfit for farming or housing, and the silk purse was RTP, developed by Hodges and other visionaries. It is now a base of operations or a research facility for IBM, CISCO, the National Humanities Center, the Research Triangle Institute, GlaxoSmithKline, Cree (pioneer in LED lighting), and many more of the world's most innovative enterprises.

The Vision and People behind RTP

At the end of World War II, the nexus between great institutions of higher learning and research/technology/growth in the American Century was clear. Cutting-edge research was already taking place in Boston, anchored by Harvard and the Massachusetts Institute of Technology, and in California around Stanford University and the University of California, Berkeley. Some of the first to think the same magic could be worked in North Carolina were Governor William B. Umstead (serving as governor only two years in 1953 and 1954), Dr. Howard Odum of the University of North Carolina (UNC), and Romeo Guest of Greensboro. When Lieutenant Governor Luther Hodges succeeded Umstead, who died in office in 1954, it was Odum and Guest, among others, who encouraged Hodges to help capture the synergies and resources offered by three great North Carolina institutions—UNC, Duke University, and State College (now North Carolina State University). Karl Robbins, and later Watts Hill, purchased or secured options on several thousand acres of pinewoods for RTP in the late 1950s, mostly in southwestern Durham County. At the same time, the three universities helped to ferment the idea of merging academia with progressive corporations into a unified vision benefiting the universities and the state. The promise, and necessity, of the idea behind RTP was underscored in 1957 when the Soviets launched Sputnik. In 1959 Governor Hodges declared the park open for business.

In the years before RTP opened, some of the most creative minds from each of the area's universities became involved—including UNC professors Arthur Rowe and George Simpson (executive director and sparkplug for the enterprise); Marcus Hobbs of Duke; and Malcolm Campbell and Arthur Menius at North Carolina State. The involvement of academia was critical, but the ultimate success of the enterprise also required the buy in of many of North Carolina's business leaders and visionaries, including Robert Hanes, William C. Friday, Karl Robbins, Watts Hill, Elizabeth Aycock, and Archie K. Davis. It was not lost on anyone that the three institutions formed a triangle—thus the name Research Triangle Park.

The Geological Event

It dawned on me several years ago that the movers and shakers who created RTP probably never knew the geological history of what would become some of North Carolina's priciest real estate. To find out why the land under RTP was not suited for agriculture or homes, and how it evolved into one of the world's great corporate and research landscapes, you have to go back over 200 million years. It was the time when much of the land on Earth was still lumped together into a supercontinent that geologists today call Pangaea. Much of the northwestern African coastline from today's Mauritania and Morocco was crunched up against what is now the East Coast of the United States. It was the beginning of the Mesozoic age, which is divided into three parts—the Triassic, Jurassic, and Cretaceous periods. Our kids know this time as the Age of Dinosaurs, the heyday of the largest land animals to ever roam the Earth. Dinosaurs diversified in the Triassic, but most disappeared forever in the Cretaceous following a mass extinction event approximately 65 million years ago.

It was during the Triassic period, around 220 million years ago, when Pangaea began to crack and separate into today's continents. Most of the land in the Piedmont and the Mountain region of today's North Carolina were already in place when northwestern Africa and the eastern United States of today began to pull apart. The pulling apart of continents is a violent event, even though it takes place over millions of years. In late August 2011, an earthquake measuring 5.8 on the Richter Scale shook buildings from Atlanta to Boston. We were told that such quakes and their aftershocks were rare in the East. This may be true today, but 220 million years ago, North Carolina was a quake zone with relatively frequent tremors caused by the ripping and slipping of continents occurring just east of Raleigh.

As the continental tectonic plates tugged against each other, "stretch marks" developed near the lines of separation (called rifts or faults) from the state of Georgia to Canada's Nova Scotia. Near the continental seams, where land was stretched and pulled like taffy, there were long rift valleys with steep cliffs on either side. Over millions of years, the Appalachians to the west eroded, and the great valleys filled with conglomerates, silt, organic materials, and sediments carried by rivers flowing to the southeast. On the edges of the basin, conglomerates (a sedimentary rock formed when gravel and small boulders are bound together) indicate where streams and rivers entered. The basins themselves are filled with deep layers (up to 7,000 feet) of sedimentary red clay, mudstone, siltstone, carbonaceous shale, and even thin layers of coal—all hallmarks of the Triassic basins in North Carolina. The red color is essentially rust that came from iron oxides in the soil. The surface soils over North Carolina's Triassic regions are highly variable and actually include some good farmland next to rivers and even some large wetlands, including those in the upper reaches of Jordan Lake and the wetlands of the Pee Dee National Wildlife Refuge near Wadesboro.

There are two major rift basins, or areas filled with Triassic sediments, in North Carolina. One is the Dan River basin extending south from Virginia to Mayodan, North Carolina; the other is the much larger Deep River basin, made up of several subbasins extending from Durham southwest to Wadesboro. In this larger Triassic basin, you will find much of Durham County, RDU International Airport, Research Triangle Park, Jordan Lake, Sanford, and Wadesboro. Most of Chapel Hill lies on the west side of the once-great rift valley, while Raleigh is located just to the east.

The next time you leave Raleigh going west on Interstate 40, take a long look at the Triassic basin stretching out before you when passing under the overpass at Harrison Avenue (Exit 287). At the bottom of the hill, you will soon see Lake Crabtree on the left and the exits to RDU International Airport on your right: you have arrived in the Triassic basin. Another landmark marking the top of the *east wall* of the Triassic basin is Raleigh's well-known

(top) Red sedimentary rock, known as mudstone or siltstone, is found throughout the Triassic basins of North Carolina. This photograph was taken near the intersection of the Durham Freeway and Interstate 40 during a road-construction project.

(bottom) This is a 200-million-year-old view looking east on Interstate 40 from mile marker 268 outside of Chapel Hill. Few motorists are aware that they are driving on the western wall of the Triassic basin and looking into an ancient rift lake.

Angus Barn Restaurant located on U.S. Highway 70. If you are driving from Hillsborough heading east on Interstate 40, you'll drop almost 400 feet between Hillsborough and the N.C. Highway 54 exit (the most precipitous drop occurring between mile markers 268 and 269) as you journey down the *west wall* of the ancient basin. For me, however, the very best view from the west side of the basin is from Gimghoul Castle in Chapel Hill looking southwest toward Jordan Lake.

Before the success of Research Triangle Park, others had tried to turn a profit from North Carolina's Triassic landscape, sometimes with tragic results. Tar Heels are often unaware that until 1925, North Carolina was, like Pennsylvania and West Virginia, a coal-mining state, though with a much lower quantity and quality of coal. Most of the mining took place around Sanford in Lee and Chatham Counties in mines named Egypt, Cumnock, and Coal Glen. Mining had begun before the signing of the Declaration of Independence in 1776, continued through the Civil War, and was going strong through the start of the twentieth century. Although Triassic coal deposits are still present, the future of coal mining in North Carolina was dealt a near fatal blow on May 27, 1925, when fifty-three men were killed in the Coal Glen Mine disaster—the worst industrial accident in the history of the state. Because of this tragedy, and perhaps because the quantity of Tar Heel coal resources was much smaller (and less profitable) than the resources of states to our north, coal mining had essentially ended by the early 1950s.

In recent years, a new king of energy wealth has been touted for the Triassic basin around Sanford and Wadesboro: natural gas. Potential, viable natural gas deposits in Triassic shale have been located in North Carolina, but to release it, a process known as hydraulic fracturing, or "fracking," must be used in which chemical compounds and large amounts of water are injected into carbonaceous shale deposits, fracturing it to release natural gas. Only time will tell if North Carolina becomes a natural gas producer, because a state and national debate is currently under way over the safety of fracking and its long-term effects on groundwater supplies. New energy supplies are important, but even more essential to North Carolina's future are water resources (see chapter 13). Like North Carolina's modest, low-grade coal deposits, our shale gas deposits are also small in comparison to almost any other North American gas fields. Estimates have ranged from a forty-year supply for the state to a paltry five years. Lawmakers must weigh carefully the potential of long-term damage to water sources in the region before succumbing to the allure of short-term gas profits through fracking.

Brick made with Triassic clays were used to build many of the iconic buildings of the region, including Old South Building at the University of North Carolina at Chapel Hill (begun in 1798). The manufacture of brick is still a very important industry along the basins.

Here my father would counsel caution: it is possible to turn a silk purse back into a sow's ear!

The best-known traditional industries in the Triassic basin today are the clay-mining and brick-making operations around Durham, Sanford, and Wadesboro. Excellent brick clays are found in the North Carolina Piedmont and even in the mountains, but none is more accessible and abundant than the clay sediments of the Triassic basin. Brick making in North Carolina was part of the state's economy long before Luther Hodges nudged business and education leaders to create RTP. Beginning in precolonial times and well into the twentieth century, bricks were made and fired by hand; you can see North Carolina red brick in the century-old Textile Mills at Saxapahaw, in the restored buildings of the American Tobacco Company in Durham, and in the oldest structures—Old East Dormitory (1793) and South Building (1814)—on the UNC–Chapel Hill campus. There is another part of the Triassic clay economy, however, that I find far sexier and more aesthetically pleasing than any other enterprise occurring in or near the Triassic basin.

Potter-Farmers of the Triassic

In the fall of 1964, I was a freshman at Davidson College—excited, but sorely lacking in preparation for the academic rigors of college life. One of the

(left) Ben Owen was one of many extraordinary potters who helped turn a region known for small farms and poor soil into a destination for pottery collectors. This photograph was taken by Bayard Wootten, who became one of North Carolina's preeminent photographers, especially for her work from the 1930s. (Photo courtesy of the North Carolina Collection, UNC–Chapel Hill)

(above) Almost every potter signs or marks his or her work. This seal, "Ben Owen, Master Potter," was used by Owen after his departure from Jugtown Pottery.

great assets offered by a small college like Davidson for kids like me was an advisory system in which experienced professors were assigned to mentor a handful of new students during the critical first year. On Sunday evenings, advisees were often invited to the homes of their mentor/advisor for refreshments.

It was at a faculty house during a Sunday evening visitation in October that I focused on a gleaming collection of pottery—teapots, bowls, plates, pitchers, and vases—in warm earth tones of green, brown, orange, and speckled gray. As an eighteen-year-old, I had never looked twice at a piece of pottery and had no interest in it as art. Yet I remember spending much of that evening looking at earthenware and asking my advisor, Professor William McGavock, about its origin. He explained that the collection had come from the Sanford/Seagrove area. Much of it was attributed to one man, Ben Owen, but McGavock also mentioned other famous pottery names from the region—Cole, Teague, Hancock, and Owens—who also came from families with potter-farmer traditions.

Within a month of my chance encounter with North Carolina pottery, I got directions from Professor McGavock to Ben Owen's place of business near Seagrove. On a Saturday in early November 1964, I thumbed several rides from Davidson to Asheboro and then toward Seagrove before arriving at Owen's studio just as he was closing for lunch at about 1:00 P.M. Even though I had never met Ben Owen, within an hour he had me crawling into a "groundhog" brick kiln with his assistant to remove finished pottery that had cooled for several days. I remember being petrified that I would drop a piece of his work.

That was my first of dozens of trips in the coming decade to visit Ben Owen and neighboring potters. All of the potters of the region could talk in depth about clay, "nature's plastic," a material that can be molded into items of utility and art. Each potter had his/her sources for a variety of clays in Lee, Moore, Durham, Chatham, and Montgomery Counties.

The Properties of Clay

Even though I learned much about the extraordinary properties of nature's plastic from the men and women who work with it daily, it was many years before I learned about the mineral, geological history, and properties of clay. Why was it so slick? What makes it malleable, and from where did it come?

Clay is a mineral formed by the weathering of silicate minerals (including quartz, feldspar, and mica) over long periods of time. Clay particles are among the smallest inorganic soil components as defined by the geologists. Clay (particles less than .00015 inches) is up to 133 times smaller than medium sand (particles not exceeding .02 inches), up to thirty-three times smaller than very fine sand (particles not exceeding .0049 inches), and up to fifteen times smaller than silt (particles not exceeding .0025 inches). Although the smallest silt particles can be close in size to clay particles, they do not have the same plasticity as clay when mixed with water.

Under a microscope, clay particles appear to be flat plates. When water is added to dry clay, a surface tension forms between the flat surfaces, making

BEN OWEN, MASTER POTTER

Ben Owen's story is a little different from that of most potters. At Jugtown, where he worked for thirty-five years, he was mentored by Jacques and Juliana Busbee. Much has been written about the Busbees, who did more than any other individuals to publicize and revitalize North Carolina's pottery heritage. Just after World War I, they brought in Charlie Teague as the first Jugtown potter, who was assisted by young Ben Owen starting in 1923. The Busbees marketed Jugtown Ware in New York and out of their shop and residence between Seagrove and Robbins. Jugtown earned a loyal clientele; many customers came to purchase the distinctive candlesticks, tea sets, bean pots, and pitchers, but people also gravitated to Jugtown just to talk with the artistic—and eccentric—Busbees and their star potter, Ben Owen.

On one visit, Owen showed me a tattered notebook of drawings he had made while visiting museums in New York with Jacque Busbee. The Busbees knew that in addition to utilitarian American shapes, classic pottery design and colors from China and Korea were needed to enhance sales of Jugtown Ware in New York. Owen and Busbee observed not only shape and proportion, but thickness and delicacy. To go with the new shapes from the Orient, new glaze colors were added, including a "Chinese blue," the rarest of the original Jugtown Ware colors, which was not produced again after Jacque Busbees death in 1947. The moniker of "artist" was uncomfortable for Ben Owen because he believed deeply that he was using the shapes, colors, and designs of American and Chinese potter/artists who had created the original works. He preferred the term "craftsman."

After Jacques Busbee's death, Owen worked at Jugtown for another dozen years before leaving reluctantly in 1959 to start his own pottery enterprise following legal squabbles over how to save Jugtown and its mark "Jugtown Ware." Only after his departure from Jugtown did Owen begin to mark his pottery "Ben Owen, Master Potter." Apart from the Busbees, Ben Owen was a celebrity in his own right—a fact that I didn't fully appreciate until one Saturday when I found Owen in an animated conversation with a tall, courtly man in a tweed sport coat. Ben introduced me to John Kenneth Galbraith, the renowned Harvard economist and ambassador to India during the Kennedy years. Galbraith said warmly, "Whenever I'm in the area, I come to visit and learn from Ben."

Although I majored in history at Davidson, I felt that during those four years, I had earned a second major in "earth science" from "Professor" Owen, alchemist of clay. In addition to coming to understand something about the properties of clay and the physics of the firing process, I learned from Owen that the life of even an established potter was not easy. Like many potters of the time, his hands and fingers were twisted by arthritis from years of working with cold, damp clay. Being a potter meant staying with a hot kiln for long periods of time to add wood while trying to maintain a desired temperature. For Owen and other great potters of the region, it also meant throwing away work that wasn't perfect.

In 1969, just after my first year in law school, I decided to drive from Chapel Hill to Owen's shop for a Saturday afternoon visit. When I got out of the car, the only sound I heard was the sickening crack of breaking pottery. Alarmed, I ran behind his shop to see Owen methodically examining and then lobbing perfectly good pieces of salt-glaze pottery against a kiln wall. He quietly explained that he was grading and destroying pottery with any defects—bubbles, blemishes, uneven glazes, or variations in shape. I told him that his "seconds" looked pretty good to me, and that it hurt to see his pottery broken. His response has stayed with me for years: "Would you put your name on something that *you know* is not right?"

the tiny plates in clay particles stick together—thus creating the plasticity. Unlike larger soil particles that do not adhere together like the tiny sheets of silicate, clay can be molded, dried, and even fired to become a ceramic—an inorganic, glass-like solid. The same plastic properties of clay that allow it to absorb water and swell (the water between tiny flat surfaces) make it easy to form a delicate bowl on a potter's wheel and difficult to remove a stuck car from a slippery, clay-filled ditch.

Clays can form in place as rock formations weather. The thickest deposits occur, however, in low-energy environments such as lakes and other bodies of water with little current. The Triassic basin areas of North Carolina were the perfect low-energy locations for the deposition of clay particles. Over several million years, deep rifts and cracks filled in with eroded sediments of the Piedmont and the Appalachian range to the west. As layers of inorganic clay particles settled in rift lakes while the continents were pulling apart some 210 million years ago, they created dense seams of clay almost impervious to water. Again, this is why the Triassic basin has been generally marginal for farming and good for potters and brick makers who turned "plastic soil" into clay pots and building materials.

In addition to the red clays found in much of the Triassic basin, potters use a variety of kaolins, which are white and gray clays with a finer texture. Part of the work of each potter was digging and then preparing the clay—cleaning, grinding in "plug mills," mixing with other clays, and curing for weeks—before it was portioned, weighed, kneaded, and placed on the potter's wheel. Properly mixed clay, formed into pitchers, jugs, and bowls, holds its form without cracking or shrinking. After an item is removed from the potter's wheel and air dried, it is ready for firing.

Pottery aficionados soon learn the difference between earthenware and stoneware. The softer earthenwares, primarily made with red-clay mixtures, are fired to approximately 1,800 degrees Fahrenheit and removed with an unglazed flat bisque finish. After a glaze or design is applied to the bisque pottery, it is fired a second time to the same 1,800 degrees. Stoneware, considered harder and more durable than earthenware, is usually made with the gray or white kaolin clays and fired only one time to a much higher temperature of around 2,300 degrees Fahrenheit. During this single firing, salt is sometimes poured into an opening in the kiln, which bonds with the superheated clay to create a speckled salt-glaze finish. To achieve the higher temperatures for firing stoneware, wood that burned hotter and faster, including resin-rich pine, was used.

It should be clear by now that the farmer/potters of the Triassic basin

Stoneware, fired only once at a higher temperature, is considered more durable. The salt-glaze (gray) tea set with blue markings on the top glass shelf is stoneware. Much of the other pottery, including the orange and brown ("tobacco spit") pieces, are examples of twice-fired earthenware.

wore many hats. They were manual laborers (digging, cleaning, and grinding), chemists (mixing the right clays and additives), thermal engineers (maintaining a wood fire at the right temperature for the right length of time), and craftsmen/artists (creating forms with utility and beauty).

Without the continental separation, the rift valleys, and the clay particles deposited over millions of years, there would be no Triassic basin. Without the thick gooey clay of the Triassic, there may not have been the great potter Ben Owen or as many as seven generations of potters whose "marks" include the names Cole, Auman, Teague, Craven, Owens, Luck, and Hancock. Ben Owen and his neighbors were blessed by soil that wouldn't perk and by land that contained too much clay for easy farming. Rather than bow to their misfortunes, the farmer/potters of the Triassic basin turned clay-laden soil into utility and beauty by making bean pots, butter churns, teapots, vases, and candlesticks, which are now regarded as art on every continent.

Like fans of barbecue and basketball, I have discovered that pottery collectors in North Carolina can never agree on their favorite "mud slinger." Just as I appreciated Ben Owen's work, others today are equally passionate about the pottery of Mark Hewitt (Pittsboro); Vernon and Pam Owens (Jugtown); Frank Neef (Seagrove); Ben Owen III, the grandson of Ben Owen (Seagrove); and many others living near the ancient clay-filled crack in the Earth's crust.

You should know one more thing about North Carolina's Triassic basins—a fact that is little known, or appreciated, by the leaders in RTP and the potters of the Seagrove/Sanford area. Under their feet, in that same poor Triassic-clay soil, are world-class fossil deposits. This is the final segment of the Triassic trilogy.

Fossil Fields

Almost every weekday between 8:30 A.M. and 5:00 P.M., the basement of the North Carolina Museum of Natural Sciences sounds like a multichair dental office: one hears the screech of high-speed drills . . . then silence . . . then more whirring, ear-splitting drills. And just as in a dental office, there are bright lights and steady hands at work. But there are no dentists around, only scientists, graduate students, and volunteers removing stone from bone in the museum's paleontology laboratory. The specimens from this state's Triassic terrain are easy to distinguish from others in the laboratory because the stone is typically a rusty-red siltstone over 200 million years old. Some fossil-bearing stone comes from quarries still used by brick companies between Raleigh and Sanford, while other fossils have been found in Triassic-age sedimentary rock encountered during highway construction.

Whenever I entered the museum laboratory, I would instinctively ask the men and women operating the drills the same question: "What kind of dinosaur are you working on today?"

The answer was almost always the same: "I'm *not* working on a dinosaur. This is a type of phytosaurus, and the specimens across the table are rausuchids."

If you know much about these animals, you are in a distinct minority. They lived in the time before the very large dinosaurs (although there were dinosaurs in the Triassic), when other tetrapods (vetebrates with four legs) called archosaurs ruled the land. The top land predators included a

variety of carnivorous rauisuchians, up to twenty-five feet in length, and phytosaurs, semiaquatic crocodile look-alikes. I was reminded that at the beginning of the Triassic, over 250 million years ago, the supercontinent of Pangaea had experienced a mass extinction of plants and animals. The early Triassic period was a time when nature conducted innumerable experiments, as new life forms appeared in every nook and cranny.

When the Pangaean land mass began to burst at the seams and stretch some 220 million years ago, great rift valleys and lakes appeared. Land that would become North Carolina lay near the Equator for much of the Triassic. For millions of years, the edges of warm lakes witnessed the evolution of an enormous variety of plants, reptiles (the first turtles), early mammals, dinosaurs, and insects, including beetles and dragonflies. There were forests of fern, horsetail (looking like giant bamboo), and cycads (palm-like plants with an evergreen leaf top). It was toward the end of the Triassic period that both the rauisuchians and phytosaurs became dominant before most of them disappeared from the fossil record.

The Triassic was a time during which several groups of similar plants

Archosaurs such as the rauisuchian (foreground) ruled the land during much of the Triassic period, while the waters of rift-basin lakes were patrolled by crocodile-like phytosaurs. Steep-walled Triassic rift valleys, as shown in this diorama at the North Carolina Museum of Natural Sciences, were eventually filled with eroded sediments from the west.

(top) Vince Schneider, curator of paleontology at the North Carolina Museum of Natural Sciences, has been a pioneer in the study of Triassic fossils. Here, Schneider is preparing to remove a fossil from mudstone between Durham and Sanford.

(bottom) Bones and teeth from North Carolina's Triassic basins, such as this rauisuchian tooth, are unearthed and studied by museum scientists.

and animals evolved side by side, a process called parallel evolution. The phytosaurs, for example, looked like early models of today's crocodiles or alligators and fed on the same things, yet their branch on the tree of evolution withered and died. For reasons still being sought by scientists, their reptilian cousins (modern crocodiles or alligators) were better able to adapt and are still going strong. The existence of many animals that lived in proto–North Carolina around 200 million years ago are known only because their fossil remains exist in Triassic clay and siltstones.

Dinosaurs soon evolved in size and number, ruling the land through the Jurassic period and until the end of the Cretaceous period (covering the span from approximately 190 million to 65 million years ago). Because nature can be a tough landlord, there was another mass extinction 65 million years ago, which abruptly ended the Age of Dinosaurs and cracked open the door for mammals to rule. North Carolina does not have many exposed geologic formations from either the Jurassic or Cretaceous periods, but in Tar Heel Triassic sediments, we are rich in fossil deposits.

■ I have thought on more than one occasion that activity in the Research Triangle Park today is not much different from that which occurred toward the end of the Triassic over 200 million years ago. Fearsome species evolved and grew in much the same way that corporations evolve and compete in the modern world. Never-ending competition continues in the Triassic basin, pitting the fittest and strongest—creatures or corporations—against each other. Natural history teaches us that through the trials of adaptation and evolution, most animals will eventually become extinct. We also know that many corporations will fail as they compete head-to-head with others in the same businesses (parallel evolution?), or as a result of mass casualties during recessions and depressions (mass extinctions).

The faces frozen in stone and the work being done in the Museum of Natural Sciences should remind us that we are all—living species and businesses—in an evolutionary crapshoot with few guarantees. I am also reminded by Governor Luther Hodges, Ben Owen, and my father that each of us has the ability to make something good happen, even when life throws boulders, or slippery mud, in our way. We can get stuck in Carolina red clay and curse our fate, or we can "turn a sow's ear into a silk purse." Just look at the promise of Research Triangle Park, the work of generations of potters, and the discovery of ancient animals by talented scientists: all were accomplished in soil that wouldn't grow pine or kudzu.

■ The Tar Heel landscape holds one of the most complete rock collections to be found anywhere. Precious stones, bright minerals, and even gold nuggets found in our Piedmont and Mountain region are a result of violent continental collisions during the last 1.2 billion years. Understanding what we are made of, how it arrived, and when our mountains, rivers, and beaches were formed helps explain the past and anticipate opportunities in our future.

4

TAR HEEL TIME

I would like to know if there is a more frequently asked question than "how old is it?" We are all interested in age. It is *the* question asked by archaeologists, paleontologists, geologists, and cosmologists—but most of all, by children. Kids want to know the age of their dog in "people years," the age of dad's baseball glove, the age of the family cat and of mom's old Volvo. But then the questions get more difficult. How old are the Great Pyramids? How old are the mountains?

My kids loved to hear that our thirteen-year-old Labrador, Lulu, was ninety-one in people years. My son did not like to hear that his dad's baseball glove was almost forty years old. I found the age of the Volvo from its registration card, and I could guess at the age of Sydney, the stray cat who had taken up residence with us ten years earlier. I could bluff my way through the ages of the Great Pyramids of Egypt, but the age of mountains and things geologic always elicited wild speculation on my part.

As a child, I had the same questions about the age of the arrowheads I had picked up in fields and of the rocks from which they were made. I was, and still am, a totally indiscriminate collector of rocks—crystals of every kind (clear quartz, purple amethyst, and red garnet), smooth pebbles from favorite streams, cubes of brittle pyrite (fool's gold), sheets of mica, lumpy sapphires, low-grade coal, and chunks of iron ore. My mineral "treasures" were transported in pants pockets, trout-fishing vests, and the trunk of my car. They are displayed on bookshelves, mantles, and desktops and in the window ledges of my office. My largest rocks, colorful rounded boulders found along mountain streams over many years, now encircle wildflower gardens in our yard. Although a few specimens were picked up in other states, countries, or continents, most of my mineral hodgepodge, which could easily be mistaken for highway gravel, was plucked from the soil in North Carolina. In this assemblage—hardly a collection—there are no items of great value. I pick up stones because they are colorful or have a pleasing shape—but most of all, because they provide a direct connection to the places I love.

Just as each valley in our southern Appalachians and each river basin of the Piedmont have unique plants and creatures, splendid diversity in the rocks and minerals can be found a few miles, or a few yards, apart. In the same way that fauna and flora illustrate North Carolina's status as a crossroads, or a natural boundary, representing northern and southern ecosystems, the variety of gems and minerals occurring within Tar Heel borders bespeak an ancient and complex geologic history.

Many of us are deficient in knowledge of the living things around us; too many of us also have a minimal knowledge of local geology. It was only as the number and variety of North Carolina rocks and minerals increased on my shelves that I dug deeper into the history and origin of Tar Heel minerals. For example, I knew little about the "Carolina Gold Rush" of the 1820s, which preceded the 1849 gold rush in California by a quarter century. Mining operations, most located to the east of Charlotte, made North Carolina the leading gold producer in the nation. The history of Tar Heel gold began in 1799 in the sediments of Little Meadow Creek south of Concord (Cabarrus County), where a seventeen-pound nugget was discovered. The remarkable discovery was eclipsed by a twenty-eight-pounder from the same creek in 1803. In the 1830s, North Carolina was the sole source of gold for the U.S. mint in Philadelphia. This new wealth, and the coinage it produced, was so important to a young nation that an official U.S. mint was opened in Charlotte in 1837.

Gold was not the only underground treasure to be found in North Carolina. Also around 1800, one of the largest iron-ore deposits in North America at the time was discovered in Avery County and became known as the Cranberry Iron Mine. Its ore would provide the Confederacy with much of the iron for its cannons in the Civil War. Beginning in 1855, the Ore Hill Mine, near Jefferson in Ashe County, was a major producer of American copper, along with significant amounts of gold and silver. Add to this list the precious and semiprecious stones still being unearthed today, including high-quality emeralds from Mitchell and Alexander Counties, rubies and sapphires from Macon County, aquamarine from several northwest counties, and a host of other gemstones—even some small diamonds. Throughout the Mountain region and the Piedmont, North Carolina is a destination for serious collectors.

Although there are no active coal mines in the state today, Chatham, Montgomery, and Lee Counties were major coal producers during the nineteenth and early twentieth centuries. As was mentioned in chapter 3, North Carolina's coal-mining operations bore little resemblance to the mammoth coal operations seen today in West Virginia, Pennsylvania, and Wyoming. Although important at the time, the amount and quality of North Carolina coal would be considered low in today's market.

Mining is still big business across North Carolina, starting with extensive coastal deposits of phosphate, high-quality clays (for bricks and porcelain) in the Triassic basin, and some of the finest granite for buildings and monuments found anywhere. The largest open-faced granite quarry in the world, supplying monument-quality granite, is located near Mount Airy. In at least eighty of our 100 counties, quarries supply stone aggregate from a variety of stone types—granite, gneiss, greywacke, and limestone. Stone aggregate is crushed stone and rock used in construction and public works (highways, airports, dams, etc.).

Perhaps the best-kept secret of Tar Heel mineral diversity and mining allows North Carolina to remain at the geological epicenter of technology. Much of the world's high-quality quartz is mined in North Carolina—quartz that is indispensible in the making of silicon chips for the world's computers and mobile phones. Just how important is quartz from our northwestern mountains? A story prepared and aired by the British Broadcasting Corporation (BBC) in August 2009 ended with this conclusion: "The world runs on computers, we all know that now. And if we locked the gates to Mitchell County, they could not make any more computers."

The fact that separates North Carolina from better-known mining states is this: we have never been dominated by only one or two sources of mineral wealth. Here, there are no iron ranges like those in Michigan; no Texas-size oil fields; and no mountains of easily accessible coal, as in Wyoming, Pennsylvania, and West Virginia. Rather than being a one-mineral, boom-or-bust location, North Carolina has been bestowed by nature with a generous sampling of many of the world's rocks and minerals. Perhaps because of the diversity of our geology and landscape, the North Carolina economy and the talents of its people are also more diverse.

As a young rock collector, I loved the quest more than the discovery, but it was years before I concluded that to truly know North Carolina, or any other state, a person must have more than a casual knowledge of rocks and minerals. They help explain soil types and what grows here, how mountains and rivers are formed, the industries in our past, and the opportunities in our future. My assortment of crystals, ore samples, pebbles, and rocks introduced me to the basics of geology and helped provide the answers to some questions, but they raised many more. How were they formed in the Earth's crust, and how long had they been there? Perhaps the most vexing question posed by my pile of stones: how can one location, North Carolina, hold such a wide array of the world's minerals and gems? With more than a little help from geologist friends and a few good books, I delved into the questions of geologic age and origin.

North Carolina: A Geologic Crazy Quilt

Most of us never see the stone underpinnings of North Carolina. Whether from the air or from interstate highways, we only catch glimpses of stone beneath soil and vegetation. Only in a few places do we see large protrusions of rock. There are stone outcrops on hillsides, highway cuts, stones exposed by rivers, and a few western mountains that are entirely stone, including Stone Mountain in Alleghany County, Whiteside Mountain in Jackson County, and the ancient rock faces in Hickory Nut Gorge. In the Piedmont are a number of rocky, stand-alone mountains called monadnocks, which include Pilot Mountain, Hanging Rock, and Kings Mountain (near Charlotte).

These visible stone outcrops are only the proverbial tip of the iceberg, because under thin layers of tree roots, topsoil, and clay, most of North Carolina (especially in the Mountain region and the Piedmont) has a foundation of stone. If we could lift this mantle of green, we would see what scientists describe as a geologic "crazy quilt" comprised of rocks and minerals formed at different times and in different places. By understanding the composition of this quilt and how its various pieces—the types of stone making up the North Carolina tableau—got here, it is possible to determine their age. Geologic age and composition can vary dramatically from region to region, from county to county, and from one side of a hill to another.

Because I am not a geologist by training, geological time does not come easily to me. Changes in rivers, mountains, and continents do not take place over months, seasons, years, or even centuries—but over spans lasting millions, tens of millions, or even hundreds of millions of years. To help make

Although most of North Carolina is covered by forest and fields, we know that a stone crust lies beneath the Piedmont and mountains. Stone Mountain in Alleghany County offers a glimpse of what lies beneath. Fortunately, the mountain belongs to all of us as part of Stone Mountain State Park. (Photo by Mike Dunn)

sense of the incomprehensible, geologists have divided geological time events into categories, which include eons, eras, periods, and epochs (eons being longer and epochs shorter). They have been codified by the International Commission on Stratigraphy into a geologic timescale. Almost a decade ago, I bought the Geological Time Table from Elsevier Science and Technology Books (Oxford, UK) for my office. It was intended to be a three-by-five-foot quick reference to the vocabulary of "geologic shorthand" (my term) for scientists and laypersons who work to explain the distant past of the planet and of each continent. Because there is nothing quick about geology, even quick-reference charts and shorthand can hide the big picture,

Of the many impressive rock formations in the North Carolina Piedmont, Pilot Mountain is arguably the most dramatic. The "Pilot," rising almost 1,500 feet above the surrounding landscape, is a monadnock, or a stand-alone mountain. The site is also protected as Pilot Mountain State Park.

At over 400 feet, Whitewater Falls, near Cashiers, is one of the highest and most spectacular waterfalls in eastern America. All rivers and waterfalls constantly wear away and expose the stone around them.

or at least hinder a short explanation. Undaunted, I have prepared for you, the reader, a region-by-region summary of geologic history and ages for major geographic regions of North Carolina. If you still want to know more about the vocabulary of geological time—eons, eras, periods, and epochs—as it applies to North Carolina geological history, please see the sidebar at the end of this chapter.

Appalachian Upheaval

It should come as no surprise that the oldest landscapes in North Carolina are in the far western counties, generally known as the Blue Ridge Belt, which is bordered on the east by another geologic feature, the Brevard Fault Zone. Here, in our mountains, most of the rock is *metamorphic*—squeezed, fractured, folded, heated, and *changed* within the Earth's crust. The metamorphism creating the foundations of the southern Appalachians we know today came in pulses beginning 1.2 billion years ago and ending some 300 million years ago, with each pulse lasting tens of millions of years. Because our final mountain-building event, known as the Appalachian Orogeny (also known as the Alleghanian Orogeny), was completed 300 million years ago, our mountains are very old even in geologic terms.

The earliest rocks in North Carolina's mountains date back to Rodinia, a massive supercontinent that existed some 1.2 billion years ago. As always occurs with supercontinents, Rodinia broke up into smaller landmasses, including Laurentia, which has remained the core of North American landmass. During the next several hundred million years, Laurentia (sometimes referred to as the North American craton) bounced around as part of several lesser supercontinents, which meant more tectonic-plate separations and collisions (mountain-building pulses). Our last mountain building event occurred when Laurentia and other landmasses collided to form another massive supercontinent, Pangaea, a little more than 300 million years ago.

Although the tectonic-plate movements that formed Rodinia, several lesser supercontinents, and Pangaea occurred over tens of millions of years, they were violent events in which the Earth's crust cracked and moved along fault lines. Where faults occurred, land masses rode over, or under, other land mass. In some cases, massive pressures actually caused the Earth's crust to fold. The compression caused by the collision of these land masses was so great that mountain ranges were raised. These include "young" mountains like the Himalayas, the Rockies, the Andes, and the Alps and much older ranges like our own southern Appalachians.

The early Appalachians were high and rugged, with peaks thought to reach 20,000 feet or more in altitude. It was only after more than 250 million years of erosion (wind, water, ice, and plant roots) following the last mountain-building event that the Blue Ridge and Smoky Mountains we now love, with their lush valleys and ancient rivers, were sculpted. By comparison, the younger peaks of the Rockies in the American West were pushed up between 50 and 100 million years ago. Still younger, at an estimated 30 million years old, are the easternmost peaks of the Andes in South America, with numerous peaks over 20,000 feet—mere toddlers compared to North Carolina's ancient Blue Ridge.

To put all this in perspective, the first multicellular life on Earth also appeared around 1.2 billion years ago, the first ferns and treelike plants didn't evolve until about 375 million years ago, and the Age of Dinosaurs ended about 65 million years ago. The rocks anchoring North Carolina in our western counties have witnessed a lot.

Hawksbill Mountain on the east wall of Linville Gorge offers a rare view of the enormous pressures that cause the earth's crust to fold and buckle during continental collisions and separations.

The Exotic, Suspect Piedmont

More than any other landscape in North Carolina, the Piedmont is cloaked in mystery. Much of the western half of the Piedmont (the Inner Piedmont) has long been referred to by geologists as "suspect terrain," while a wide swath of the eastern Piedmont is simply referred to as "exotic terrain." This is in contrast to older "basement rock" in the western mountains, part of original North America. "Suspect" simply means that geologists are not sure where it came from—only that they are most likely "nonnative" lands added to North America during continental collisions.

Geologists are certain, however, about the origin of exotic land known as the Carolina Terrain, which stretches from southern Virginia across North Carolina and well into South Carolina. Like the islands of Japan, and the Aleutians extending from present-day Alaska, the Carolina Terrain was once a separate volcanic island arc before being pushed into the Carolinas by the forces of plate tectonics. It seems strange to use the word "exotic" to describe a volcanic island chain that formed in a distant ocean almost 600 million years ago and slammed into North America more than 300 million years ago. Contained in these volcanic remnants are the cores of old volcanoes, which can be seen as part of the Uwharrie Mountain range in Stanley, Davidson, Montgomery, and Randolph Counties. Perhaps the most important volcanic stone in the Uwharries is igneous rhyolite, the extremely hard stone of choice for early stone-tool makers (see chapter 2). The best known mountain from this ancient island arc is Morrow Mountain, now the focal point of a North Carolina state park that bears its name.

Whether exotic, suspect, or native, all Piedmont rocks are very old, forming between 800 and 200 million B.P. Among the oldest, quartzite rock, in the range of 800 million years old, is a primary component of the Sauratown Mountains, which include both Hanging Rock and nearby Pilot Mountain. The Sauratowns and several other stand-alone mountains (monadnocks) of the Piedmont rise above the landscape to elevations exceeding 2,300 feet (Pilot Mountain). Quartzite—metamorphosed sandstone (changed under pressure and heat) from an ancient ocean—is more erosion resistant than surrounding rock formations. Fortunately, we celebrate these "little mountains" in the Piedmont: in addition to Morrow Mountain, North Carolina state parks are also built around Hanging Rock and Pilot Mountain.

As in our western mountains, many other types and ages of metamorphic rock are to be found in the Piedmont mix, including gneiss, schist, and slate. Along with the igneous formations in the Uwharries, there is newer

North Carolina's many types of rock weather at different rates. Harder rock formations, including volcanic rhyolite in the Uwharrie Mountains of the southern Piedmont, and the quartzite of the Sauratown Mountains above Winston-Salem do not erode as quickly as softer rocks. Here, the quartzite of Hanging Rock (also a state park) still defies the elements hundreds of feet above the surrounding Piedmont terrain below.

igneous rock in the Piedmont, molten material extruded from the Earth's crust and little changed over time. The most common igneous rock in the region is granite (granites can also be changed or metamorphosed). The granite from the earlier mentioned Mount Airy open-faced quarry—and several other granite quarries across the Piedmont—come from granite plutons, rock formed when plumes of magma cooled underground just over 300 million years ago.

North Carolina's Piedmont, our "middle third," also holds large deposits of sedimentary rock (formed when particles settle and accumulate), including mudstone, siltstone, and shale. They were laid down when our fault-bounded Triassic basins began filling with eroded material over 200 million years ago (see chapter 3). Because of the complexity, multiple origins, and geologic age of rock underlying our Piedmont region, we should be grateful to the unheralded geologists who help the rest of us make sense of the pieces of the crazy quilt called North Carolina.

Origins of the Coastal Plain

Finally, the youngest real estate in North Carolina, the Coastal Plain, is made primarily from eroded sediments from the Appalachians and the Piedmont Plateau. Most of this region ranges in age from 65 million years old to only a few million years old. One of the prominent features of the upper Coastal Plain is the Sandhills, extending south from Sanford and Pinehurst into South Carolina. The porous and rolling terrain began as sand dunes along the Carolina shoreline around 20 million years ago. Today, this ancient "beach" 100 miles from the ocean is a land of golf courses and Longleaf Pine.

Once you leave the hilly Piedmont and the gentle slopes of the Sandhills, the entire Coastal Plain is large and flat, comprising almost 40 percent of the state's surface area. Much of the Earth's crust, east of today's Interstate 95, was literally ripped away when the supercontinent Pangaea broke apart over 200 million years ago. The torn edges of North Carolina and much of the eastern United States can be roughly matched with the coastline of Africa between the countries of Mauritania and Morocco. It was only following the rending of Africa from North America that the Coastal Plain of present-day North Carolina began to grow, formed by eroding sediments from 20,000-foot peaks of the young Appalachians and the exotic/suspect Piedmont terrain.

If you dig into the Coastal Plain, you will quickly notice there are no naturally occurring igneous or metamorphic rocks near the surface, but there is a crust of gradual tapering sediments. As the deep deposits of sediment from the west were laid down, North Carolina's coastline was a shallow sea. What you may find in the sediments, as far west as eastern Wake County, are sharks' teeth and other fossil remnants of ancient oceans. The only resistant rock formation (hard rock) in the Coastal Plain is sedimentary rock, known as Castle Hayne limestone. The limestone was formed between 50 and 30 million B.P. in a rich, shallow sea. Organisms that lived in the sea died, fell to the bottom, and left only their shells and bones. The calcium from these remains hardened to form limestone, which still clearly reveals the impressions of the shells and creatures of our most ancient coastline. This limestone is mined today and used as crushed stone aggregate and in the making of concrete.

There is one final geologic slice of the Coastal Plain worthy of mention near where the Tar-Pamlico River flows into the Pamlico Sound. At Aurora, inorganic phosphates, used in fertilizer and other products, are mined from enormous pits sliced through several formations between 3 and 20 million years old.

By now you know many of the sources of my motley collection of rocks and minerals. It was in the valley between Blowing Rock and Boone that I picked up pieces of stone known to be 1.2 billion years old. Near Black Mountain, I have climbed over 800-million-year-old formations in the Black Mountains, which have been twisted and folded like a peppermint candy by the unimaginable ebb and flow of colliding continents. In the late 1950s, I dug crystals of quartz and amethyst and found envelope-sized sheets of mica near Spruce Pine. I climbed the ancient, weathered quartzite summit of Hanging Rock as a teenager and then again fifty years later, only to find it unchanged. As a Boy Scout, I picked up Paleo-Indian projectile points in Davidson County and found chunks of the same glass-like rhyolite from which they were made in the Uwharrie Mountains. It would be decades before I learned rhyolite was an igneous stone from the exotic volcanoes (today's Uwharrie Mountains) brought here by the same forces that pushed up the Appalachians. I have walked through quarries of Castle Hayne and the phosphate mines at Aurora and felt surrounded by the creatures from oceans past.

One cannot uncover, touch, and collect pieces of North Carolina's foundation without feeling compelled to know more about it. Above, you have read the story of our crazy quilt and how geologists think it was assembled. There is one more question: how do we know the age in years of each part,

(top) Castle Hayne limestone was formed in a shallow sea between 30 and 50 million years ago. Most layers of the Castle Hayne formation contain the imprints of ancient mollusks and bivalves that became part of the limestone.

(bottom) One of the largest mining operations in North Carolina is located near Aurora, close to the Pamlico Sound. The phosphate mines expose sections of the earth's crust between 3 and 20 million years old.

The Aurora phosphate pits are famous for dramatic marine fossils, including the teeth of Megalodon, bus-length sharks that once patrolled the North Carolina coastline.

especially when dealing with numbers large enough to be associated with our national debt?

The Story in Quarries

To get the most accurate geologic history of your part of North Carolina, there is no better place to go than to the quarry nearest your house. Why a quarry, you ask? Almost every community has at least one quarry nearby, and whether we realize it or not, each American man, woman, and child currently uses between seven and ten tons of stone products each year. Most of these products come in the form of stone aggregates used in homes, businesses, parking lots, and the schools/highways/airports we pay for as taxpayers. Because it is expensive to haul and cheap to mine, stone is seldom transported more than twenty-five miles from a quarry—meaning there are lots of quarries from Boone to Wilmington. Raleigh alone has eight active quarries around its perimeter. For geologists, these quarries are literally windows into the Earth that allow us to see fresh cuts of the stone beneath our feet.

Some of the quarries are enormous and can spiral 300 feet or more into the bedrock. Such cuts expose fractures and folds in the Earth's crust at multiple angles. Perhaps most important, fresh, unweathered (unaltered) rock samples can be aged using precise radiometric dating techniques. Through radiometric dating, geologic time lines are derived. The chemical elements we learned in high school chemistry all have an atomic number, and these elements may exist in isotopes, which from the time they are formed begin to transform or decay. Only certain elements have radioactive isotopes; not all isotopes are radioactive. By measuring the known rates of decay of *certain* isotopes, actual dates and ages can be obtained. (See the discussion of radiometric dating in chapter 1 measuring the decay of the isotope carbon 14 in organic material. Carbon dating is now indispensible in determining actual ages of *organic* matter from archaeological sites.)

In rock, there are no organic materials containing carbon 14, but there are a number of isotopes that can be measured. For example, where the common mineral zirconium silicate (zircon crystal) is found in rock formations (igneous, metamorphic, or sedimentary), its age can be determined using uranium-lead geochronology. By measuring the decay of uranium-235's to lead-207, rocks containing zircons can be aged with extraordinary accuracy even in samples of rock more than 2 billion years old. Other techniques are available that can be used to determine the age of rocks of even older rock formations. Potassium-argon radiometric dating, measuring the decay of potassium-40 to argon-40, can be used to determine the actual age of the rocks even if they are as old as the Earth itself (4.5 billion years). Suffice it to say, these are simple examples of extraordinary techniques in geochronology available to geologists who determine the age of the rocks comprising our landscape.

Because researchers must use *unaltered* rock sources to get accurate ages, fresh rock from deep within a quarry is ideal. Through the use of one or more radiometric dating techniques, the ages of stone in many quarries have been determined. Knowing the accuracy of these techniques, geologists can determine with certainty the age of the granite from Wake Stone Corporation's quarries in Knightdale and Mount Airy: just over 300 million years old. At the Hedrick Industries quarry in Black Mountain, geologists showed me deposits of greywacke, highly metamorphosed sandstone pushed up during the formation of the Appalachians that is known through radiometric dating to be 700 to 800 million years old.

It is also through radiometric dating that "basement rock" formations near Blowing Rock and Grandfather Mountain were found to be 1.2 billion years old. This technique has given us the age of the volcanic island arc we now call the Uwharrie Mountains. By determining the absolute ages of rock types from a road cut or a quarry, adjacent rock formations above and below can often be assigned a relative age. Although relative ages are not

The granite from Wake Stone Corporation's Knightdale quarry (top), east of Raleigh, is just over 300 million years old. Two hundred miles to the west in Black Mountain, much of the Hedrick Industries quarry (bottom) is composed of greywacke, which was formed almost 800 million years ago. Because of complex geology, the age of the underlying terrain across North Carolina varies greatly.

precise in the same way as dates determined through radiometric dating, it is possible to determine the sequence of appearance. For example, the layers of rock found beneath materials with a known actual age are deemed to be older by relative dating, but there are exceptions.

There is another technique utilized by scientists that doesn't rely on the radiometric measurements and the decay of isotopes. "Index" fossils can tell us much about the age of the sedimentary rocks in which they are found. Extinction is a fact in the life of virtually all species; remember the missing megafauna of the Ice Ages, the giant sharks and whales found in the phosphate pits at Aurora, the dinosaurs of the Cretaceous, the archosaurs of the Triassic, and all of the others plants and smaller creatures that vanished with them. Although hard to comprehend, 99.9 percent of all species of living organisms that have lived on the planet are now extinct. In some rock formations of a known age, scientists can identify and even classify extinct species, as well as when their fossils first appear on the geologic time line. When the species ceases to exist in sediments, we can infer that it is extinct.

It was near Wilmington at the Castle Hayne limestone quarry, owned by Martin Marietta Materials, that three professional geologists, including a company geologist, showed me the impressions of several species of extinct mollusks of a known age in the limestone stratigraphy. Such fossils are known as "index species." When fossil remains of species known to have lived between 30 and 35 million years ago are found in rock stratigraphy at another location, the same age can be assigned to the rock formation based on the *known age* of index fossils. By knowing the time span during which an index species lived, the three geologists at Castle Hayne were able to assign with confidence an age range to bands of limestone. Thus, whether through radiometric dating, relative dating, or with the aid of index fossils, modern science has many tools to tell us the age of the rock around us.

■ Having read the material above, you won't have to sweat anymore when your children or grandchildren begin asking the question, "How old is it?" You already knew how to give the age of cars, antique furniture, and even the age of the Pyramids of Egypt. You could even convert dog years into people years.

Now, when a child asks you how old the oldest mountains in North Carolina are, you can ask her which range—the Uwharries, the Sauratowns, or the Black Mountains? When she asks, "How old is North Carolina?," just let her know that she lives on a very interesting crazy quilt of different ages. And be prepared to convert all age ranges from people years to dog years.

THE VOCABULARY OF TIME

When you have the time, take a leap into the unfamiliar and learn the terminology of geology. You may already know some of it. The current eon on the geologic timescale, covering the present day all the way back to 542 million years B.P., is called the Phanerozoic eon. It marks the moment in time when the Earth's hard-bodied animals and terrestrial plants first began to increase exponentially. It was preceded by the Proterozoic eon, which covered the span of time from 542 million years B.P. all the way back to 2.5 billion years B.P. It marked the gathering of oxygen in the atmosphere, the first complex organisms, and the first supercontinents. There are only two more eons, the Archean and the Hadean, which extend back to the formation of the planet Earth approximately 4.5 billion years ago.

There are ten geologic eras covering the same period of time—from the present day to 4.5 billion years ago. I'll only mention the first three, beginning with the Cenozoic era (beginning today and extending back 65 million years ago). The Cenozoic marks the extinction of the great dinosaurs and the beginning of the Age of Mammals. It is also the time when the continents we know today fell into place. You may have already guessed that the earlier Mesozoic era (65 million to 250 million years B.P.) is the Age of Reptiles. It also marks the formation and breakup of the supercontinent Pangaea. The last era I will mention is the Paleozoic era (250 million to 542 million years B.P.), which began with the largest mass extinction known to have occurred. It should be remembered, however, for the explosion of modern life forms that followed the extinction event.

As you have surmised by now, "eras" are further subdivided into a third category, "periods." A few examples will suffice. The modern era, known as the Cenozoic, is broken into three periods: the Quaternary, Neogene, and Paleogene. The Quaternary period, the period in which we now live, is the geological time marked by repeated cold and warm periods resulting in as many as twenty glacial and interglacial episodes (extending from the present to 2.5 million years B.P.). It is this period that has witnessed the extinction of the Ice Age megafauna and the rise of man as Earth's dominant creature. The Neogene period spanned the gap from 2.5 million to 23 million years B.P. During this period, the modern forms of birds and mammals now with us evolved on landforms that looked very similar to those on the planet today. Also during the Neogene, North and South America joined together at the location of present-day Panama, cutting off an important connection between the Atlantic and the Pacific (later reopened with the Panama Canal). The final period of the Cenozoic era is the Paleogene, which began 65 million years ago and ended roughly 23 million years ago. It was during this period that large mammals evolved (following the extinction of dinosaurs). There was also considerable tectonic-plate movement, the time during which much of the Andes, the Rocky Mountains, and the Himalayas were formed (all "young" mountains).

Going further back in time, the Cenozoic era was preceded by the Mesozoic era, better known as the Age of Reptiles. It contains three periods on the geologic time table: the Cretaceous, the Jurassic, and the Triassic. If you aren't familiar with each of them, ask your dinosaur-loving children. You should recall that the Cretaceous period (65 to 145 million years B.P.) was made famous by Tyrannosaurus Rex (or simply T. Rex); was a time of high sea levels and a warm global climate; served as the launching pad for deciduous trees and many species of mammals; and ended with another global extinction event closing the curtain on the Age of Dinosaurs. The Jurassic period (145 million to 200 million years B.P.) is the easiest to remember: just think of the movie *Jurassic Park*. It was the time when dinosaurs were at their zenith during the Age of Reptiles, but, more important, it marked the breakup of the supercontinent Pangaea and the outlines of today's continents around 200 million years B.P. The final subdivision of the Mesozoic, the Triassic period (200 million to 300 million years B.P.), saw the formation of the supercontinent Pangaea and the last mountain-building events in the Appalachian chain. The Triassic period included the evolution of new plant and animal species, especially reptiles, following the great mass extinction marking the end of the Paleozoic era and the beginning of the Mesozoic era. During the Triassic period, the land that would become North Carolina was situated on the Equator in a warm, wet environment in which life could flourish. For North Carolina, the Triassic is memorialized by the great Triassic basins (see chapter 3), the ancient rift valleys near the line where Africa began pulling away from North America some 220 million years B.P.

Finally, the same slices of geologic history carved above into eons, eras, and periods are sliced once again on geological timescales into smaller units called epochs. You should have the gist of the process by now. Our current period, the Quaternary, is divided into two epochs: the Holocene and Pleistocene. The Holocene epoch (10,000 years B.P. to the present) marks the beginning of the impact of human beings on our planet. It also marks the end of the great Ice Age mammals known as megafauna. Preceding the Holocene is the Pleistocene epoch (from 2.5 million to 10,000 years B.P.). You already know this epoch as the Ice Ages, the series of glacial and interglacial climate activity before modern humans. There are many more epochs subdividing the longer geologic time spans known as periods. And as you have no doubt surmised, even epochs are further subdivided into geologic time lines applying specifically to regions and continents.

I hope that this crash course in geologic timescales is useful to your understanding of the age of the Earth, with special emphasis on the patch of land called North Carolina. Geologic time shorthand is wonderful for those that work in geology, paleobotany (the study of ancient plants), and climatological history, but it can be confusing to nonscientists if you don't happen to have a three-by-five-foot chart to fall back on.

Although as a nonscientist, I still prefer knowing the age of our landscape in absolute or relative numbers, a check of my wall chart tells me that we are living in the Holocene epoch. The Holocene marked the end of the Pleistocene epoch—the Ice Ages—and the beginning of the impact of humankind on the planet Earth. How long will this current epoch last? Some scientists are now arguing that the Holocene, which began 10,000 years B.P., maybe be extremely short-lived by geological standards. They propose that we may have already entered a new epoch, the Anthropocene, which marks the profound influence on and change (some call it destruction) of the Earth's surface and atmosphere wrought by modern man. These scientists contend that the Anthropocene epoch began with the Industrial Revolution in the eighteenth century. A few argue a new epoch began earlier at the time when widespread farming and forestry practices changed landscapes. Whether a new epoch, the Anthropocene, will be included in the Geological Time Table available to my great-grandchildren a century from now, I will never know. Personally, I hope we learn to become kinder, gentler stewards of the planet Earth—starting with North Carolina—while remaining in the Holocene epoch for millennia to come.

PART II.
DIVERSITY AND
BOUNDARIES

■ In some North Carolina towns and neighborhoods, you won't see the large array of butterflies, moths on porch screens, or fireflies at sunset that were present just a generation ago. You may also miss the sound of familiar songbirds or the buzz of cicadas on a summer's eve. Too many of us have replaced native vegetation—one yard at a time—that is required by insects and birds with fast-growing, problem-free plants and trees. North Carolina is now a divided land of natural and exotic landscapes.

5

BUTTERFLIES — WITHOUT THE WORMS

I graduated from high school in 1964, but I never heard or used the terms "species diversity" and "ecosystem" until I took college biology or even later than that. The Environmental Protection Agency and the Endangered Species Act didn't exist yet. Even though many years passed before I fully appreciated the extreme diversity of life found in North Carolina, the seeds of recognition of such unusual bounty were planted at my family's summer cabin on Bearwallow Mountain in the 1950s. We were at 3,000 feet in the Upper Hickory Nut Gorge just east of Asheville. Like so many children, then and now, who live on farms or in rural areas, a subtle biology lesson awaited every time I walked out the door.

Much of my time was spent on, or in, the water. In the tiny creek behind our cabin, every rock was home to a salamander, and each stair-step pool was guarded by a crayfish. I found them all. Just down the hill, a one-acre pond held Bluegill, Redbreast (Long-Eared Sunfish), and Largemouth Bass. I knew every inch of the pond and the lair of every bass over two pounds. The pond's Bullfrogs and Leopard Frogs always produced a summer's worth of excitement in the form of tadpoles. Snapping Turtles, Muskrats, Blue Herons, and plenty of water snakes were also at the pond to pick up the slack when the fishing was slow.

On the rare occasion when the pond failed to entertain, there was another "water park" just a few hundred yards away. At the base of Bearwallow Mountain, Hickory Nut Creek ran through the tiny community of Gerton. If you watched carefully on a summer's day, you could see wild Rainbow Trout, scarcely nine inches long, picking off mayflies and caddis flies as they danced over ripples. It was in a bend of this creek in front of Roy Owenby's house that I caught my first trout with a grasshopper for bait during my eighth summer.

Although the watery playgrounds were magnets for a fish-obsessed kid, there was much more to see on the mountain. A constant image in my memory is the lush green canopy of Chestnut Oak, Basswood, Sweet Birch, Yellow Buckeye, Tulip Poplar, and White Pine. The most interesting trees on Bearwallow Mountain, however, were dead, though many still stood tall, gray, and straight, like stone pillars. In the early 1950s, ghostly trunks were all that remained of the great stands of American Chestnut, killed by the "blight" (an introduced Asian fungus) between 1910 and 1950. Ironically, the old road in front of our house was still called Chestnut Hill.

Every community needs a naturalist Pied Piper who children will follow and who never tires of answering questions. Chestnut Hill had Mrs. Asbury, better known as "Aunt Winnie," although she was not related to any family on the mountain. With white hair and bulging eyes, and by then well into her eighties, Aunt Winnie lived year-round in a cottage at the top of the hill with her husband, "Uncle Jinks." She was proud of the neat rows of hydrangeas and boxwoods in her yard, but she also tended several patches of wildflowers, including Mayapple, Solomon's Seal, Jack-in-the-Pulpit, and several types of trillium in the shade along her rock walls. She would show you orange Butterfly Weed, scarlet Fire Pinks, and head-high Turk's-Cap-Lilies in an open space behind her house. Sitting on her porch, she would tell her young fans about the birds on the mountain, but mostly she talked about the Ruby-Throated Hummingbirds that came to her feeders. She was the first to tell me the common names of various groups of butterflies on Bearwallow Mountain—sulphurs, swallowtails, fritillaries, and skippers. In the eyes of all the eight-to-ten-year-olds on our mountain, Aunt Winnie knew everything there was to know about nature.

With all that the mountain had to offer during the day, the real diversity show took place at night on our front porch. A warm summer's night sparkled with fireflies, which we called lightning bugs, and was filled with the sounds of unseen cicadas, crickets, tree frogs, and owls. If the light on our porch was turned on for even a few minutes, delicate mayflies, fearsome dobsonflies (with long mandibles), and beetles in every size and color appeared on the screen door. There were noisy, large-bodied sphinx moths

Of all the night visitors that appeared on the porch on Bearwallow Mountain, none were more welcome than the magnificent Luna Moth (top) and the giant Cecropia Moth (bottom). Luna moths require specific native "host plants," including Black Walnut and several species of hickory and birch. With its six-inch wingspan, the Cecropia is the largest moth in North America. Its native host plants include Sassafras, Black Cherry, and Red Maple. (Photos by Mike Dunn)

(several species) that looked like jet fighter planes with wings folded. Summer nights meant lots of bats in the yard—and frequently, to my mother's disgust, in our house.

The most welcome night visitors were several species of giant silk moths called Saturnids. These magnificent creatures with a four- to five-inch wingspan and fern-like antennae included the Cecropia and Polyphemus. Their wing patterns of brown, red, and gold were more elegant than any oriental rug. As a boy not yet in my preteens, I found the true superstars of a July night to be the lime-green Luna Moths. They were surreal creatures, with deep, feminine curves in their long-tailed wings, which mesmerized every visitor on our porch. On more than one occasion, however, the spell was broken when a bat swooped across the porch just over our heads and snatched a Luna out of the air in midflight.

Although the term "biodiversity" wouldn't become established in the national vocabulary until the 1980s, I now know that I experienced it in the forests on Bearwallow Mountain, in the pond, in the creeks, at the feet of Aunt Winnie, and during those summer nights on our cabin porch, so rich in sounds and sights. Unfortunately, fast-forwarding fifty years to today, a number of plant and creature populations have diminished in many areas of North Carolina and the nation. As our population has grown dramatically in the last half century, forests have been cleared for towns and subdivisions. Such change is understandable, but with it has come another troubling development that may have escaped your notice.

A Desert of Flowers and Trees

As you drive through almost any small town or big city in North Carolina—down "Main Streets" or through parks and subdivisions—you will likely encounter an ecological desert of flowers and trees. The use of the word "desert" is appropriate, even though many species of trees with shiny green leaves and flowers in brilliant colors can be found in such areas. Look closer: our yards and parks are frequently devoid of much of the native plant and animal life that would have been found at the same location only a couple of generations ago.

A change has occurred, and it has almost escaped notice in a sea of sprinklers and green vegetation. My family and I have observed a distinct decline in biodiversity in the Raleigh neighborhood where we now live. A few years after we moved into our house some twenty years ago, we enjoyed the same lightning bug show that I used to see in the mountains. On a summer's night, all over our neighborhood, a silent fireworks display could be seen hovering in low spots and around bushy thickets. Now, as our son and daughter are heading off to college, my wife and I still watch closely for fireflies, but there are few. There are wild night sounds, but not the symphony that entertained us during the first few years in the neighborhood. An occasional bat will buzz our front yard, but less frequently than in the past. We have several species of butterflies, but not the numbers we once observed, despite our efforts to attract them. Three years ago, there was a minor celebration when a lone Luna Moth clung to the screen on our back porch.

Before you accuse me of trying to resurrect a fantasy world that never existed or of preaching doom and gloom, let me emphasize that most of the wild things from my memory can still to be found in North Carolina, and I see them regularly as I travel across this state. Breathtaking biodiversity still flourishes in every geographic region within our borders. It remains possible to be surrounded by numerous owls, woodpeckers, and migratory warblers in the hardwood bottomlands of the Chowan and Roanoke Rivers in the northeast corner of our state. Concentrations of both common and unique plants and animals can still be found in the remnant Longleaf Pine forests in the Sandhills and in the southeastern lowlands near Wilmington. Stretches of wilderness in the Uwharrie National Forest east of Charlotte and in the Sauratown Mountains above Winston-Salem are as stunning as any landscape in the Piedmont of the southeastern United States. Across the Mountain region of North Carolina are cradles of diversity as rich as any found in the temperate latitudes of our planet. You can immerse yourself in the best of the natural world in Linville Gorge and on Grandfather Mountain, in the Great Smoky Mountains National Park, and in the 3 million acres of the Pisgah and Nantahala National Forests.

You are probably confused by now. How can a growing state and region be the location of numerous "ecological deserts" and also be home to a multiple listing of naturalists' paradises?

Although most of us, especially our kids, know the meaning of the terms "biodiversity" and "ecosystem," knowing does not necessarily equate to understanding. I have come to believe that many of us regard diversity in nature as a mere curiosity, something of interest to scientists, naturalists, and a few others but not worthy of celebration. It is easier to regard the loss of a few species and the destruction of critical habitat as someone else's problem and not a crisis that ultimately affects each of us. After all, much of the loss of plant and animal diversity about which we read and hear involves distant rain forests or tropical reefs that we may never visit. We also like to take solace in the thought that most ecological damage is done far away by nameless "big corporations" responsible for clear-cutting whole forests and stripping away mountaintops.

Think for a moment about the habitat damage that may be occurring in your own yard. In many small, often insidious ways, each of us has played a part in making dramatic changes to the fauna and flora around us. As I indicated earlier, in North Carolina and much of the developed world, large patches of urban and suburban land, including yards, highways, and most parks, have evolved into ecologically challenged landscapes.

How could this have happened? After all, many of us have large, lush green lawns and live near parks, soccer fields, golf courses, or greenways. We buy our plants and trees at the local lawn-and-garden center. What about the huge patches of flowers along our interstates and the magnificent flowering trees lining the entrance to subdivisions? Even our shopping centers have beautiful trees with shinny leaves separating parking lanes. So what's the problem?

Somewhere along the way, we bought into the idea that form and appearance of our lawns, neighborhoods, and parks is more important than ecological function. We like our songbirds, but not the insects that many of them require. We were convinced at the lawn-and-garden center, or by recurring television ads, that we needed an herbicide or fungicide in our fertilizer to kill all those grubs and pests infesting our lawns, but no one told us that those grubs were next summer's lightning bugs and ladybugs. Many of the trees, flowers, and shrubs bought at the lawn-and-garden center were advertised as "pest resistant," and that, too, sounded like a good idea. Just as pharmaceutical ads on the evening news have heightened our awareness of many previously unknown infirmities, such as "restless leg" and "got-to-go-right-now" syndromes, as a nation of suburbanites, many of us have unwittingly become yard hypochondriacs. We will pay whatever is necessary to engage in mortal combat with patches of crabgrass or a stray dandelion.

This desire for "beauty without bother" was underlined for me by Bill Reynolds, an entomologist at the North Carolina Museum of Natural Sciences who minces few words. He frequently hears how much people love butterflies and moths, but he is disturbed by what else he hears. As curator of entomology at the museum, Reynolds is often asked variations of two questions that pose an environmental conundrum. "Visitors frequently ask, 'What can I do to attract more butterflies?'" Reynolds says. "But some of the same people also ask, 'How can I eliminate the ugly worms in my yard that eat my flowers and strip the leaves off maples and oaks?' Even well-educated people just don't understand that you can't have butterflies without the worms—caterpillars!"

Reynolds and his staff tell summer visitors to the museum that good populations of Lepidoptera (moths and butterflies) require nectar plants and host plants. Nectar is the sweet liquid sought by adult butterflies, bees, other insects, and some birds. But even with an abundance of favored nectar plants, butterflies cannot survive in your neighborhood or subdivision without host plants. These are the flora on which butterflies lay their eggs and that provide the food for hungry caterpillars.

With few exceptions, host plants are *not* the same plants as nectar plants. To attract and hold populations of moths and butterflies, you must have both plants in your yard, but there is a hitch: nectar plants that attract one or two species of butterflies often are not sought out by any other species. The same is true with host flora: host plants that serve as egg sites and food for the caterpillars of several species of moths and butterflies may be totally unsuitable for others common to your area. Consequently, to attract a variety of Lepidoptera, yards and neighborhoods must have a wide diversity of native plants. It would be nice to think that merely having a colorful yard with numerous species of trees, flowers, and shrubs would guarantee nectar and host plants suitable for a variety of Lepidoptera. Twenty-five years ago, when native flora in most areas was the norm, this may have been true, but not today.

Try to name the flowers and flowering trees that you see in your neighborhood and yard from late spring to early fall. I'll bet there are white and pink azaleas, forsythia, daffodils, wisteria, roses, geraniums, day lilies, and ornamental cherry/pear trees like the Bradford Pear. Think of the trees, vines, and plants on your street that might serve as host plants for ravenous caterpillars. Especially if you live in a newer neighborhood or subdivision in North Carolina and the Southeast, chances are pretty good that you can find Bradford Pear (a variety of Callery Pear), Mimosa, English Ivy, Crape Myrtle, Deodar Cedar, Sawtooth Oak, Japanese Zelkova (the elm without problems), and Norway Maple. All are readily available from local nurseries and garden centers.

Now think carefully: how many butterflies have you seen getting nectar from your roses, azaleas, or Crape Myrtles? Have you seen caterpillars munching on your Deodar Cedar, Sawtooth Oak, or Ginkgo? No question about it, these are beautiful, often fast-growing, hardy plants and trees that can be a lovely addition to any yard. Some are even "well behaved" and stay where they are planted without spreading their unwanted progeny. Unfortunately, with few exceptions, most of these commonly planted trees are not suitable nectar or host plants for North Carolina Lepidoptera. Many of the commercially available plants introduced by the developer of your neighborhood or purchased at your local garden center are alien to this region. Crape Myrtle, Mimosa, Ginkgo, and Sawtooth Oak, for example, are exotics, natives of China and Southeast Asia. Deodar Cedar is native to northern India and the Himalayas. (See chapter 12 for more about exotic and invasive species in your neighborhood.)

Generalists and Specialists

We must remember that to insects and other animals, not all plants are created equal. Just because they are "plant eaters" doesn't mean they can eat, or survive on, just any plant. Many exotics evolved in a country or region that has a similar climate to North Carolina. The "taste and texture"—actually the chemical content—of plants alien to a particular region is frequently unacceptable to local insects that evolved over thousands of generations with other plants. The fact that they are exotics is the very reason they are frequently "pest resistant." When alien plants are introduced to a new region, the insect herbivores that dined on them are left behind.

Many insects, especially moths and butterflies, are specialists, meaning that they require specific plants to provide them nectar or to host their eggs and larvae. Some become generalists and are able to eat or utilize a wider variety of plants. Think about your own plant-eating habits. You may enjoy green beans, watercress, broccoli, celery, and lettuce. But you can't eat oak leaves, tulips, ivy, or the grass in your front yard. If you could not get the food that you wanted or needed, you would have to move elsewhere. Like the caterpillar of a Zebra Swallowtail or a Luna Moth, our sensory systems and digestive systems have evolved to be attracted to and digest specific plants.

Plants also have needs. During the evolutionary process, many plants, as links in the food chain, become dependent on the animals that eat them or require their nectar; the important services provided by these animals include pollination, seed distribution, and fertilization. Simply stated, many of the butterflies and moths (along with many other creatures) native to your region of North Carolina or America have coevolved with their nectar and host plants and have literally become dependent on them for survival. Thus, when the Sweet Gums, Red Maples, Tulip Trees, Pawpaws, Sweet

What happens when we substitute alien (exotic) plant biomass for the native species with which our fauna evolved? No author has better connected the dots between the loss of native plants, insects, and birds with the choices we make in our cities and yards than Douglas Tallamy of the University of Delaware. In his 2007 book, *Bringing Nature Home*, Tallamy eliminates any doubt about the connection between the displacement of native vegetation by exotics and the decline of native fauna. Tallamy cites previously unpublished experimental evidence from a study he performed in Oxford, Pennsylvania: "In a survey of insect herbivores found eating woody native and alien species . . . native plants produced over four times more insect biomass that alien plants produced. This difference resulted entirely from the inability of insects with chewing mouthparts to eat alien plants." In a related study, also done in Oxford, Pennsylvania, Tallamy found that, "in a comparison of Lepidoptera larvae produced on native and alien woody plants[,] . . . native plants supported 35 times more caterpillar biomass, the preferred source of protein for most bird nestlings, than alien plants supported."

Douglas Tallamy's findings support what many of us have known intuitively for years: small changes—actions by a single landowner—can make a difference. Do we need any more compelling reasons why we should plant and maintain native vegetation in our yards and communities?

Shrubs, Button Bushes, and Black Willows that once made up the forests and understory where your subdivision is located were replaced by rows of Bradford Pear, Sawtooth Oak, and hybrid hollies, the fundamental needs of many specialist butterflies and moths were removed. As more subdivisions, shopping centers, and even parks are developed and native plants necessary for the survival of Lepidoptera are replaced, moths and butterflies will continue to decrease as they are pushed into smaller and smaller pockets of suitable habitat.

Not long ago, I spent a week in London in the middle of July with my wife and daughter. During a sightseeing tour of Buckingham Palace, we were struck by many acres of formal, manicured flower beds alive with blooms of red geraniums and several blue flowers. However, on a rare eighty-degree English day with bright sun, something was missing. We saw no butterflies, no insects of any kind, and not a single species of bird—except for pigeons. We wondered aloud if Queen Elizabeth or Prince Charles, heir to the throne and an ardent naturalist, would approve if they knew that royal public gardens contained no native flowers attractive to any of the more than sixty species of butterflies found in the United Kingdom. During the same trip, we had seen plenty of butterflies in other parts of London and England, but in the Queen's own front yard, among thousands of blossoms, there appeared to be no nectar plants of interest to England's butterflies. Whether in a royal residence or a more humble North Carolina home, none of us are exempt from the laws of evolution. We cannot simply remove those things with which we coevolved without consequences.

If You Plant It, They Will Come

I admit that for much of my six decades, I have been oblivious to the elimination of important ecosystems in my own yard and in the neighborhoods in which I have lived. I now find it difficult to be both quiet and passive as large pieces of our landscape are being altered for short-term aesthetic gain. The biodiversity that has long characterized North Carolina and our region is part of our legacy to the next generation, no less than a good system of public education, a sound highway–public transit infrastructure, a strong economy, and clean air. The natural world has remarkable recuperative powers when given a little help and time. I have witnessed such regeneration in stream-improvement projects, in badly eroded hillsides, and at once-blighted industrial sites. Perhaps that is why I have always been an optimist when it comes to the natural world. I believe that the efforts of each property owner and municipality can make a huge difference in reestablishing and maintaining ecological diversity, a critical component of a high quality of life. I also want to believe that all of us, when properly informed, will make the right decisions.

Several years ago, I was traveling in the mountains near Boone with videographer and friend Joe Albea. We were looking for butterflies to photograph on a warm day in July. Moving along fifty miles of back roads, we stopped several times to film small numbers of butterflies on isolated patches of Joe-Pye Weed, Passion Flower, and Butterfly Weed. We stopped next to a small creek to record several dozen Tiger Swallowtails competing for the same small cluster of bright red Bee Balm. At about 4:00 P.M., we rounded a curve and watched as a cloud of butterflies hovered over a fifty-foot stretch of right-of-way. There were literally hundreds of fritillaries, monarchs, swallowtails, sulphurs, skippers, and hairstreaks. An individual flower frequently held a dozen butterflies, causing plant stems to bend under the weight. Along a roadside ditch were plenty of sweet-smelling Common Milkweed plants in full bloom, six-foot Turk's-Cap-Lilies, and billowy pink Joe-Pye Weed. In the field behind the ditch were other nectar plants, including Bull Thistle and Ironweed.

Joe and I had a similar experience in eastern North Carolina earlier that same summer when we came upon a line of Button Bushes covered with white blooms along a ditch bank east of Tarboro. There, also, we were treated to squadrons of butterflies, mostly Zebra Swallowtails, rising in unison as we disturbed their nectar gathering.

In both instances, there were varied native host plants nearby. In the mountains, we saw native maples, cherries, different oaks, and several birches. Near Tarboro, we saw Black Willow, Sycamore, Water Tupelo, White Ash, Sweet Gum, Red Bay, and numerous Pawpaw trees (the key host plant for Zebra Swallowtails).

These wild, seemingly random explosions of butterflies were not random at all. Even to a nonbotanist like me, it was clear that both locations had all of the elements for a perfect butterfly garden: a variety of native nectar plants and the right mixture of native host plants. If there is a rich and varied native plant community, there will be a large number of butterflies of several different species.

You may be surprised when I tell you that such rich concentrations of life can be attracted within a few years, even in the most unlikely places. Not long ago, a thirty-five-acre tract of land, formerly a pasture, lay within a few hundred yards of the large arena where the North Carolina State Wolfpack play basketball and the Carolina Hurricanes play ice hockey. After several controlled burns to get rid of invasive weeds and trees, parts of the tract were replanted with dozens of tree and shrub species native to North Carolina. The rest of the land was planted in native wildflowers and grasses that dominated the Tar Heel Piedmont just a few generations ago. Some of these flowers and grasses stood more than six feet tall by midsummer. A small pond was also built in a natural hollow.

As I write this seven years after this site, called the Prairie Ridge Ecostation, was established, the explosion of wildlife has been nothing short of phenomenal. The native vegetation has attracted a plethora of birds, butterflies, and beetles. Katydids, crickets, and a splendid assortment of grasshoppers cling to long blades of prairie grass from late spring until the first frost. The pond is now home to thirteen species of frogs, salamanders in several shapes and colors, and a host of aquatic insects, my favorites being gaudy dragonflies. As in any productive ecosystem new or ancient, the plants and animals of Prairie Ridge are species that evolved with each other and depend on each other. I have visited this miracle of restoration dozens of times with family members and by myself. It is a long-term project of the North Carolina Museum of Natural Sciences and is open to everyone.

Encounters like these across this state have assured me that good stewardship of the land, even of small patches in suburbia, will be rewarded.

Throughout the summer, the pond at Prairie Ridge Ecosystem is alive with many species of gaudy dragonflies. These agile creatures, which date back to the Triassic period, can be found in almost every slow-moving body of water in North Carolina.

I now count a number of people as friends who "went native" long before I thought about it. Their successes on ecologically challenged landscapes prove that yards and neighborhoods can be revived.

Breaking Bad Habits

I am under no illusion that breaking old lawn-and-garden habits is easy. As our computers, smart phones, drive-thru fast-food restaurants, and coffee/latte windows have improved technologically and gotten faster, so have lawn services. Developers and landscapers have given us what we want: instant green. Turf carpets can be purchased and unrolled in an afternoon, so why should anyone wait for seeds to grow? We can have instant shade with fast-growing fifteen-foot Bradford Pear trees or Zelcova planted with a forklift, even in the middle of the summer.

In this climate of instant gratification, how do changes come about? In our market economy, suppliers will adjust their products to meet changing demands. Just as our demands for instant green have been met, a demand for native plants will also be met by the marketplace—but only after our buying habits have changed.

It is both unrealistic and expensive to make major changes all at once. The half acre my family and I live on came with Dogwood, Red Oak, Red

If you have a stream or moist area in your yard, plant a Button Bush. Few native plants attract more species of butterfly. Their unique "starburst" flowers and lush green foliage make it an interesting yard plant.

Maple, Tulip Poplar, Loblolly Pine, Southern Magnolia, and a mixed bag of exotics. When our children were born, my wife and I planted an American Beech for each of them. When Hurricanes Fran and Floyd dropped several of our large trees and ripped the limbs off others, we viewed the open spaces as opportunities. It took some looking, but we found Swamp White Oak, Eastern Hemlock, Sourwood, Pawpaw, Sassafras, Bald Cypress and Longleaf Pine. Very slowly, we have replaced many of our exotic bushes and understory plants—including azalea, nandina, and privet—with native shrubs. My favorite natives include Witch Alder (Fothergilla), Button Bush, and Fringe Tree (Graybeard). All three of these have lovely white flowers, and no plant is more fragrant than the Fringe Tree. Each of these is either a nectar plant or a host plant for various Lepidoptera. We have also encouraged several volunteer natives that the wind or birds brought to our yard, including Red Bud, Black Cherry, Black Willow, American Holly, and Willow Oak.

Over the past decade, I also have fought an ongoing war against English Ivy that wants to choke every tree, climb the house, and cover the ground. I have mowed it, pulled it, attacked it with a hatchet, and poisoned it with careful applications of herbicide. A most wonderful native vine, Coral Honeysuckle, has now completely replaced the English problem child in our backyard. This is a North Carolina native with beautiful coral trum-

(top) Coral Honeysuckle is a magnet for hummingbirds and, by any measure, one of the most beautiful of our native flowering vines. The honeysuckle shown here, located in the author's yard, adds beauty and serves as a "lunch stop" for Ruby-Throated Hummingbirds and many other creatures.

(bottom) If you have always thought this was a large species of bee, join the club! This native Clear-Winged Hummingbird Moth, which flies like a hummingbird and looks like an exotic bumblebee, will come to your Coral Honeysuckle or, as shown here, to native Bee Balm. Wouldn't your yard be more interesting if it hosted such creatures? (Photo by Mike Dunn)

One of the most resilient and heat-resistant native flowers of midsummer is the Purple Coneflower. While in bloom, and when it dries and goes to seed, this species from the genus *Echinacea* attracts butterflies and birds, including the Goldfinch shown here.

pets that are magnets for hummingbirds and a fantastic daytime moth, the Clear-Winged Hummingbird Moth (a species of sphinx moth).

In the sun and semishade where shrubs once grew, we have also planted wildflowers. Although the mix has changed from time to time, we have established plantings of Purple Coneflower, Black-Eyed Susan, orange Butterfly Weed, Common Milkweed, Joe-Pye Weed, Turk's-Cap-Lily, Cardinal Flower, and Blazingstar. In the shaded areas, we have Trout Lily, Blood Root, and Red Columbine. We acquired these slowly and in small numbers from native-plant nurseries, from the North Carolina Botanical Garden in Chapel Hill, and through plant swaps with friends.

You may have wondered how so many different trees, shrubs, and flowers can fit in a half acre. The truth is that as we have added more trees and shrubs, the amount of grass that my son and I mow has shrunk dramatically. Our yard is green but far from being all grass. It is an equal-opportunity lawn, where clover, dandelions, mushrooms, and patches of violets are welcome. We have not used pesticides and have used only the occasional herbicide (on the ivy). A thing of beauty, probably not, but it is definitely interesting!

The thing we are most proud of in our yard are "munch marks," the leaves chewed by caterpillars and other yard critters. Though we are in the middle of Raleigh, we have a healthy population of rabbits, squirrels, and lots of chipmunks. The odd mix of trees and shrubs have also attracted many

WHERE TO START?

The list of trees, vines, shrubs, and especially wildflowers native to your region of North Carolina is long, so ask questions about them. Think "out of the box." A White Ash, Sassafras, American Beech, Black Willow, Sweet Birch, Tulip Tree, Basswood, Sycamore, or one of thirty species of North Carolina oak can provide food or habitat for native insects and birds that coevolved with them. Don't forget the "fruit and nut" trees that feed animals and once fed American Indians and many of our grandparents. Persimmon, Pawpaw, hickory (six species), Black Walnut, and Pecan (part of the hickory family) may be "messy" plants when the fruit and nuts fall, but all of them make interesting additions and great critter habitat.

Plant Corral Honeysuckle, and within a couple of seasons, your yard will become a magnet for hummingbirds and cool moths. Pipe Vine and Trumpet Vine will grow well in much of the state. Another summer vine that you will want to consider is the native Passion Flower, an intricate purple and white flower that rivals the most beautiful offerings of a tropical rain forest. It also happens to be a critical plant in the life of several species of fritillary butterflies.

In place of exotic hollies, try Winterberry (red berries) and Beauty Berry (lavender berries), hardy, colorful plants native to the Southeast. My mother had two favorite shrubs that grow in much of North Carolina. One was Sweet Shrub, with burgundy flowers and a spicy smell. She also liked the bush called Heart's 'a Burstin', locally known as the Strawberry Tree. For great spring/summer colors, go for some of the azaleas native to the Southeast—Flame Azalea, Pinkshell, and Pinxterbloom—in place of common exotic nursery stock.

As you have already surmised, there are literally hundreds of native Tar Heel wildflowers from which to choose. Although there are some species found statewide, many have special requirements or restricted distribution. Do you want spring color (violets), summer hardiness (milkweeds), or fall blooms (astors)? Is your yard sunny (Butterfly Weed) or shady (Columbine), wet (Jewell Weed) or alkaline (Yellow Lady Slipper)? Do you prefer long-lasting blooms (Purple Cone Flower)?

Always get your plants from reputable native plant dealers and growers or swap with friends. Wild plants should stay in the wild, especially those on public lands that are protected by law.

species of nesting birds, including Cardinal, Wood Thrush, Robin, Catbird, and Eastern Towhee.

Before you think I am romanticizing my wild, native yard, think again. It is sometimes ragged, and native plants don't always "fill out" properly, grow quickly, or have the perfect shape of readily available exotics or hybrids. Mine is not the yard or plant selection for those of you who prefer a more formal setting. But I really don't care whether your yard is formal or casual as long as you make room for more native plants and trees. By replacing or adding a few native trees, shrubs, and flowers to your yard each year, you will have taken an important step toward reestablishing diversity in our urban and suburban flora.

You don't need to dump all of the exotics that you have grown to love or tolerate. As much as we appreciate native vegetation, my wife and I are not purists. We have no plans to remove our Japanese maples, or the Norway spruce that once served as a living Christmas tree, from our Raleigh yard. My wife insists on red geraniums in planters on our front steps in the summer and the daily blooms of bright red and pink hibiscus in our backyard. There is still a mixed side-yard hedge of invasive privet (*Ligustrum*) and olive (*Elaeagnus*)—both useless plants, but I am too lazy, or too sentimental, to eliminate them. However, because we have included many native plants in our home landscape over the last two decades, we feel little guilt.

If you now have a slight twinge of angst and feel the need to plant more natives, I have succeeded. Know that you will be challenged by an army of nonbelievers—friends, landscapers, and nursery salespeople who will continue to preach the benefits of fast-growing, shapely exotics. I have been told that "native trees grow too slowly" and that I will "sell my house long before I can enjoy them."

I have politely stood my ground and explained that White Oaks, Walnuts, American Beech trees, or Longleaf Pines can live several hundred years. Such native plants may not leap out of the ground like a Princess Tree, a Mimosa, or a Tree of Heaven, but they will be around for a long time. Try to think of native plants as "value added" to your property, which future buyers and homeowners will cherish.

Soil and Fertilizer

Finally, more native plants in your yard will yield an extra bonus of *soil and fertilizer*. First, all leaves should be mulched or composted and turned into topsoil. Native plant leaves that served as host plants to caterpillars and other critters will also contain natural fertilizer in the form of frass, the proper term for caterpillar poop. If you ever watch closely while a hungry caterpillar munches leaves, you will see brown or dark-gray granules of caterpillar frass. The combination of native leaves and natural, free fertilizer will provide a nutrient base well tolerated by other native plants. Think about the last time you walked in an old forest of mature trees and felt rich spongy soil beneath your feet. Such soil is an integral part of a native landscape. Save your leaves and use them as mulch around shrubs and in your flower beds.

This leaf litter deposited by trees quickly creates a base of rich soil. In November, I rake up the leaves in our yard and deposit them in shrubs,

There is no better natural fertilizer than caterpillar poop, called frass. If you are fortunate enough to have caterpillars like this Monarch munching on plants in your yard, thank them—it means you have useful host plants. Also, leave the "worms" alone, because without caterpillars, you won't have butterflies or moths.

forested areas, and plant beds. It has also become a tradition at our house to take leaves raked to the street as yard waste by neighbors and drag them to our house to make more soil. An eighteen-inch layer of leaves will become perhaps an inch of rich, organic material by summer.

The decaying leaves will serve at least two other important functions in your yard. First, organic soil acts like a sponge and holds a tremendous amount of moisture. You will not have to water as often, even during a drought. Second, but equally important, this leaf litter will also be a home for many living creatures, such as insect grubs and earthworms. In this soil, the larvae of future lightning bugs and ladybugs will live and grow. And have you noticed that numerous birds forage in leaf litter, picking out seeds, worms, and grubs? So why would you throw away such a valuable commodity? Yet every fall in towns and cities across America, we blow or rake future topsoil—the leaves of our oaks, maples, and poplars—to the street, where giant vacuums suck them up. Keep your leaves and future topsoil in your yard!

■ When I visit my brothers and sisters-in-law, who are retired and living on Bearwallow Mountain in the Upper Hickory Nut Gorge, I find that ecological time has stood still. Most of the same trees still greet me—and like me, they have developed a thicker trunk over the decades. The same pond still holds Bluegill, Longear, and Largemouth—along with some exotic catfish and a few Rainbow Trout released by well-meaning anglers. There are still mayflies and small, wild trout in Hickory Nut Creek. Lightning bugs still dance in the shadows, and the giant silk moths perform when porch lights are turned on. And about Aunt Winnie: she departed Bearwallow Mountain near her 100th birthday a number of years ago, but I am certain that she is still showing off her hummingbirds and wildflowers to another herd of children somewhere in Hickory Nut Gorge.

North Carolina is now a divided land of natural and exotic landscapes. Unfortunately, many young people and newcomers to North Carolina did not grow up on a landscape punctuated by native plants and the creatures that depend on them. It is difficult to miss something if you have not experienced it. Across much of the state, previously common interactions with nature have become rare. The delicate bloom of Trout Lily is followed closely by the stark white flowers of Bloodroot; both short-lived events occur at fewer locations as forest habitats are transformed by development. Many North Carolinians will not witness the frantic beauty of dozens of large butterflies fluttering in a small space or see the erratic flight of a pale-lime Luna Moth. The distinctive whistle of Bobwhite Quail from the forest edge; children giggling at twilight as a swarm of fireflies dances around them; and the whir of a hummingbird, suspended in a motionless blur, sipping nectar from the trumpets of native Coral Honeysuckle, are sweet sounds and tiny pleasures missing from too many lives.

I have experienced *both* North Carolinas—complex ecosystems of interdependent plants and animals, and creeping green deserts largely devoid of native life. I prefer the former.

■ The Carolina landscape is home to such an astonishing number of plants, insects, fish, shellfish, birds, reptiles, and fungi that we were a prime destination for early naturalists. In the late 1700s, one French explorer correctly observed that within his sight in one southern Appalachian valley lived a greater variety of plant life than could be found in all of Europe. This biodiversity still abounds here, but regrettably, we have sometimes forgotten that each plant and creature has a role in the smooth functioning of nature's systems.

6

CANADIANS, MECHANICS, AND BIODIVERSITY

I was informed that we had entered the "Carolinian Life Zone." The forests looked familiar, with beech, maple, oak, ash, pine, and even Pawpaw. The ferns and wildflowers looked like those near our family cabin in Hickory Nut Gorge. Around me, there were Tar Heel birds like the Tufted Titmouse and some of my favorite neotropical visitors, including Hooded Warblers and Prothonotary Warblers (also known as the Swamp Canary). I was told to look for turkey, White-Tailed Deer, and Black Bear, in addition to common Carolina residents like the Gray Squirrel and the Opossum. The frog sounds were familiar, and the salamanders in seeps and creeks looked like those on Bearwallow Mountain, east of Asheville. If I were lucky, I would also see a Spiny Softshell Turtle or a Hognose Snake. And there were warnings not to step on the Eastern Prickly Pear Cacti.

So what's the big deal about plants and animals seen by North Carolinians every day? I was in Canada!

Extending southwest from Toronto along the north shore of Lake Erie is a zone of great natural diversity known and celebrated by Canadians as the Carolinian Life Zone, or Carolinian Canada. Largely because the temperatures of the region are moderated by the waters of three of the Great Lakes (Erie, Huron, and Ontario), Carolinian Canada is one of the northernmost deciduous forests in North America and has more frost-free days than virtually any other part of Canada. This relatively small sliver of land with London, Ontario, at its center holds a substantial percentage of the rare plants and among the greatest number of animal species (including reptiles and amphibians) found in all of Canada. For its incredible natural diversity, the region received its "Carolinian" designation—a recognition of the even greater diversity found in North and South Carolina.

Long before Canadians had named their most biologically diverse region for our landscape, the rest of the world had long recognized the natural environment of the Carolinas, and especially North Carolina. Three zones (four if you count the Sandhills as a separate category), including the Coastal Plain, the Piedmont, and the southern Appalachian Mountains, hold some of the largest and most diverse plant communities found in the temperate world. These plant communities—specific assemblages of plants best adapted to the soil-moisture-temperature cards dealt by nature—in large part dictate the types of animal life found there. At various times while writing this book, I have been tempted to rattle off the astonishing number of species found in North Carolina, but I have restrained myself . . . until now.

If you are a Tar Heel, you are surrounded by over 4,000 species of herbaceous plants, including a combined 500 native trees, shrubs, and woody vines. In the air around you are over 450 species of birds, including residents and seasonal visitors. You live in an amphibian hot spot, with close to thirty kinds of frogs and toads and sixty species of salamanders. We have some 265 species of freshwater fish, forty-five types of crayfish, and about sixty-three freshwater mussels. Our land is home to thirty-eight good-neighbor snakes, a dozen lizards, and twenty turtles. If you thought we had just red and black ants, consider that North Carolina is home to over 200 ant species. Add to this 175 species of butterflies and an estimated 3,000 types of moths. All of these pale in comparison to our estimated 8,000 species of fungi, which is believed by the North Carolina Museum of Natural Sciences to be the most found in any location of comparable size. Please note that I have left out North Carolina's beetles, spiders, aquatic insects, worms, tardigrades, mosses, and lichens. As mentioned in the prologue, these numbers are constantly changing as new species are added and others disappear (that is, are extirpated) from the region or become extinct.

Because I write and appear on a television show, *Exploring North Carolina*, which features the state's wild things and places, I get a lot of questions about the natural world. My formal education (history and law) did not equip me to address these questions, but my long associations with scientists and trained naturalists have given me an increased level of understanding. I can handle the inquiries about places (parks and natural areas), superlatives (the highest, the deepest, the oldest), and the numbers of species of plants and animals. One group of questions, however, always makes me shudder. These are the "so what?" questions: So what is the big deal about losing a few species of mussels, a couple of fish, a snake, a turtle, or a seldom-seen tree? Extinction is part of evolution; so what if we are missing a few parts?

Biological diversity is not just a numerical tally of the species in a particular area; it is generally considered to be a measure of the health, or vitality, of communities and ecosystems. The greatest diversity is found in communities of plants and animals that have gone through an extended period of succession. These include "climax forests" and other mature ecosystems where plants and animals have reached a place of equilibrium over a long time. These are stable systems in which plants and animals have adapted to each other and their surroundings, including rainfall, soil type, and temperature. Across North Carolina, mature, diverse ecosystems can still be found in old stands of Piedmont hardwood, mountain bogs, spruce-fir forests above 5,000 feet, Longleaf Pine savannahs, and Appalachian coves. In these systems, every organism has a "job," and each is important to the smooth functioning of the whole, from the lowliest insect to the top predators.

Many of our mature ecosystems have become isolated as humans have dammed rivers and cleared forests for farms and cities. We have changed the soil by removing native vegetation and replacing it with carpets of turf with shallow roots, often composed of a single species of grass, and numerous nonnative trees. In a misguided effort to protect ourselves and our livestock from harm, we have removed (and in some cases extirpated) predators, including wolves, raptors, and snakes. Most of the old forests and tallest trees are now gone, trees that once formed the uppermost canopy of mature forests and protected several other layers of vegetation beneath. We have diminished the number of native shellfish in our inland rivers and added new finfish species with the ability to displace native fishes. Our urban areas and transportation corridors are often so large that they form barriers restricting the movement of native plants and animals; this has the unwanted effect of creating isolated wild places disconnected from others. Perhaps most alarming of all, too many Americans, and especially our children, do not have a personal connection with remaining mature and complex ecosystems. Without such contact, it is easy to forget that all advanced plants and animals (including humans) are beholden to the organic stew beneath our feet, beginning with bacteria, fungi, lichens, worms, and tiny grubs. Because we have become a society connected to each other with machines, devices, and "systems," it is easier to understand the importance of biodiversity in the natural world in these terms.

Keep All the Parts

For the last fifteen years, I have taken our family cars to John, an independent mechanic at one of the few full-service gas stations left in Raleigh. John has worked on everything we have owned—Fords, a Chevy, Volvos, a Honda, and my prized Volkswagen. He can fix anything—tires, brakes, air conditioners, transmissions, and suspensions. On several occasions, I have gone to his garage "office" before the job was completed only to find dozens of parts from my vehicle laid out carefully on cardboard. At those times, John has reminded me that good auto mechanics follow two rules: "Rule number one: Never lose or throw away any part. And rule number two: The only things remaining after the job is completed should be the worn/broken parts that were replaced with compatible substitute parts. Break either of these rules, and you've got a big problem!"

John never intended to be profound, and he was not using the mechanical world as a metaphor for anything, especially nature. In thinking about John's words of wisdom as they relate to the living world around us, however, I have concluded that his rules are also applicable to nature's "mechanical systems"— complex communities composed of literally thousands of diverse plants and animals found across North Carolina. For those of us who are not mechanically inclined, it is difficult to distinguish between parts and "systems" in our motor vehicles required merely for our comfort and convenience and those that are necessary for the car to run.

A similar analogy was made in the late 1940s by ethicist, conservationist, and writer Aldo Leopold when he said that the "intelligent watchmaker keeps all of the parts." In *A Sand County Almanac* (1949), Leopold challenged readers to live with the land, not as a "conqueror" but as a "biotic citizen." He knew that if the wrong species is eliminated, a trophic cascade can occur, causing entire ecosystems to collapse. By implication, it is clear from his writing that he knew that not all species are critical—but which ones are? If Leopold was with us today, I think that he would agree that the many systems in a modern automobile—some critical and some not—are quite analogous to the complex ecosystems in nature.

A generation ago, watches and automobiles were almost entirely mechanical, a series of gears and wheels powered either by a windup spring or a gasoline engine. A single broken or missing part could stop everything. In those simpler times, a watchmaker or auto mechanic could identify and replace the part. Now that modern automobiles are half computer and half machine, even John cannot always immediately tell whether a problem is caused by a missing/worn part or by a computer glitch. Much of what happens in a car is now controlled by tiny, unseen microprocessors. We no longer have just brakes for stopping and a steering column for turning the wheels, but "braking systems" and "steering/handling systems" controlled in large part by signals sent from onboard computers. A defective part or a software problem can have system-wide implications.

Fortunately, in modern automobiles, as in nature, there is some built-in redundancy—dual headlights, double-layered safety glass, tires capable of running for miles when punctured, and more than one braking system. Although comparing today's cars with the natural world makes for an appropriate analogy, nature's redundant systems are far more complex. The monumental loss of an estimated one-fourth of forest canopy in the Appalachians caused by the American Chestnut "blight" in the first half of the twentieth century did not doom all of the animals that fed on that tree's nuts, munched its leaves, and sought grubs under its bark. However, its near extinction did seal the fate of some moths and at least seven butterflies that were directly dependent on it. Most animals that had thrived on the annual chestnut mast—squirrels and other rodents, bears, grouse, and turkeys—initially declined in numbers but eventually adapted to other foods. Just as a twenty-first-century automobile can continue to run because of redundancy in its systems, living things can also adapt when ecosystems contain a diversity of fungi, insects, birds, grasses, trees/shrubs, and even apex predators. Think of the options in nature provided by great biodiversity as a form of redundancy.

In the conservation community, we often focus too much on the "parts" that are already missing or in decline—the "stressed, threatened, or endangered" species of a region. We should also pay more attention to John's rule number two regarding the worn/broken parts and their replacements. No competent mechanic would install a replacement tire that is a different diameter from the other three tires, replacement spark plugs different from the originals on the car, or fan belts of the wrong length. In the natural world, especially in our urban areas and waterways, we have too often installed the wrong substitute parts, such as plant species from other parts of the world.

Both the missing parts and the nonnative replacement parts in our state's landscape should be of concern. Who among us can know with certainty when we have left out, tampered with, or replaced too many of nature's original parts? With the looming decline in numbers of the Carolina and Eastern Hemlock (from infestations of the introduced Hemlock Wooly Adelgid) in our mountains and the Redbay Magnolia under attack (from the newly arrived Redbay Ambrosia Beetle) across the Southeast, will birds, animals, and even fish adapt to their loss, or will some also become victims?

We should also remember that for every part of an ecosystem that we see, there are hundreds, even thousands, of tiny unseen parts—the "microprocessors" that fine-tune and even control the visible world. Bacteria in soils perform the herculean tasks of fixing nitrogen and other elements so that it can be used by plants. They dwell in the guts of humans and most animals, enabling the digestion of food. Without bacteria to help break down decaying plant and animal matter, the planet would soon drown in its own organic debris.

Equally important is the world of fungi, which most of us recognize only in their mushroom, or fruiting, stage. Largely unseen is the mutually beneficial relationship between plants and fungi, which are neither plant nor animal but part of their own Kingdom Fungi. The symbiotic relationship between fungi and the roots of plants is called a mycorrhizal association—with "myco" being the fungus and "rhiza" the plant roots. In this mutually beneficial relationship, the fungus is provided carbon from the plant, while the plant benefits from increased water uptake and absorption of nutrients from the soil. This special relationship with fungi also makes soil habitable for many vascular plants, including most orchids. Certain types of wood-decay fungi also work in nature's garbage disposal unit by helping to decompose wood. Without this service provided by fungi in breaking down wood (fallen trees), our forests would soon become impassable. When topsoil is washed away or organic soil removed, we lose key bacteria and fungi, unseen "microcomponents" critical to all ecosystems.

Ecosystems, like machines, have only a limited amount of redundancy, or room for error, before a system failure. Let us hope that native plants, animals, and the organic microprocessors are allowed to adapt, and we again avoid a trophic cascade. Just ask all of the megafauna that disappeared from the Carolina landscape after the last Ice Age—the elephants, the saber-toothed cats, the giant tortoises, the bison, and the sloths. What caused the systemic failure? Did these animals become doomed when the atmosphere became warmer and drier? Did paleohumans eliminate one

The symbiotic relationship between many fungi and the roots of specific plants is called a mycorrhizal association. Other fungi play an essential role in our forests by helping to decompose fallen trees. North Carolina is estimated to have over 8,000 species of fungi; be very thankful for the services they provide. (Photo by Mike Dunn)

too many species, causing a domino effect? As intelligent as we are, we still don't know all of the answers to the great Pleistocene extinction some 12,000 years ago, nor can we isolate the tipping points that occurred just 100 years ago leading to the extinction of the Ivory-Billed Woodpecker and the once-abundant Passenger Pigeon. I suggest that until we are more certain about the complex systems with which we are tinkering, we must, like John the mechanic, do our best to keep all the parts.

The Not-So-Dismal Swamp

Not long ago, on an eighty-degree day in early May, I visited the Great Dismal Swamp State Park on the North Carolina–Virginia border. This land is not greatly different from many other coastal wetlands found from eastern Virginia to Georgia. During my visit in near perfect weather, I was compelled to stop and watch enormous "puddle parties" of butterflies in the ruts of an old logging road. Many were large, showy butterflies—Tiger, Zebra, Spicebush, and Palamedes Swallowtails—but there were plenty of the smaller Question Marks, Orange Sulphur, Gray Hairstreak, and Common Buckeye. Every few hundred yards, another puddle party would be disturbed and take flight; the sheer numbers would have been astonishing even in a tropical setting.

While being entertained by the butterflies, I could hear the distinct songs of several birds that had just arrived from Central and South America to start new families. Within moments, a "swamp canary," the magnificent Prothonotary Warbler, landed in a Red Maple twenty feet above me. This is a common bird from spring to late summer in southeastern coastal hardwood forests, but they are often difficult to see in thick vegetation. The Prothonotary is not just yellow but a "Roman Catholic" yellow-orange. Like a cardinal with his brilliant red vestments, a prothonotary apostolic (alter-

Whenever you see a cluster of butterflies, such as these Zebra Swallowtails, grouped together on the trail or beside a brook, they are said to be having a "puddle party." From moist ground, butterflies are able to extract the water and mineral nutrients they need.

The magnificent Prothonotary Warbler, also known as the Swamp Canary and Golden Swamp Warbler, is the favorite neotropical songbird of many birders. The Prothonotary is very common near coastal rivers and swamps, and it even ventures into the Piedmont along slow-moving rivers. It raises its young and spends summers here but migrates to Central and South America during the winter.

Another neotropical warbler sharing forest thickets with the Prothonotary Warbler is the Hooded Warbler.
(Photo by Walker Golder)

nately spelled "protonotary") is also an important church official serving the pope, but his robes and hoods are a vibrant yellow. In keeping with their Vatican namesakes, Prothonotary Warblers occupy a visible seat of prominence in swamp ecosystems.

Over the next half hour, I heard, and then saw, an all-star supporting cast for the Prothonotary, including a Red-Eyed Vireo, a Yellow-Billed Cuckoo, a Wood Thrush, and a Hooded Warbler—all neotropical spring migrants. Regular birders and visitors to North Carolina's eastern state parks, including Great Dismal Swamp, Merchants Millpond, Lake Waccamaw, Lumber River, Goose Creek, and Pettigrew, know that such bird and butterfly concentrations are not uncommon. These parks support immense natural diversity year-round, and the same is true of other state and federal parks, forests, and refuges in the Piedmont and Mountain region.

Diverse, abundant flora supports diverse, abundant fauna. Each plant and animal in the forest is part of a food web, with the success or failure of each species tied to another. My experience at the Great Dismal Swamp State Park provides a case in point. The large concentration of butterflies could not have existed without the right mix of host plants for butterfly larvae (caterpillars) and nectar plants (supplying nutrition to adult butterflies). The numerous Zebra Swallowtails exist *only* because the swamp is dotted with "Pawpaw patches" along the forest edges. Pawpaw, which can be a large shrub or a small tree, is the *sole* host plant used by Zebra Swallowtails, although they can take nectar from a variety of flowers. Palamedes Swallowtails primarily depend on Redbay Magnolia (mentioned earlier) as their host plant, which is a species common in bottomland soils of eastern North Carolina. The swallowtail, called Spicebush, was well supplied in the swamp with one of its few host plants, Sassafras. Finally, the Tiger Swallowtails that I saw in the Great Dismal are found across much of the state—and probably in your neighborhood—because the species can use a larger variety of host plants, including Black Cherry, Tulip Popular, and Black Willow. All of these trees are in abundance on higher ground.

There are dozens of species of butterfly common to every park and natural area in our region. For example, in Duke Forest (six tracts totaling some 7,000 acres owned by Duke University), over eighty species of butterflies have been recorded by the Duke naturalists. As in the Great Dismal, there is a specific host plant, or just a few plants, on which each butterfly depends. Some butterflies are attracted to "nontree hosts" such as the milkweeds (Monarch Butterfly), violets (several species of frittilary), and even clover (sulphurs). It is therefore a safe assumption that the more species of native

The Zebra Swallowtails shown in an earlier photograph depend on a *single* host plant: the Pawpaw Tree. The Pawpaw used to be very common in the forest understory and on forest edges but is now much depleted. Without the Pawpaw, there is no Zebra Swallowtail; and without the Zebra Swallowtail's caterpillars, there would be fewer migratory warblers.

trees, shrubs, and flowers there are in the wetlands, fields, and forests, the greater the variety of butterflies and moths you will see.

What attracted the neotropical songbirds—the vireos, warblers, and cuckoos? Why did they travel thousands of miles, cross the Gulf of Mexico, and return to their natal wetlands? These birds are all primarily insect eaters, with both vireos and cuckoos being especially fond of caterpillars. The arrival of the birds and the availability of insects is no coincidence. The parts of any ecosystem, in this case that of the Great Dismal Swamp—the marshy soil and the plants, insects, and birds—are best understood when viewed as parts of a whole. The right soils and temperatures support a variety of host plants. These plants are in turn both nursery and "salad bar" for caterpillars of all sizes from spring to early fall. Caterpillars and mature insects are the preferred foods sought by migratory songbirds as they arrive to raise their young.

That day, as I left the magnificent swamp we Tar Heels share with Virginia, I saw a Black Racer cross the road ahead of me. It is a beautiful snake, up to seven feet in length and one of the most efficient tree climbers in the forest. During the visit, I had also seen a fast, agile Red-Shouldered Hawk streaking through the canopy. These two predators brought my visit full circle, because they, too, would not exist without the Pawpaw and Redbay . . . that served as the host and food for butterflies/caterpillars . . . that attracted and fed the birds from the tropics . . . that fed the snake and the hawk. A system with all of its parts!

Flying Bluefin

North Carolina has numerous ecosystems of varying complexity. The biodiversity in some is limited primarily to resident animals and plants. In others, parts of an ecosystem can come from far away, such as the neotropical birds that are integral to the cycles of the Great Dismal Swamp. Still other players from North Carolina ecosystem dramas have even more dramatic parts that make waves all the way to the Mediterranean Sea and even to Japan. My final example of interconnected Carolinian biodiversity, with a distinct international flare, occurred on the coast; it also provided a teaching moment I will never forget.

It was the Thanksgiving holiday, and my son, Izaak, was turning nine years old that week. I was with my family at Harkers Island, behind Cape Lookout, for the holiday meal and to fish for speedy False Albacore, known locally as Little Tunny. On previous trips, I had told Izaak to watch for the birds because they would direct us to fish. We were on a tide line near Barden's Inlet. Sure enough, we found lots of birds, including Brown Pelicans, Northern Gannets, and several species of gulls diving into pods (tight schools) of finger mullet and small Menhaden. We also found several large "bait balls" of sardine-like minnows just outside the "Bight" southwest of the Cape Lookout Lighthouse. The smaller, minnow-sized bait was marked by different birds—a variety of terns, gulls, and petrels. Izaak liked it that I called all of the small fish "foods in the cafeteria line" for bigger fish. He mused that the only things missing were "customers" for our cafeteria.

Suddenly, all the birds grew more excited as Striped Mullet, Menhaden, and various minnows began to break the surface 100 yards from our boat to escape voracious schools of False Albacore ripping through the bait from below. As one school of albacore moved closer, I told Izaak to get ready to cast his lure. Then without warning, the predator became prey, and the False Albacore, averaging eight to twelve pounds each, began to fly through the air in total disarray. It was clear that the silvery albacore near our boat were panicked, but why?

Without warning, just twenty-five yards from our skiff, a giant Bluefin Tuna, in pursuit of a meal, exploded from the water. The tail of the great fish cleared the surface by at least three feet, where it remained airborne with Michael Jordan–like "hang time." The eight o'clock morning sun was behind Izaak and me, while the great fish hung suspended between sea and sky. I've caught a couple hundred species of fish, but never a Bluefin Tuna, and I can only guesstimate its length and size—perhaps nine feet long and in the 500-to-700-pound range. With its silver-blue mass in direct sunlight, it looked more like a military jet than a fish. At the pinnacle of its arc, the fish and I made eye contact, if such interspecies connection is possible.

Bluefin Tuna are world travelers. The same fish that winter in the rich waters off of North Carolina's Capes Lookout and Hatteras may be found at other times during the year off of Cape Cod, in the Gulf of Mexico, swimming near New York's Montauk Point, or in Canadian waters. Some of the same fish tagged off the North Carolina coast even cross the Atlantic, pass the Rock of Gibraltar, and enter the waters of the Mediterranean off the coasts of Spain, France, and Italy. Surely, there is no more erudite, sophisticated, and well-traveled fish than the Atlantic Bluefin.

There are also Bluefin (the same species) in the Pacific, and unfortunately the stocks in both oceans are at dangerously low levels due to overfishing. The flesh is so prized by Japanese sushi lovers that the carcass of a *single* 750-pound Bluefin recently sold for a record price of $40,000 at dockside—over $500 per pound—at a time when other individual fish frequently sell for over $10,000. By the time you read this story, I am certain the prices mentioned will have been eclipsed.

When the waters settled that Thanksgiving weekend, the high price of tuna hadn't crossed my mind; I was simply awestruck. Izaak was impressed, but he was still too young to know what an uncommon happening he had just witnessed. The entire chain of events, from diving birds, startled baitfish, and marauding albacore to the surprise appearance of a giant Bluefin—a rock star of fishes—took place within a three-minute period about 100 yards off the beach. It was a great time to talk with Izaak about food chains, the "cafeteria line" of life. Neither of us expected that the usual customers at the cafeteria—the albacore—would be eaten by even larger guests. Even more startling to Izaak was that such a powerful, apex predator as a Bluefin Tuna could itself be on a menu—in faraway Tokyo.

Izaak then asked, "What makes the baitfish, False Albacore, and Bluefin Tuna show up here at the same time?"

I explained to him that all the parts in a complex system must be working or the cafeteria will close. It all begins with the marsh grass lining our estuaries called Eastern Spartina (or Smooth Cordgrass). When it dies in the fall and winter, it looks like golden wheat before becoming detritus that serves as food for the planktons that feed tiny crabs, shrimp, and larval fish. In the

Everything is connected in a forest ecosystem. Trees depend on certain fungi; caterpillars of many butterflies need specific host plants; migratory birds stay when there are enough caterpillars; and larger predators like the Black Racer (top) and the Red-Shouldered Hawk (bottom) thrive only if small birds and mammals are abundant.

spring and summer, Spartina grows to three feet or more as it goes through several shades of green while serving as incubator and nursery for snails, shrimp, crabs, and juvenile fish of all kinds. These watery fields also provide food and shelter for a diversity of shellfish (clams, snails, whelks, and oysters), birds (egrets and terns), and finfish (Spotted Weakfish, Red Drum, and myriad forage fish). Then in September and October, with falling water temperature and a lower angle of the Sun, the forage fish leave the shallow estuaries and are squeezed through the bottlenecks of nature: inlets. At the mouths of inlets, when forage fish are most concentrated, large predators assemble for their Thanksgiving feasts. When conditions are right, inlets along our coast are alive with Spanish Mackerel, Bluefish, and False Albacore looking for a meal. Then on rare occasions, giant Bluefin Tuna show up in the cafeteria line.

Changes—unchecked pollution or destruction of habitat—in our coastal ecosystem can alter the cycle at any point, but it all starts with protecting the salt marshes. It was a good time to remind Izaak of the bumper sticker he had see many times: "No Wetlands, No Seafood!" Believe it.

■ Long before the terms "biodiversity," "biotic community," and "ecosystem" were coined, well-traveled visitors knew that the Carolinas, and especially North Carolina, were different. John White knew it when he drew and painted the vast numbers and types of fish in the waters around Roanoke Island in the 1580s. John Lawson appreciated and documented the forests, prairies, birds, reptiles, and mammals when he made his C-shaped journey across the Carolinas in 1701—beginning in today's Charleston, swinging as far west as present-day Charlotte, then along a route that would later be marked by Salisbury, Hillsborough, New Bern, and Bath. Two decades later, in the 1720s, Mark Catesby, working in Virginia and the Carolinas, painted a stunning collection of animals and the plants with which they were most associated.

At the end of the colonial period and after the American Revolution, North Carolina and our adjacent sister states continued to be a Mecca for plant and animal enthusiasts, including some of the famous botanists and naturalists of the eighteenth and nineteenth centuries (see chapter 11). They included John and William Bartram, André Michaux, Asa Gray, and John Muir (founder of the Sierra Club). These plant experts collected samples and seeds and sent their discoveries to universities in New England, to herbariums, and to private collectors in Europe. They were also among the first to classify and assign Latin names to the plants of the Carolinas.

All were impressed by what they found, but none more so than the French botanist Michaux. Charles Kuralt, CBS correspondent and a favorite son of North Carolina, spoke on the 200th anniversary of the Frenchman's ascent of Grandfather Mountain—which Michaux believed to be the highest peak in North America—on August 28, 1794. Michaux turned out to be wrong about the mountain's altitude in comparison with others, but he was right about something far more consequential: the diversity of life he observed around him. Kuralt told this story near the summit of the mountain in a stirring address celebrating the accomplishments of the French botanist:

> When André Michaux reached the summit of Grandfather Mountain, he knew that within his sight on this mountain and in this valley, in a circle of a few miles, exists a greater variety of plant life than can be found in all of Europe, from the arctic capes of Scandinavia to the shores of southern Greece. He found plants and roots which exist—amazingly—only in the southern Appalachians, or only here and in Tibet, or only here and in China. This place was his Eden. No wonder he sang the "Marseillaise" that day up on the top of Grandfather, and shouted in exultation, "Long live America and the Republic of France! Long live liberty!"

Healthy Spartina marshes are essential for North Carolina's coastal ecosystems to work properly. These marshes provide food and shelter for a diversity of living things. You've seen the bumper sticker: "No wetlands, no seafood." It's true!

Few of us can compete with the writing skills of Charles Kuralt, and no one could match his elegant baritone voice and perfectly paced delivery. I can only echo Kuralt's enthusiasm, not only for Michaux the man but also for the treasures of biological diversity Michaux identified in rich cove forests, in mountain bogs above 4,000 feet, on the dry soils of rock outcroppings, and in boreal spruce-fir forests atop the highest peaks of the southern Appalachians.

To the floral treasures witnessed by Michaux, add the discoveries of others—a seemingly endless parade of wildflowers in Longleaf Pine ecosystems; a voracious assemblage of carnivorous plants (including the Venus Flytrap) growing in acidic, nitrogen-starved soils; the Bald Cypress, Water Tupelo, and White Ash of coastal bottomlands; and the Live Oaks and Cabbage Palms of Baldhead Island. Remember the amphibians, arthropods, reptiles, birds, and mammals that coevolved with this matchless trove of temperate region flora. It should make us all want to stand on a mountaintop or a tall sand dune and sing the "Marseillaise"—or better yet, a few bars of James Taylor's "Carolina in My Mind." We should not have to wait for Canadians to put a spotlight on the uniqueness of the Carolinian Life Zone.

For André Michaux, the southern Appalachians in North Carolina were a contemporary "Eden." Few places in the temperate world could compare in diversity and beauty, then or now. (Photo by Mike Dunn)

■ The transition from the high peaks and conifer forests of the Blue Ridge to the rolling hills and stands of White Oak in the Piedmont and the long, flat vistas and cypress-lined rivers of the Coastal Plain indicate changes—natural boundaries—that most of us recognize. Perhaps more important are the subtle, almost invisible transitions where ecological communities begin and end and our greatest biodiversity can be found.

7

NATURAL BOUNDARIES
AND COMMUNITIES

If you have ever traveled overseas, you may have experienced a moment of joy on the return trip when the pilot announced that the plane had just entered U.S. airspace. How many times have you returned home from distant travels and felt a sense of relief when you crossed the North Carolina state line, then passed the highway sign marking entry into your home county or the city-limits marker for your town? Even the turn into your driveway marks the crossing of a safe and familiar property line. Since we are acutely sensitive to political boundaries and property lines, it has always seemed strange to me that we are often oblivious to nature's boundaries. Learning in the fourth grade that our state is divided into the Mountain region, the Piedmont, and the Coastal Plain is, for many of us, the extent of our knowledge of nature's physical transitions. Natural boundaries on the mainland or along the coast can be subtle or very dramatic, and North Carolina has them all.

On numerous occasions, I have traveled by small boat fifteen to twenty-five miles offshore of Capes Lookout or Hatteras over clear, dark-green coastal waters, only to cross a distinct line into the eerily clear, inky-blue Gulf Stream. With your boat's bow in blue water and its stern still in green, it is a boundary line you will never forget. All coastal mariners know that the Gulf Stream water temperatures are warm year-round and that fish and flora can change abruptly there.

Have you noticed that the rivers in our eastern counties are different from those in the rest of the state? In the Coastal Plain, there are no deep valleys or easily discernable basins. As if by magic, there are no more waterfalls and riffles, and no more rocky banks to constrain water within narrowly confined quarters. Here, once-corseted rivers widen into shallow, flat ribbons only a few feet lower than the lands through which they flow. Even floodplains adjacent to rivers, which can be several hundred feet wide in the Piedmont and the mountains, are frequently several miles across in the Coastal Plain. Trees next to coastal rivers, which frequently stand in water for weeks at a time, develop thick trunks and large, shallow root mats. Finally, at some point many miles from the ocean, the freshwater of the Roanoke, Tar-Pamlico, Neuse, White Oak, and Cape Fear Rivers begins to turn salty. There is no "Begin Saltwater Zone" sign on the riverbank, but nature marks it with a new mix of plants, animals, fish, and birds found at such zones of change.

In western North Carolina, change happens abruptly, even on a single mountain. At lower elevations, diverse forests made up of oak, maple, hickory, birch, poplar, pine, buckeye, beech, and numerous other tree types are common. By going higher on the mountain (generally above 4,500 feet), the diversity of trees in deciduous forests will often diminish to fewer species, including Northern Red Oak, Striped Maple, American Beech, Mountain Ashe, and Yellow Birch. On our tallest peaks—the "Islands in the Sky"—another change can often be seen above 5,000 feet, where forests of northern hardwoods transition into dense stands of Fraser Fir and Red Spruce.

Less dramatic but ecologically important are the almost invisible lines, which are boundaries nonetheless, that separate our state into seventeen river basins (see chapter 13) and many subbasins. Though their boundaries may be subtle, basins often contain species of salamander, shellfish, finfish, and crayfish that are found in no other locations. Equally nuanced lines occur in the hills of the Piedmont and mountains of the southern Appalachians, where changes in vegetation and fauna are found on north- and east-facing slopes when compared to the plants and animals found on south- and west-facing slopes.

Whether in a boat or in an air-conditioned automobile going seventy miles per hour, most of us never know we have crossed a natural border, which can be every bit as important as political boundaries and property lines to our social and economic well-being. Ecological communities begin and end at such transitions, and our great biodiversity occurs in these changing habitats.

(opposite) There is a location near the terminus of all coastal rivers at which freshwater and saltwater meet. Nature marks such transitions with a new mix of plants and animals; it is a natural boundary. These giant Bald Cypress lie near such a natural boundary. (Photo by Mike Dunn)

Why Natural Boundaries Occur

In the prologue to this book, I mentioned several factors that make North Carolina a climatological boundary, a geological boundary, and an ecological crossroads of the temperate world. Our favorable location between latitude N 33°50′ to N 36°35′ placed us beyond the reach of multiple Ice Age glaciers that swept the Northern Hemisphere for over 2 million years and still ensures North Carolina's four distinct seasons. The absence of glacial ice also meant long periods without disturbance for species to adapt and evolve, especially when compared with the frequently glaciated terrains to the north. The moderate temperatures of our latitude are further buffered by our proximity to two ocean currents, the warm Gulf Stream and the colder Labrador Current.

With prevailing winds from the southwest and moisture from the Gulf of Mexico, every area of North Carolina—an occasional drought not withstanding—has a generous average annual rainfall (averaging almost 100 inches to slightly less than forty inches). This supply of freshwater is fairly evenly distributed across the state in our seventeen river basins. Several of these basins are home to unique species (shellfish, finfish, salamanders, and crayfish) endemic to (that is, found only in) that basin. Further adding to the ecological diversity of our land is the Eastern Continental Divide, an invisible line cleaving the southern Appalachians and directing some of our rivers toward the Gulf of Mexico and others to the Atlantic Ocean. These rivers, flowing both east and west, and their corridors serve as highways for species movement.

Since our state is only 180 miles from north to south at its widest point, the coldest temperatures and extreme climatic variations occur not because of latitude but altitude. With forty-three peaks in excess of 6,000 feet in altitude (over fifty such peaks if you count mountains with twin summits) and more than 100 additional summits over 5,000 feet, temperatures and weather conditions can change quickly over a few miles. Again, as in the prologue, I mention the simple formula: every 1,000 feet in altitude is the equivalent of traveling 200 miles to the north (in the Northern Hemisphere). Thus, with approximately 150 peaks that are 5,000 to more than 6,000 feet in altitude, the temperatures and ecosystems found on many mountains and ridges are roughly the equivalent of traveling 1,000 miles (200×5) or 1,200 miles (200×6) to the north. It is worth mentioning again that some authorities, including the North Carolina Museum of Natural Sciences, say that 300 miles for every 1,000 feet is the appropriate estimate.

How does this show up in temperature variation between locations? For Wilmington, at slightly above sea level, the monthly normal high and low temperatures are 56 and 36 degrees Fahrenheit in January and 90 and 72 degrees Fahrenheit in July. Contrast this with the average highs and lows for the same months at Mount Mitchell at 6,684 feet: 34 and 17 degrees Fahrenheit in January and 67 and 52 degrees Fahrenheit in July. The temperature variations are just the beginning of the differences between Mount Mitchell (and other peaks over 6,000 feet) and the lowlands of the Piedmont and Coastal Plain. Mount Mitchell has an average annual precipitation of almost seventy-five inches (including an average snowfall of 104 inches). Rain and snow are not the only sources of moisture; dense fog in the summer and thick frosts in winter (known as "hoarfrost") add additional inches of water to the ecosystem. Winter temperatures as low as −34 degrees Fahrenheit have been recorded, as have winds as high as 178 miles per hour. In 1993 a single snow event dropped fifty inches on the mountain. Needless to say, the mix of living things found just 275 miles apart (the distance from Mount Mitchell to Wilmington) also reflects these extremes.

If you drive the relatively easy day trip from Baldhead Island (just south of Wilmington) to Mount Mitchell—with 85 percent of the journey along Interstate 40—you will never leave North Carolina, but ecologically, you will effectively travel from central Florida to the southern end of Hudson Bay in Canada. You will leave a land defined by plants, fish, reptiles, and birds common to the subtropics and arrive in another world where the creatures and vegetation are the same as those you would encounter in northern Maine, Minnesota, and Canada. In between, the entire state of North Carolina is a billboard for biodiversity and the intersection where North and South meet.

Where the Arctic and Tropics Meet

The Tar Heel landscape is the effective northern or southern end range for many species. Although some examples have been listed in other portions of this book, a short list is instructive here. Let's start with Cabbage Palms that make it as far north as Baldhead Island, just above the South Carolina border. Largely because the Longleaf Pine's historic range ran across the border into southeastern Virginia, North Carolina is also the effective northern reach for nesting Red-Cockaded Woodpeckers and the magnificent Pine Lily (also called Catesby's Lily). The Yellow Rat Snake, Pigmy Rattlesnake, and Diamondback Rattlesnake are found only as far north as

the southeastern counties of North Carolina. Another reptile, the American Alligator, has its current northern boundary in eastern North Carolina. Also extending north through all coastal counties and into southeastern Virginia are stands of Bald Cypress, Pond Cypress, and Water Tupelo. And let us not forget my favorite North Carolina spider, the Golden Silk Orbweaver, and our largest grasshopper, the Lubber Grasshopper, both of which are found no farther north than the Neuse River.

The list of plants and animals with effective southern boundaries in North Carolina is equally impressive. A short list includes the Eastern Hemlock and White Pine that extends through the southern Appalachians of North Carolina (including a few pockets in the Piedmont) and barely touches South Carolina, north Georgia, and Alabama. There are the spruce/fir forests above 5,500 feet where Northern Red Squirrels, Saw-Whet Owls, and Cedar Waxwings are at their southern/eastern breeding limits. The Bog Turtle, found only in the cold-water wetlands of eastern America, survives only as far south as the high-altitude bogs of North Carolina and

Endless Longleaf Pine savannahs once covered the majority of eastern North Carolina. Few large tracts now exist north of the North Carolina–Virginia border. Hidden in the apparent sameness of the savannah, which often went on for miles, were unique species that depended largely on the Longleaf—and regular fires—for survival. Note the charred trunks of pines in this photograph.

(clockwise from top left)

This endangered Red-Cockaded Woodpecker builds its nest in the trunks of living Longleaf Pines. (Photo by Mike Dunn)

Few wildflowers are more stunning than the rare Pine Lily, also found primarily among Longleaf. Only through the preservation of Longleaf savannahs can we be assured of retaining these uncommon parts of our heritage.

The American Alligator, which can reach more than twelve feet in length, is at the end of its northern range in North Carolina. (Photo by Mike Dunn)

The Golden Silk Orbweaver is found no farther north than the southeastern counties of North Carolina. They are fine weavers and good neighbors. (Photo by Walker Golder)

The high mountains of North Carolina and Tennessee are the effective southern limit for breeding resident populations of the Northern Saw-Whet Owl.

The high mountains of the Appalachians also mark the southern reach of the Northern Red Squirrel.

Tennessee. Along with the Appalachian Brook Trout, with its southern end range in the high-altitude creeks of western North Carolina, several other cold-water fish have their native end range in our far western rivers, which are part of the upper Mississippi drainage. They include the elusive, and often very large, Muskellunge and the popular Smallmouth Bass.

The plants and creatures above represent only a fraction of the known and unknown species found along the natural boundary that is North Carolina. Think also of biota too often classified as "lesser things," including species of ants, beetles, beetles, spiders, moths, mosses, tardigrades (also called water bears or moss bears), fungi, lichens, and even bacteria that are at their end ranges but seldom noticed.

North Carolina at Ground Level

I have made the journey from Raleigh to Asheville many times, especially the four-hour leg on Interstate 40 before turning north onto the Blue Ridge Parkway toward Mount Mitchell. I admit that I am usually more concerned about schedules and meetings than about ecological and geological boundaries along the way. However, it is seldom that I pass through Chapel Hill or go near Mount Mitchell that I don't think about one of the most extraordinary scholar/naturalists in North Carolina history, Elisha Mitchell, "professor of everything" at UNC between 1818 and 1857. Perhaps more than any other early observer in North Carolina history, Mitchell understood the extraordinary mix of geology and biology and the dynamic boundaries that occur in nature.

After fulfilling his teaching and administrative duties each year at Chapel Hill from 1818 to 1857, Mitchell still had the energy and curiosity to travel the state at ground level to work for the Geological Survey of North Carolina. During the early decades of his travels in North Carolina, there were no east-west railroads and no bridges spanning large rivers, such as the Yadkin and Catawba. Much of the commerce of the time was built around the naval stores industry in the pinewoods of the east and the water-powered factories on the Haw River in the Piedmont. Roads were built . . . out of wood! From 1836 until the beginning of the Civil War, over 500 miles of plank roads were built in this state, most constructed of two layers of pine or hardwood lumber. The road from Fayetteville to the Moravian village of Bethania (Forsyth County) covered 129 miles and was one of the longest wooden roads ever constructed. Mitchell certainly traveled on some of the superhighways of his time, but trips of any substantial distance were measured in days, not hours.

At the speed of a horse or of his own two feet, Mitchell saw a North Carolina none of us can envision. His words describe a physically demanding life requiring the fording of rivers, weeks of grueling travel, and sleep in the most inhospitable conditions. His travels took him to Atlantic shores, to a Piedmont landscape abuzz with gold fever in the 1820s and 1830s, to iron mines near present-day Boone, and to high mountains that begged to be measured. Perhaps no person in our state's history has seen more of North Carolina at ground level than Elisha Mitchell. In a diary entry dated December 1827, part of a collection of entries to his wife, Mitchell wrote about travels along the southeast coast of North Carolina to Swansboro ("a village of 4 tolerable houses") and his crossing of the New River and the White Oak River before turning west toward New Bern. The trip would have taken him through virgin savannas of Longleaf (in today's Croatan National Forest) that covered most of eastern North Carolina.

Just seven months later, in July 1828, Mitchell wrote in detail about high mountains; changes in temperature, soil, rocks, and minerals; and changes in plant species. His skills as an observer and scientist are obvious, but the professor clearly appreciated the beauty and grandeur around him. In Jefferson on July 9, 1828, he wrote: "The soil of Ashe at least on this side of New River is certainly fertile as is proved by the size of the trees that spring up from it. A ride in the deep valleys of such a country with the blue tops of mountains appearing everywhere, then around a stream as clear as crystal dashing over its rocky bed . . . and a cloudless sky overhead, in a summer evening cannot be unpleasant except that those whom one loves may not be present to partake of the enjoyment."

It is easy to forget that in the 1820s and 1830s, there were still virgin forests across North Carolina. Almost a quarter of the entire canopy in the western Piedmont and the Mountains was formed by "great forests of American Chestnut and oak." Even the amazing Dr. Mitchell could not have foreseen that the chestnut forests, stretching from Maine to Alabama, would disappear forever within a century. The peaks of the Black Mountain (and other high peaks) and their north-facing slopes were covered by tall stands of spruce and fir, reported to be 100 to 125 feet tall, with thousands of acres remaining uncut through the first decade of the twentieth century. These, too, exist today only in photographs.

In his summertime trips on foot or on horseback to Grandfather Mountain, Roan Mountain, and the peaks of the Black Mountain, Mitchell would

THE AMAZING PROFESSOR MITCHELL

Most North Carolinians learned in grade school that the tallest mountain in the state is named for Elisha Mitchell. We also learned that he died tragically on the mountain. What few of us learned, however, was that the story of the tenacious Mitchell and his mountain was an epic stretching over several decades, utilizing high-tech (at the time) scientific instruments and ending with a valiant struggle to save his reputation.

Just after sunset on June 27, 1857, a thunderstorm formed over the Black Mountain thirty miles northeast of Asheville. Traveling alone, sixty-three-year old Elisha Mitchell had, on that day, covered over twenty miles of the steepest terrain in North Carolina. He was trying to reach the safety of cabins in the Cane River community (near present-day Burnsville) northwest of the mountain when the streambed (Sugar Camp Fork of the Cane River) that he was following through a dense thicket of rhododendron suddenly fell away into a waterfall. In his haste, and enveloped by the sound of thunder and of the rain striking the dense canopy around him, the old hiker likely did not detect the watery precipice in front of him. If Elisha Mitchell wasn't killed instantly in the twenty-five-foot fall, he quickly succumbed to the frigid waters of the deep pool below at around 8:19 P.M., the time when the pocket watch he was carrying stopped. It would be eleven days before a search party led by the legendary bear hunter and guide Big Tom Wilson would find the body of one of the most famous scholars and teachers of his time. News of Professor Elisha Mitchell's death spread quickly through mountain cove towns and villages and across the young agrarian state to his university community in Chapel Hill.

Over 150 years later, we still marvel at the breadth of the intellectual curiosity and physical stamina of Elisha Mitchell. When he arrived in Chapel Hill from Yale in 1818, he was one of about a dozen professors overseeing barely more than 100 students. Even when compared to other multitasking scholars of his day, Mitchell was unusual—a professor of mathematics, chemistry, geology, natural philosophy, mineralogy, and much more. His daily work plans also show that he studied Greek, French, and Spanish. He was the bursar of the university, an ordained minister, an avid astronomer, and the head of the North Carolina Geologic Survey. Mitchell even served a stint as acting president of the university. Oh yes—did I mention that he was also an excellent botanist who collected specimens around Chapel Hill and communicated with other experts of the region?

Like others of his time, Mitchell had believed that the tallest mountain in North America was Mount Washington in New Hampshire (now known to be 6,288 feet) and that Grandfather Mountain was the tallest in North Carolina. During the professor's first trips to the Blue Ridge in 1827 and 1828, he began to suspect that some peaks of the Black Mountain were taller than the Grandfather. In the collection of letters to his wife, Maria, which became known as the "Diary of a Geological Tour," Mitchell made this observation: "It was a question with us whether the Black and Roan Mountains were not higher than the Grandfather. . . . I very well recollect that when I was in Morganton last year a mountain lying towards the westward (the Black Mountain) appeared higher than it (Grandfather) and the same impression was made by the Yellow and Roan mountains. . . . There can be no doubt that the country around the base of the Grandfather is higher than any other tract along these elevations but I suspect the Black and Roan to be higher peaks." (In Mitchell's time, the "Black Mountain" referred to the ridge and a series of high peaks.)

By 1835 Mitchell, using the latest technology of the day incorporating barometers and mathematical formulas, was able to measure accurately several locations on the Black Mountain over 6,000 feet—

all taller than Grandfather Mountain. In 1838 he reported the measurement of peaks close to 6,600 feet in altitude. By 1850 locals were already calling the highest point on the Black Mountain "Mount Mitchell." Trouble came in 1855, when one of Professor Mitchell's former students, Thomas Clingman—politician, amateur geologist, and promoter—ascended the high ridge of the Black Mountain, measured the tallest outcrops, and claimed that he and not Mitchell had discovered the tallest peak on the Black Mountain complex. The ensuing controversy was public and bitter. Clingman was a competent explorer and geologist, and there was some room for doubt as to whether Mitchell had measured the tallest of a dozen closely grouped 6,000-foot peaks in the 1830s. Unfortunately, on that ill-fated day in June 1857, while trying to reestablish his claim as the man to measure the tallest mountain in eastern America, Mitchell lost his life, and the university lost one of its greatest teachers and leaders.

Within a year of his death, Mitchell was buried on the tallest peak of the Black Mountain and portrayed as a martyr by his many admirers. With the professor's passing, no one doubted that it was Mitchell who had established the heights and fame of the Black Mountain range with its multiple peaks over 6,000 feet in altitude. In spite of Clingman's guile and possible skullduggery, his name was given to the second-highest peak in the East: Clingman's Dome on the North Carolina–Tennessee border.

have passed through displays of summer wildflowers not found in the Piedmont or coastal counties—Turk's-Cap-Lily, Dutchman's Breeches, and Flame Azalea. On the bald of Roan Mountain, Mitchell would have seen Gray's Lily mixed among the grasses and sedges. Near the rocky summit of Grandfather Mountain, Mitchell probably saw flowers now considered rare, including Turkeybeard, Heller's Blazing Star, Death Camus, and Blue Ridge Goldenrod. Among ancient stands of Fraser Fir and Red Spruce on the Black Mountain, fallen trees would have created space for small Purple Fringed Orchids and the blooms of Red Raspberries. Although a fine botanist, the professor was not afraid to admit when knowledge failed him. In the summer of 1828, he confessed to his wife: "Saw a good many plants that were new to me, dug a root of ginseng for you, a small one with my own hands."

On that same trip in 1828, Mitchell's diary entries describe dramatic change as he crossed a natural boundary during his first ascent of Grandfather Mountain: "We passed on over one ridge after another winding through the woods over logs and rocks, and through laurels, walking when we could not ride. . . . [We] arrived at the foot of Grandfather, where we were obliged to leave our horses. . . . The ascent of the mountain is rough, thickety, and disagreeable. Steep, perpendicular cliffs in places but in general not very difficult. About half way up we met with a Fir-Balsam tree. It

(left) During Elisha Mitchell's summer trips to the mountains, he would have seen an unmatched assemblage of undisturbed wildflowers—including the Flame Azalea, which most assuredly would have been among the most common flowering plants in early summer.

(right) In late June, Elisha Mitchell would have also seen plenty of Purple-Fringed Orchids. This specimen was photographed by the author near the summit of Mitchell's mountain.

is sometimes a foot and a half in thickness and pretty tall." In a later entry, dated July 20, 1828, Mitchell continued: "The vegetation of the summit of the Grandfather is peculiar. Carexes [sedges found in moist soil] constitute the principal grasses, the trees are the Balsam Fir—and one or two others which I did not know. . . . The climate of the summit must be considerably colder than that of Chapel Hill."

Understanding Natural Communities

In the 250 years from the first English colony in the New World to the mid-nineteenth century, the Southeast in general, and North Carolina in particular, was a must-see destination for explorers, scientists, and naturalists. The work of Mitchell and the publicity surrounding his measurement of high mountains enhanced the state's reputation even more in the decade before the Civil War. Implicit in Mitchell's writing and observations is that changes in location, soil, altitude, and temperature—even in a small geographic area—generally result in new and different combinations of living things, combinations that are known today as "communities."

A contemporary of Elisha Mitchell lured by the legendary peaks and flora of this region was Asa Gray, a distinguished Harvard University professor who ranks among the most important nineteenth-century American botanists. During a trip in 1841, not long after Mitchell's measurements of the peaks of the Black Mountain, Gray was one of the first to state clearly, in his *Notes of a Botanical Excursion to the Mountains of North Carolina*, what Mitchell observed and what we know today: North Carolina's high mountains hold unique plant communities. On Grandfather Mountain, where Mitchell had observed cooler temperatures and a dramatic change of flora, Gray determined that conditions and plants at the summit were the same as those of New England and Canada:

> The next day [July 9] we ascended the Grandfather, the highest as well as the most rugged and savage we had yet attempted; although by no means the most elevated in North Carolina, as had been supposed. . . . It is entirely covered by trees, except where the rocks are perpendicular, and towards the summit [are spruce/fir forests]. . . . The earth, rocks, and prostrate decaying trunks, in the shade of these trees, are covered with Mosses and Lichens; and the whole presents the most perfect resemblance to the dark and somber forests of the northern parts of New York and Vermont, except that the trees here are much smaller. The resemblance extends to the whole vegetation; and a list of the shrubs and herbaceous plants of this mountain would be found to include a large portion of the common plants of the extreme Northern States and Canada. Indeed, the vegetation is essentially Canadian, with a considerable number of peculiar species intermixed.

The observations of Mitchell and Gray should make each of us want to slow down and take a ground-level tour of our remarkable land. Although the virgin stands of Longleaf, American Chestnut, and Red Spruce and Fraser Fir that once defined North Carolina from the Green Swamp in the east to Roan Mountain in the west are distant memories, many natural communities are still with us in a reduced size. Today, communities are defined by the North Carolina Natural Heritage Program as "a distinct and recurring assemblage of plants, animals, fungi, and bacteria, in association with each other and their physical environment."

Recognizing "Community" Boundaries

Recognizing changes in the mix of flora and other living things tells us we have crossed a boundary into a new community. Recognizing these boundaries does not come naturally, however; it takes a little practice. A good place to start is with a visit to the dioramas of the North Carolina Museum of Natural Sciences in Raleigh. There you will see such communities as "Salt Marsh," where fields of Common Cord Grass, Spartina, anchor the food chain for finfish, shellfish, turtles, and birds. "Maritime Forests" on higher ground of barrier islands are combinations of Live Oak, Yaupon Holly, Loblolly, and Red Cedar that thrive and survive in salt spray and high winds while providing food and shelter for a wide array of critters. The museum has depictions of "Longleaf Pine Savannas" with extraordinary diversity of plants and animals—many of which *actually need* fire at regular intervals to survive. A favorite diorama for children is the "Bottomland Hardwood Forest," an ecological community anchored by Bald Cypress and Water Tupelo where turtles, water snakes, owls, and unique fish (like the air-gulping Bowfin) abound. At the Museum of Natural Sciences, you can also learn about "Piedmont Hardwood Forests," "Pocosins," and "Spruce-Fir Forests." These dioramas will inspire you to visit the real thing.

Each of these living communities is composed of plants, animals, fungi, and bacteria connected through symbiotic relationships. For example, while collecting food in upland forests, ants (over 200 known species in North Carolina) spread the seeds of many plants, including violets, ginger, and trilliums. In a symbiotic relationship with many trees, fungi (over 8,000 species estimated to be in North Carolina) help extract nutrients from the soil. Fungi and bacteria help to break down organic material (logs and leaves), creating new soil. Communities flourish only when the right combinations of soil (minerals, acidity/alkalinity, and permeability), water, temperature, wind, and even fire are present. When similar conditions occur even miles away, you can expect to find similar communities.

You will quickly learn that wild places you have known and observed for years are in fact communities with plants and creatures distinct from the lands and communities around them. It was decades before I learned that the rich forest behind our cabin on Bearwallow Mountain—with dozens of tree species, thick beds of fern and wildflowers, countless songbirds, and spring lizards (salamanders)—was a "Mountain Cove Forest." When I played on the cliffs and outcrops in Panthertown Valley (Jackson County), I did not know the wildflowers, "spikemoss," lichens, and creepy "rock tripe" (also a type of lichen) were members of a rare community known as "High-Elevation Rock Outcrops." I also had no idea that the unusual plants—mosses, liverworts, and ferns—found next to and behind some of my favorite waterfalls in Jackson and Transylvania Counties have now been classified as "Spray Cliff" communities. Finally, for much of my adult life I have known there were high, mucky swamps called bogs in Pisgah National Forest near Brevard, but no one told me that "Mountain Bogs" were also special natural communities.

Each natural community is a repository of biodiversity. Some members of a community are mobile and flexible and can be a part of several communities. Pileated Woodpeckers, Eastern Box Turtles, White-Tailed Deer, Carolina Anoles (or "Chameleons") and Raccoons are all very adaptable. Some trees, like American Beech, Red Maple, and American Sycamore, can also do well in varied conditions and communities. Other living components of natural communities have very specific requirements and, therefore, limited ranges and adaptability. Venus Flytraps, for example, have such specialized requirements that they are found naturally only within a ninety-mile radius of Wilmington in "Wet Pine Savanna" communities. Wildflowers like Oconee Bell, Heller's Blazing Star, and Gray's Lily are only found in a handful of locations—natural communities that meet their strict requirements. Also picky about its surroundings is the Red-Cockaded Woodpecker, which prefers nesting cavities in living trees, preferably mature Longleaf Pines. The Diamondback Terrapin thrives primarily in salt-marsh communities, and the diminutive Bog Turtle is found only in mountain bogs of the southern Appalachians or cold-water bogs of the northeastern United States.

As you have already figured out, natural communities are complex and take a long time, sometimes thousands of years, to become established. Certain communities requiring cooler air have been around since the Ice Ages, when forests of northern conifers reached as far south as Atlanta 18,000 years ago. When the glaciers, which had stopped several hundred miles north of the Carolinas, retreated, pockets of cold-weather plants were left on mountaintops and in "remnant forests." Such remnant or "orphan" populations are generally found on steep, north- and east-facing slopes with little direct sun, and they are said to have their own microclimates. In my home county of Wake, there is no better example than the steep slopes over Swift Creek, known as Hemlock Bluffs Nature Preserve. At this preserve in the Piedmont are naturally occurring communities of Mountain Laurel, Chestnut Oak, Eastern Hemlock (some over 400 years old), and glossy-leaved Galax—species typically found in the mountains more than 100 miles to the west. At Hemlock Bluffs, in the shade of a fifty-foot, north-facing bank, you can actually feel the difference in temperature and humidity and see the boundary line between a "mountain forest" and the Loblolly, White Oak, and Red Maple common to the Piedmont. Other Piedmont microclimates with mountain flora on north-facing slopes are found at White Pines Nature Preserve (Chatham County) and in the Morgan Creek Valley in Chapel Hill. It goes without saying that such isolated remnants are communities worth protecting.

How do you reestablish the conditions that led to a Longleaf Pine Savanna once the ax or the blade of a bulldozer removes key vegetation and fire is suppressed for decades, allowing competing vegetation to dominate the landscape? How do you replace the lost diversity from a Mountain Bog drained to make way for a new vacation community? How do you replace the lost biodiversity in spruce/fir communities, which once covered thousands of acres of the Black Mountain range and other high peaks across western North Carolina? The short answer is that we can't replace such losses—although nature is resilient and will heal given time and attention. Preserving surviving communities is our best option.

Of the millions of acres of Longleaf Pine that once draped the U.S. Southeast from southeastern Virginia to central Florida and east Texas, 97 percent have been erased or replaced. Of an estimated 5,000 acres of mountain bogs in our southern Appalachians a century ago, less than 500 acres survive. Virtually all that remained of *uncut* Red Spruce and Fraser Fir on Mount Mitchell, a paltry 525 acres, was purchased in 1915 to create North Carolina's first state park. We have been rapacious in our use of the natural bounty we were given. We now know that we removed not only trees but whole communities of living things.

■ We are in a race. In the next two decades, North Carolina's population will increase from roughly 9 million to over 12 million. Natural communities will be competing with planned communities in every region of the state for space. New and expanding businesses employing the next generation of Tar Heels will also have to have space. To get my kids and yours to newly created job opportunities in the year 2030, multilane highways will require more rights-of-way through forests and wetlands. The winners

UNSUNG HEROES OF THE LAND

Throughout this book, I have mentioned the importance of public lands—state parks, national parks, state and national forests, wildlife refuges, and national seashores—and their importance in enhancing critical habitat, biodiversity, and quality of life in North Carolina. This state has also been involved in the protection of land in other ways through the establishment of several trust funds. The first, founded in 1987, was the Natural Heritage Trust Fund, which was followed later by the Parks and Recreation Trust Fund and the Clean Water Trust Fund. Many important places have been saved for future generations because of these funds, and North Carolina has earned the reputation as a national leader in conservation.

None of us can or should expect government to be the only protector of the land. Many North Carolinians are familiar with the work of the Nature Conservancy, which through its membership has protected land and river corridors around the world. The Nature Conservancy in North Carolina, established in 1977, has a shining record of working with private, willing landowners to protect wild rivers, threatened forest ecosystems, and critical habitats across the state. Protection has taken many forms, including conservation easements and even direct purchase. Whether you enjoy time on the cypress-lined Black River, photographing woodpeckers among the Longleaf Pine of the Green Swamp, or experiencing the wildflowers on Roan Mountain, you have the Nature Conservancy to thank.

For almost all North Carolinians interested in preserving special places for future generations, there is a local option in the form of two dozen land trusts/conservancies across the state. They include large organizations, such as the North Carolina Coastal Land Trust (encompassing our coastal counties from the Virginia border to the South Carolina border), the Piedmont Land Conservancy, the Land Trust for Central North Carolina, and the Catawba Lands Conservancy. Some are focused on specific areas of the mountains, including the Carolina Mountains Land Conservancy, the Blue Ridge Conservancy, the Land Trust for the Little Tennessee, and the Southern Appalachians Highland Conservancy. Several smaller, equally effective land trusts focus on a specific river or a specific land area; these include the Eno River Association, the Lumber River Conservancy, and the High-Cashiers Land Trust. If you are a landowner with an interest in protecting acreage for others to enjoy or a volunteer with time and a few skills, there is no better way to get involved with the protection of important habitats and living communities in your area than through a local trust or conservancy. If you don't know the organization nearest you, contact the Conservation Trust for North Carolina in Raleigh.

These organizations have protected literally thousands of acres across North Carolina. They are the personification of stewardship in a modern, increasingly urban state and make it easy for anyone to get involved in the nitty-gritty of land conservation. The trademarked slogan of the Nature Conservancy is "Protecting Nature. Preserving Life." This wonderful sentiment also applies to the network of local unsung heroes preserving the best of North Carolina.

in tomorrow's economy will vacation in communities requiring still more space near coastal and mountain wetlands, in maritime forests, on high-altitude rock outcrops, and in cove forests. Will we have set aside enough rare and representative natural communities to provide a wilderness experience and preserve important biodiversity for future generations? Will the natural boundaries marking the transitions between diverse flora remain distinct, or will they disappear in a homogenized landscape of easy-care alien vegetation?

Natural communities and the quality of life they represent are a major part of our heritage and will be our legacy to future generations. These communities arose out of the geologic, climatological, and topographic variations in the Carolina landscape. If you have believed up until now that we only had three natural transitions—the Coastal Plain, the Piedmont, and the Mountain region—think again. You now have several dozen (and counting) types of natural communities with which to get acquainted. Celebrate our communities of carnivorous plants in the nutrient-poor, acidic soils near Wilmington in the same way that you celebrate the giants of Joyce Kilmer Memorial Forest.

Since the creation of Mount Mitchell State Park in 1915, many natural communities have been given protection in North Carolina's three dozen state parks and natural areas, national seashores, national wildlife refuges, national forests and national parks. Some of the most significant saves and acquisitions, however, have been made by the Nature Conservancy, the Blue Ridge Parkway Foundation, and many unsung heroes of North Carolina's network of land trusts. Such investments in our remaining wild things and places are not just good environmental policy; they are also smart economic policy.

State and city boundary lines are supposed to tell us that we have arrived safely at our destination. For me, however, homecomings are never complete until I cross one of North Carolina's natural boundaries—into the twisted beauty of Live Oaks on Core Banks, a maze of Water Tupelo and Bald Cypress on the lower Roanoke, the awe-inspiring beauty of high-altitude rock outcrops over Linville Gorge, or the "Canadian landscape" on the summit of Mitchell's mountain. Like Professor Mitchell, it behooves all of us, especially our leaders and policy makers, to slow down and observe North Carolina from ground level. There are no more 6,000-foot peaks or virgin forests to discover, but the state's unrivaled natural communities offer every North Carolinian, old and young, the opportunity to experience the rush of discovery.

■ Frogs, tuna, turtles, cicadas, and even delectable mushrooms have internal calendars and clocks, though they do not always adhere to the twelve-month, 365-day Julian calendar. Native honeysuckle must bloom at the right time to feed migrating hummingbirds. Neotropical songbirds know that caterpillars will be on the menu when they return to nest in Tar Heel thickets. Just like the return of giant sea turtles on a high tide in June, every man, women, and child is connected by events written long ago on nature's calendar.

8

UNDERSTANDING NATURE'S CALENDAR

During the second week of September, my kids and I stood on Fayetteville Street, Raleigh's "Main Street," looking westward and skyward. Gathering high over the old Briggs Hardware Building was a swirling cloud of winged creatures. As the sky turned shades of deep pink a few minutes after sunset, we watched as the "cloud" became a tight, dark vortex and disappeared into the roof of a ten-story building a couple of blocks away.

A tripod-mounted video camera, a pair of binoculars in hand, and a Nikon camera around my neck were more than enough to attract the attention of two Raleigh police officers on bicycles. As my preteen son and daughter began to slink away, certain that their dad was getting busted, one of the officers asked, "What are you doing, sir?"

I pointed to the sky and explained that I was filming birds—and not just any birds, but Chimney Swifts assembling for a return trip to South America. Without hesitation, one of the officers corrected me and said, "Sir, those aren't birds, they're bats. I've seen them over Raleigh for years."

Not wanting to embarrass my kids further, I thanked the officers for the information, and they shook their heads and peddled away. They were mistaken, although in fairness, the darting creatures twenty stories above street level could easily be mistaken for bats. What we were observing was an ancient ritual on nature's calendar, a gathering that occurs in September in many cities across North Carolina and North America. Chimney swifts numbering from a few hundred to thousands magically select one chimney (or several across a city) as their roost, or staging area. For perhaps three weeks, the evening "cloud" will grow larger and larger as new swifts join the roost. At night, they literally hang, like bats, on the inside of their chosen chimney and then depart around sunrise to feed on high-flying insects over the city.

Then one morning during the last week of September, often coinciding with a spike of cool autumn air, the swifts will depart en masse, not to be seen again until March. Their annual journey to the rain forests of eastern Peru is staggering to contemplate and a story for another time. It begins here, however, with the formation of a vortex high over an industrial chimney—a fall occurrence just as certain as a new school year and football Saturdays. You can count on the appearance of Chimney Swifts over your city, and you need not put it on your Blackberry or iPhone.

It is one of thousands of events already scheduled on nature's calendar, proving that humans are not the only living things hardwired to schedules. Both animals and plants have things to do and appointments to keep. I first understood this in the North Carolina mountains with the help of mayflies, tiny aquatic insects with vertical wings like a small sail. Their primary habitats include lakes, rivers, and fast-moving streams with clear, cool water. Because there are so many varieties, sizes, and colors of mayflies (almost 700 species in North America alone), "hatches" of adults occur from early spring through fall. Each hatch, or emergence, is distinct and often lasts for no more than a couple of days. This family of insects is appropriately known as "ephemeras" because their lives are so brief.

After an adult mayfly lays its eggs on the water's surface, the eggs sink and yield tiny nymphs, also called naiads, which will molt (split open) up to twenty-five times as they grow and develop in beds of gravel among submerged plants and under rocks. This process of incomplete metamorphosis (there is no pupal stage, only molting nymphs) goes on for an entire year and, at exactly the right moment on nature's calendar, results in a magnificent winged creature that will live for a few hours or days. The adults have no working mouth parts or digestive system; the sole purpose of their one-day life is to reproduce.

The thing to remember is that a mayfly's passage from egg to adult takes one year (and in a few species, two). The emergence cycles of mayflies in streams around the world are well known to trained observers and ardent

The appearance of the Green Drake, one of the largest North American mayflies, or the predicable appearance of other significant aquatic insects is, for many trout fishermen, a major holiday. The event is so important that some anglers are reputed to have missed their children's graduation or their sister's wedding to participate in "the hatch." (Photo from Heath Cartee of Davidson River Outfitters)

fly fishers in the same way that they know their own wedding anniversary or their children's birthdays. Knowing the time of emergence, anglers festooned with tiny hooks dressed (tied) to look like mayflies eagerly await the arrival of specific mayflies so they can match wits with trout awaiting the same creatures. Feeding trout are then forced to choose between newly emerged mayflies or the mayfly imitations offered by anglers. Few creatures have a life as fleeting or as choreographed as the magnificent mayfly.

I have experienced hatches of mayflies on several continents. Although they are similar everywhere, an estimated 3,000 species worldwide have evolved to fill niches based on temperature, the pH of water (whether the water is acidic or alkaline), gravel composition, and available food for the nymphal stage. Some of these aquatics are small, barely the length of your little fingernail, while other species are over two inches in length. In many U.S. states, and in countries with cold-water lakes and rivers, there are hatches so famous that two events occur at the same time: a momentous emergence of mayflies and a deluge of highly motivated anglers.

One such event occurs on the Davidson River (near Brevard) in the Pisgah National Forest. If you are fortunate enough to attend this happening, known as the Green Drake Hatch, you will witness one of the most marvelous annual displays that nature has to offer. Everything rises to the occasion—feeding trout, barn swallows, bats, and anglers—when Green Drakes (*Litobrancha recurvata*) emerge from the sediments of the Davidson around the last week in May. For fisherfolk who are devotees of the fly rod, it is "March Madness" and the Super Bowl all rolled into one. For trout and countless other creatures, it is a smorgasbord unlike any other in the southern Appalachians. *Before it happens*, both trout and anglers wait patiently. *When it happens*, stretches of the Davidson spring to chaotic life over a period of three or four days. It is a natural event of such epic proportions that trout of all sizes (Rainbow, Brown, and Appalachian Brook Trout) feed together, experienced anglers fumble and drool, and nonfishing spouses wonder if their marriages have ended. The Green Drake Hatch is nothing short of a spiritual event for which weddings and funerals should be postponed. For the chosen few who experience this event at its peak, the hatch will be remembered longer than a World Series no-hitter or a hole-in-one in a hailstorm.

Phenology

It is easy to get excited about Green Drakes if you are an angler, or to know when Chimney Swifts depart if you are a birder. The truth is that everyone I know—no exceptions—is also in sync with at least part of nature's calendar. If you are unsure about your synchronicity with wild things, here are some cues that should jog your memory. I'll bet that you already associate Easter with Dogwood blossoms, Redbud trees, and azaleas. If you live in North Carolina's Piedmont, you already expect the "yellow haze" of pine pollen on your car and front porch during the first week of April. By mid-May, most of us look forward to the familiar "jug-o-rum" harmonizing from North Carolina's most famous amphibian, the Bull Frog. You dread July when wild cherries drop and stain your car, and you fear the dents caused by acorns bouncing off your car's hood in September. Remember around the end of September, before the first true cold snap, when you saw a number of large orange butterflies in your yard? They were Monarchs on their fall pilgrimage to Mexico. You always look forward to the second or third week in October and the pallet of fall color in your area, even if you can't identify the trees. These annual plant and animal cycles—whether "blooms," "appearances," or "migrations"—fall within the study of phenology. Phenology is the study of life cycles, with special emphasis on species arrivals, departures, and emergences. (It should not be confused with "phonology," the study of sounds.)

Phenology enables us to connect species that are dependent on each other. Within days of the bloom of Coral Honeysuckle in my yard in late March, for example, I *expect* to see the first Ruby-Throated Hummingbirds

Opossums (top) are not generally ranked among the smartest creatures in the Animal Kingdom. They do maintain a calendar, however, and can be counted on to appear when persimmons (bottom) reach the peak of ripeness across most of North Carolina.

drawn to the honeysuckle trumpets during their northern migration. When our Purple Coneflowers turn to seed in early August, every Eastern Goldfinch in my part of town descends on my yard. When the persimmons turn orange and sweet across North Carolina in late October, you don't have to wait long to see a grinning Opossum. Such "connections" in the natural world are not random: nature makes them easy to predict by providing a calendar.

Phenology also allows us to reach back in time and tie threads of our lives together based on "parallel events" occurring in the natural world. I remember many days with my father because they are connected to a phenological event. Our shad-fishing trips to the Coastal Plain must have occurred in late March, the peak of the Hickory Shad migration up coastal rivers. We fished for Bluegill and Pumpkinseed in Piedmont farm ponds when these scrappy sunfish were on their spawning beds, which happened around the full Moon in May.

Among the best memories with my mother were forage trips—again, based in phenology—for wild blackberries and persimmons. In Hickory Nut Gorge, the blackberries on Little Pisgah Mountain were not ripe until mid-July, which corresponded with the arrival of the first peaches from South Carolina—making possible Mom's favorite mixed peach-and-blackberry pie. As for persimmons, she always said they would not be sweet and worth picking until after one hard frost. Since we lived in Thomasville, located in the central Piedmont, during the school year, those trips had to have taken place in early November and the first freeze. For reasons of phenology and the advice of my mother, I still won't eat persimmon pudding until after the first hard frost.

Once you start remembering your time in a certain place, especially if you lived there over a period of years, a phenological sequence begins to emerge, just like letters in the alphabet. Don't think of such events as "things that just happen" but as nature's social and survival calendar. If flowers do not bloom on time, some insects will lack a food supply. If key species of mayflies do not hatch according to plan, trout are left with a major protein deficit, and birds like Barn Swallows, which also feed on the aquatic insects, may not have adequate food for their offspring. Frogs, tuna, turtles, cicadas, and even delectable morel mushrooms (the first two weeks in April!) have internal calendars and clocks, though they do not always adhere to the twelve-month, 365-day Julian calendar. Nature's calendar includes an internal clock, specific to each plant and creature, that is constantly adjusted by the tilt of the Earth, the phase of the Moon, moisture levels, and the air temperature. Few phenological events are isolated and disconnected from those of other living organisms higher or lower on the food chain. Many naturalists and scientists, more disciplined than I, actually keep a phenological calendar. They record exact dates of the appearance of each species of migratory birds, the emergence of spring wildflowers, or the arrival of certain fish in coastal estuaries. Some "complete naturalists" record everything and can give you an all-encompassing sequence of nature's events for their area.

Although I don't write down such dates, I confess that rarely a day, and never a week, passes that I am not checking on the phenological status of something. These are small things that happen in my yard, in my neighborhood, and across Wake County. The timing of the same events will be a week earlier if you live in New Bern and perhaps a month later if you live in the mountains above 3,500 feet. What you must remember is that there are grand events, and predicable cycles, to be celebrated every day in every corner of North Carolina.

North Carolina's International Airports

Even if you have no professed interest in nature, there is one special group of travelers that deserve your attention and accolades. This is especially true since we humans have a tendency to pat ourselves on the back when it comes to travel prowess. Many of us remember a generation ago when we were at the mercy of travel agents to make all our trip arrangements. Now, we can book and pay for plane trips online with a smart phone and even choose our preferred hotel room at our destination.

What if you had to travel with your kids to South America or to the Canadian Arctic with no computer to plan your trip, no clothing or gear, no accommodations upon your arrival, and *no airplane*? Could you manage to pull it off, and would you have the courage to try?

International travel is "old news" for millions of North Carolina's seasonal guests. They do not use North Carolina's better-publicized international airports—Charlotte's Douglas, the Piedmont Triad, or Raleigh-Durham. They have had their own landing fields for years all across the state. I'm referring, of course, to Tar Heel avian international traffic: the birds of summer and the birds of winter. The birds of summer are mostly neotropicals like the Chimney Swifts, which spend half of their year in North Carolina, building nests and raising their young, and their winters in Peru and northwestern South America. You are likely familiar with many

North Carolina is home to a large variety of migratory birds in both summer and winter. Many Tar Heels are surprised to learn that Barn Swallows, which build mud nests under bridges and eaves, have been known to migrate as far south as Argentina during the North American winter. (Photo by Mike Dunn)

of them, including Purple Martins, which prefer "gourd homes" (winters in Brazil), and Barn Swallows, which build mud nests under bridges and cliffs (winters in Argentina). Other neotropical songbirds are more secretive and love dense thickets and forests—the vireos, cuckoos, buntings, and three-dozen species of warbler. These birds, all warm-weather visitors, are as much a part of the North Carolina landscape as year-round Eastern Bluebirds and Carolina Wrens.

Our best-known avian visitors are the large birds of winter—ducks, geese, and swans—but we are not always sure why they choose to spend almost half the year in North Carolina. In a nutshell, waterfowl from Canada, Alaska, and even a few from Russia and Greenland come to feed, rest, and, in some cases, mate. Unique North Carolina wetlands, especially in coastal estuaries and along coastal rivers, are critical to their survival. Each species of duck and geese has its own travel agent and phenology-based travel plan. Blue-Winged Teals are among the earliest arrivals in late September, followed by other species, including Redheads, Canvasbacks, Black Ducks, Hooded Mergansers, and Buffleheads. They are drawn to international landing fields behind North Carolina's Outer Banks from Currituck to Carteret Counties. Because of their size and numbers, the Brant, Canada, and Snow Geese and the magnificent Tundra Swans exude great star power.

If you need a "must-see" recommendation from this book, here it is: whether you are a birder, a banker, a preacher, or a teenager in love, I guarantee that you will be moved by the annual winter flying-fauna show on

(top) Snow Geese are magnificent black-and-white migrants that spend their summers and raise their young on Arctic tundra before returning to North Carolina's Albemarle Peninsula. (Photo by Mike Dunn)

(bottom) Between Christmas and the end of January, observing thousands of birds of winter in the air above Pocosin Lakes National Wildlife Refuge is one of nature's best outdoor shows. (Photo by Mike Dunn)

North Carolina's Albemarle Peninsula. The area between the Albemarle Sound and the Tar-Pamlico River includes the Pocosin Lakes National Wildlife Refuge (NWR), the Mattamuskeet NWR, and the Alligator River NWR. The display runs from early December to early March, with the peak action from Christmas through January. To see 40,000 (no exaggeration) Snow Geese in the air at one time over Pocosin Lakes NWR is as close as you will get to a truly spiritual outdoor experience. Chevrons of white geese with black wing tips, colored gold or pink by the sun, fill the skies in the morning as they depart the refuge to feed in nearby fields and then return in the evening. In another essay in this book, I suggest that the "awe" terms are overused in our daily lives—but not if they are being used to describe North Carolina's best winter extravaganza. Write down this event in your phenological calendar!

At the same time you are watching clouds of Snow Geese, you will also see families of Tundra Swans, numbering from five to twenty, strung out over winter fields. These white birds with jet-black beaks have six-foot wingspans and can weigh as much as twenty pounds. Tundra Swans, with a life in the wild up to two decades, complete multiple round-trips from North Carolina to their nesting grounds above the Arctic Circle near the Alaska-Canada border.

You might be wondering why three national wildlife refuges are located in such close proximity. Quite simply, there are few wild lands like them on the East Coast. The refuges are surrounded by large farms and a sparse human population. Wetlands, freshwater lakes, and excellent food supplies give swans, geese, and ducks a near-perfect habitat. These are also "dark sites" with few farm lights and no towns for miles. The refuges and surrounding lands also have large populations of deer, bobcat, and turkey, as well as one of the largest concentrations of American Black Bear in the lower forty-eight states—in the range of 6,000 bears over a few counties! These same lands are also home to the reintroduced Red Wolf, which was once eradicated from the wild. In a word, the Albemarle Peninsula is irreplaceable.

We do not have the same staggering numbers of wintering waterfowl that "darkened the skies from horizon to horizon" a hundred years ago, but we do have much of the best remaining waterfowl habitat on the East Coast. These are wild lands worth protecting, not just for North Carolina and the Eastern Flyway but for all of North America. This argument was severely tested in the dispute between the U.S. Navy and landowners of the Albemarle region in the first decade of the 2000s.

The navy chose a 30,000-acre site near the Pocosin Lakes NWR for an Outlying Landing Field (OLF), in large part because the area was lightly populated and not subject to encroachment by nearby cities. Navy planners also coveted the "dark nights" at the location. For these reasons, it would have been a great place for pilots to practice touch-and-go landings, especially night touchdowns on aircraft carriers. Unfortunately for the navy, the birds of winter had long used this area for the same reasons: open spaces and minimal human encroachment both day and night. In the battle of the "Birds vs. the U.S. Navy," the navy lost.

It was a gripping conservation struggle pitting admirals, the Pentagon, and members of Congress against a few farmers, a small-town mayor, Audubon North Carolina (leading the conservation community), some excellent lawyers (who did their work *pro bono*), and some tenacious individuals acting as advocates for the birds of the Pocosin Lakes NWR. The battle was waged in newspapers and in federal courts. There are a variety of reasons why the navy ultimately abandoned its plan for an OLF near Plymouth, North Carolina. In the future, only one reason will be remembered: phenology. Opponents of the navy's plans pointed out from the beginning that for five months of the year, the airspace was already occupied by thousands of large birds. From December through February, the populations of swans and geese were so large that avian squadrons would have posed a constant danger to pilots in the area. These winter dates on nature's calendar had already been taken for hundreds, if not thousands, of years. When the navy sought to co-opt the same dates over the same land, the birds of winter prevailed: two flying forces—fighter planes and large birds—cannot simultaneously occupy one relatively tight airspace.

Adding New Events to Your Calendar

You are never too old to add new events to your phenological calendar. Several years ago I was at Harkers Island the weekend before Labor Day. With a cup of coffee in hand just before 7:00 A.M., I noticed a female Eastern Box Turtle (most males have red eyes and females have yellow/brown eyes) crossing the road in front of our cottage. She was clearly on a mission. I watched the reptile stride purposely between houses heading toward the beach. Twice she stopped and pointed her nose high into the air, like a bird dog trying to detect a scent. In the minute it took me to grab a camera from inside the house, she had covered another twenty-five feet of yard.

Even Eastern Box Turtles have places to go and schedules to keep. This "turtle on a mission" at Harkers Island knew that ripe muscadines were falling to the ground in late August.

All the while, I wondered: why was she heading toward Back Sound and saltwater, only seventy-five feet away? At the point where the yard began to angle toward the water, she turned right and loped toward a tangle of Live Oak, Yaupon, and Muscadine in the southwest corner of the yard. Then it dawned on me: the native grapes were at their peak. (I had noticed Blue Jays fighting over them the day before.) In the still morning air, I could smell overripe fruit that had already fallen. Perhaps the lady turtle had just discovered this place, or perhaps she had come to these old vines for decades, drawn by the intense sweetness of fermenting muscadines. Either way, she had entered the yard to harvest my grapes. For a half hour, I caught fleeting glimpses as she moved around under the dense tangle surrounded by soft, warm fruit.

The truth be told, in more than three decades of visiting Harkers Island, I had never seen an Eastern Box Turtle on the island. What makes this even more surprising is that within two miles of the cottage, I have seen Diamondback Terrapins (a rare, salt-marsh creature), numerous Loggerhead Turtles, Green Turtles, and several giant Leatherbacks. Within hours, I had told shoppers at the Island's Billy Best Market about the visitor in my yard. Several residents confirmed that they rarely saw Eastern Box Turtles moving about Harkers Island—until the Muscadines fall. One woman declared: "It's an August thing . . . when turtles become pigs."

The world's turtles have survived and evolved since the Triassic period (that is, for over 200 million years). Just as we celebrate the egg-laying runs of giant sea turtles that come ashore on a full Moon in the early summer, little box turtles also need recognition for their annual rituals. From spring to late fall, these omnivores eat a boring diet of slugs, worms, grubs, and low-hanging berries in the Carolina underbrush. Now I know they have an end-of-summer celebration with sweet, lightly fermented grapes as the main course. Even a turtle deserves a little "buzz" every once in a while. This simple discovery is now a part of my phenological calendar. When the muscadines fall, I will start looking for North Carolina's Official State Reptile.

It is hard to add phenological events to your calendar if you don't get outside on a regular basis. If you think carefully, however, you may already be participating in an event planned by nature and sponsored by your town. Some towns and counties have long sponsored phenological festivals.

People usually loathe the "hairy worms" that eat their vegetation, but around Grandfather Mountain they celebrate them—specifically, the larva of the Isabella Tiger Moth, known as the Banded Woolly Bear. You probably know it as the Woolly Worm. Because mountain folk have long believed that

No meteorologist can predict winter weather better than a Banded Woolly Bear—or so the legend goes. This caterpillar of the Isabella Tiger Moth has its own festival in Banner Elk during the third week of October.

the width of this worm's fuzzy black-and-brown stripes can help foretell future weather, the town of Banner Elk capitalizes on the belief during a phenologically significant time: the third week in October. During the Woolly Worm Festival, caterpillars are toasted (with words), raced by children, and measured by experts. Does this sound like the celebration of *another* hairy creature with weather-forecasting skills, which searches for its shadow on February 2?

One of the most unusual events on nature's Tar Heel calendar is the Pilot Mountain Hawk Watch, which has been celebrated for three decades during the last two weeks in September. Observers are attracted to this towering monadnock (an isolated mountain) in the northwestern Piedmont to watch for individual hawks and eagles, and also to witness "kettles" of these raptors—groups, usually numbering ten to fifty, which appear to move, swirl, and rise like water boiling in a kettle as the birds ride thermals next to mountains and ridges. Some of these gatherings can be much larger: on one occasion, watchers at Pilot Mountain reported 1,800 Broad-Winged Hawks in the same kettle. This is impressive, until you compare it with the sighting of 11,000 raptors in a single day in 1993 (mostly Buteos—Broad Wing, Red-Shouldered, and Red-Tailed Hawks). The annual Hawk Watch is a human event based on phenology.

If you have the time, you could go to a different phenological festival, or event, almost every week somewhere in North Carolina. The Grifton Shad Festival (April), the Ramp (mountain onion) Festival in Waynesville (May), and the Rhododendron Festivals in Bakersville and Asheville (June) are typical of such events. Once you start looking for them, you can't get away from celebrations taken directly out of nature's packed calendar.

For many years, an angling companion of mine wrote an outdoor column for the *Baltimore Sun* newspaper. The writer, Bernard "Lefty" Kreh, loved the beauty and bounty of autumn—the color changes in leaves and fish, the abundance of acorns and tree nuts, the predictable migration of birds, and the last big "feeds" of mammals. One year, he wrote: "God's only mistake in the Creation was not making twelve Octobers." For a long time, I agreed with Lefty, because there are few times in the temperate zones of the Northern Hemisphere when nature's phenological calendar is more crowded. Perhaps this is why I have only been to a few October football games: there is just too much going on in the outdoors that time of year. Now that I am older and better traveled across North Carolina, however, I respectfully disagree with Lefty's observation. I am convinced that if he

PHENOLOGY AND GLOBAL WARMING

I'd like for the story of nature's calendar to be a happy one, but in the future, it may have ominous implications. You should not be surprised to learn that the study of phenology is being used by scientists to provide important clues about climate change. Going forward, researchers will be interested in variations from the climate norm—established patterns in moisture and temperature. They have long known that a slight rise in water temperature in the Pacific Ocean (El Niño), or a slight decrease (La Niña), can affect weather patterns, even hurricanes, in the Atlantic. They have also known that an average temperature increase of even 2 degrees Fahrenheit can produce noticeable changes in forests and agricultural output. Around the planet, there is already dramatic evidence of temperature rise in the form of satellite imagery of shrinking glaciers, smaller/thinner polar ice, and melting permafrost.

Phenological records can demonstrate changes in temperature in North Carolina and the Southeast. Records from hunt clubs, birding clubs, commercial fishermen, and wildflower lovers will show trends over time. If animals and plants begin appearing earlier in the spring and departing later in the fall, such observations may confirm a rise in temperature. Even a small average temperature increase in the Northern Hemisphere can produce earlier migratory runs of fish; neotropical birds may arrive weeks earlier; wildflowers may bloom sooner; fall colors might occur weeks later; and the swans and geese of the Albemarle Peninsula may arrive later and depart earlier. And these are relatively minor scenarios.

The real concern is that some events on nature's calendar not only may be changed but will cease altogether. A variety of plants and creatures are temperature sensitive: a year-round increase of a few degrees will eliminate some species of mayfly and trout from streams at lower altitudes. A slight temperature increase has the potential to alter, or destroy, forest ecosystems, especially spruce/fir forests above 5,000 feet. As temperatures increase, these islands of northern plant and animal diversity will diminish as boreal forests are pushed higher up the mountain—and they will disappear altogether when trees "run out of mountain." If spruce and fir are forced to exit North Carolina's high peaks, an extreme array of smaller plants and animals will also disappear—an outcome I do not want to contemplate.

Suffice it to say, North Carolina's great temperate biodiversity and varied ecosystems make us a laboratory where change, especially temperature rise, will be visible. Sensitive plants and animals will become living litmus tests. Over the next few decades, our stewardship of North Carolina and this planet will determine whether the events on nature's calendar remain largely unchanged or whether a new calendar will be needed.

were a Tar Heel, he would have great difficulty choosing just one month from nature's calendar.

How do you choose between the high-flying swans and geese at Pocosin Lakes in December and January, the shad runs of March, the Green Drake Hatch on the Davidson River in late May, the Catawba Rhododendron on Roan Mountain in June, the Eastern Box Turtle's "muscadine binge" in August, a vortex of Chimney Swifts in September, and an explosion of color in October? If you live in North Carolina, there is no need to choose a favorite month. No matter the season, nature always provides a full calendar.

PART III.
VOICES FOR THE
WILDERNESS
Saving the Best

■ You may not experience awe watching your favorite team, listening to a symphony, or visiting one of the world's great cathedrals. Awe is, however, a common reaction to sights and events in the natural world. It can be felt by any North Carolinian in Linville Gorge, on the Black River among giant cypress trees, or in your own backyard.

9

STEWARDSHIP AND AWE

When I was a child growing up in North Carolina in the 1940s and 1950s, Sunday school and church attendance were nonnegotiable. During the school year in Thomasville, located in the center of the Piedmont, my family was Methodist, but from Memorial Day to Labor Day, we were "summer Baptists" in the village of Gerton, east of Asheville. When I turned sixteen and had a steady summer job at the Chestnut Hills swimming pool near Asheville, I was faced with a spiritual dilemma. Anyone who has ever sat in a lifeguard's chair knows that the real work of lifeguards—mowing grass, picking up candy wrappers, and cleaning bathhouses—starts long before the pool opens. Even though regular pool hours were 10:00 A.M. to 6:00 P.M. Monday through Saturday, my workday started at about 8:30 A.M.

The pool was closed for church on Sundays until noon, making Sunday mornings the *only* block of time available for serious morning trout fishing. My father and mother were both very supportive of my enthusiasm for fishing, but neither would officially go on record in support of my conspicuous absence from Bearwallow Baptist Church, which was really a community church for the Upper Hickory Nut Gorge. They finally agreed, however, that I could fish a couple of Sunday mornings a month during the summer, but only if I cleared it with the preacher. Ministerial approval—an "excused absence"—was especially important to my mother since she served as the summer pianist at Gerton's only church.

The Reverend Roy Bradford was the minister at Bearwallow Baptist, a classic white-framed Appalachian church with congregation records dating back to the 1860s. Reverend Bradford was an imposing character. In between his required duties on Sunday morning and Wednesday night preaching, he also did weddings, funerals, and served as the local scoutmaster. As if this wasn't enough, he also worked a second job as a law-enforcement officer in nearby Hendersonville. I finally gathered the courage to ask the preacher for a fishing "leave of absence" as we sat on the church steps in June 1962 after his rousing Sunday sermon. I got right to the point: "Your sermons are really good, but would it be OK with you if I fished on *some* Sunday mornings? It's the only time I can drive the thirty-five miles to Brevard and have time to fish."

Just as I had feared, he answered my question with more questions.

"Tell me why trout fishing is so important to you," he began. "Where are you going to be fishing, and do those places evoke a sense of awe for the Creation?"

I wasn't at all prepared to deliver a justification for why I fished, and I didn't know what Bradford meant by "a sense of awe for the Creation." After a long pause, I began mumbling about Sunday mornings being the only time available when I could drive to the best streams and fish a few hours before other anglers disturbed the trout. As additional justification for skipping church, I emphasized that I used no bait and tied my own flies. I thought this was important, because my father and others had led me to believe that fly fishermen were more pure—and worthy—than "worm and cricket dunkers."

Preacher Bradford seemed unimpressed by my reply. He said he saw no connection between bait fishing, fly-fishing, and the condition of one's soul. He continued to press me: "I don't care how you catch fish, but tell me about what is special about the places where you fish? Are you awed by them?"

Suddenly, it was clear to me why "awe" was so important to Bradford. He didn't care if, or how, a person caught fish; he wanted to know if I was impressed with God's handiwork. I began to describe my favorite streams, which were about an hour away, near Brevard: the Davidson, North Mills, and South Mills Rivers. I told him about my "secret" water, a remote stretch of the South Mills below "Wolf Ford" where I never saw other anglers, where the fish were wild, and where wildflowers—especially Pink Lady Slippers, Crested Iris, and Flame Azalea—were common. I mentioned the Black Bear that had followed me on my last trip along the South Mills, the Ruffed Grouse that had exploded from a fallen tree by the trail, and the tracks of Wild Turkeys on the river's edge. I explained that since the fish on the South

Fishing is important to many North Carolinians, but most soon learn that the surroundings are more important. Pictured are the Fraser's Magnolia (above) and Eastern Hemlock (left), encountered by the author along the South Mills River in the 1950s.

Mills were wild and not stocked from a truck, their colors were more vivid than any hatchery trout: the Rainbow Trout had a deep pink stripe, while the Brown Trout glowed with gold and ruby-red spots. The tiny tributaries of my special water also held a few Appalachian Brook Trout, seldom more than nine inches long but more beautiful than any tropical fish I had ever seen in an aquarium.

As I began to describe the trees near the river, including Mountain Magnolia (Fraser's Magnolia), with its large leaves and white flowers, and Eastern Hemlock, with trunks thicker than three large men, Reverend Bradford began to smile and nod.

"You *are* awed by these places," he exclaimed. "You may think you go there to fish alone, but God is talking to you and showing you the best of his Creation. Since this is the case, no sermon I can preach can compete with His handiwork; no hymns we sing and nothing about the beauty of our little church can compare with the magnificence of nature found in the Davidson or South Mills valley. Time spent in the wilderness can never be wrong."

That was the first and only time in my life that a member of the clergy has granted me "absolution for fishing," and since that moment, I have never sought a second opinion! I admit to having abused this now nearly fifty-year-old license to skip church and to backsliding into my own pantheistic, prowilderness theology. Over the years, however, I have continued to struggle with the concept of "awe," which for the Reverend Roy Bradford was important enough to issue a get-out-of-church pass to a teenage sinner.

"Awe" Misapplied

Ever hear someone say they were "awestruck" by a rock star or a sports hero? Over the years, I've had a lot of time to consider what I hold in "awe" or find "awe inspiring." At the top of my list of awesome moments was the mixture of thankfulness, hope, humility, and joy that I felt when my children were born. For my wife and me, those were the most indelible, natural, and life-changing events of our lives. But with or without children, each of us can instantly recall moments of awe, and the events that caused them, which we will never forget.

Because I have been guiltier than most in the indiscriminate use of the term "awe," I have now reconsidered some of the things, places, and situations where I have applied it. In retrospect, the Parthenon in Athens, Stonehenge in England, and the Great Wall of China were all jaw-dropping, and I marveled at the ingenuity and intellect of the people who built them. The great churches and cathedrals of England and France—including Westminster Abbey, St. Paul's, Winchester, Notre Dame, and Chartres—were grand and beautiful. Great art from museums and galleries have evoked in me both curiosity and wonderment. Trips on bullet trains, hovercraft, and jumbo jets were all breathtaking. I have regarded the musical skill of Yo-Yo Ma, the acting talent of Paul Newman, or the athletic prowess of Michael Jordan as inspiring and humbling, especially since I possess no such talents. Again, in describing buildings, inventions, and talents, I have surely uttered more than a few awe phrases.

After decades of reflection, however, I have decided that in describing architecture, technical advances, athletic prowess, musical performances, and great films, "awe" and "awe inspiring" simply don't work for me. I know this is completely subjective, because thankfully, each of us is wired differently. I now regard awe terms as superlatives of description. Roy Bradford had it figured out when, on the steps of Bearwallow Baptist Church, he told me that no sermon, no music, and nothing about his church could compete with the beauty in the wild and of wild things. He understood that I was not just curious, excited, and inspired by my Sunday morning outings—I was awed! So what is it that evokes in humans this superlative in primal emotions?

Through my experiences, through the eyes of my children, and from the declarations of others in literature, I have discovered when awe is the appropriate descriptor. I'd like to think that the first humans to stare into the Grand Canyon, come across Yellowstone Falls, or descend into Carlsbad Caverns felt a sense of awe. Surely, John Lawson felt it when he saw the limbs of oak trees breaking under the weight of millions of passenger pigeons near present-day Charlotte in 1701. André Michaux's declarations of joy in his diary indicate that he found awe in the vista and the diversity of plants observed after climbing Grandfather Mountain in 1794. William Bartram had to be inspired as wrote about the impact of nature while crisscrossing the southern Appalachians in search of new plants. Elisha Mitchell must have experienced a sense of awe on peaks of the Black Mountain from the 1830s through the 1850s or he wouldn't have made the arduous journey from Chapel Hill year after year.

Fortunately, awe is not a feeling that is only experienced once or twice in a lifetime. I believe it was a common reaction to the natural world by the early explorers and writers—and for a sixteen-year-old trout fisherman who experienced awe even on fishless days. The same feeling, however, is available today to every man, woman, and child in North Carolina. Although others might, I don't find it in the Dean Dome, the North Carolina Museum of Art, or even the North Carolina Symphony. I do, however, experience awe at Wiseman's View in Linville Gorge; when a giant sea turtle (Loggerhead, Leatherback, or Green) surfaces next to my boat in Cape Lookout Bight; or during a January sunrise at Lake Mattamuskeet or Pocosin Lakes National Wildlife Refuge, when the sky is filled with layers of undulating chevrons of Snow Geese and Tundra Swans. After many visits, I still find awe in the seemingly endless Longleaf Pine savannah at the Green Swamp near Wilmington and at the sight of *wild* Venus Flytraps or clusters of carnivorous pitcher plants. For those who want it, there is awe at the backyard feeder upon the arrival of a tiny (one-tenth of an ounce) Rufus Hummingbird on a *twenty-degree day in January*. These living, changing places and things are so unique, so special, that they merit a reserved, superlative accolade for the feelings they conjure within us.

By now, you have figured out that for me, most if not all awe-inspiring experiences spring from natural events and the natural world. The places or things to which I am referring can be exotic or familiar, one-of-a-kind or common. I also know that in North Carolina, one need not travel far to be awed.

When it comes to wild places, I have come to believe that awe is the emo-

(opposite, clockwise) Locations like Wiseman's View on the west wall of Linville Gorge provide a grand view of wilderness at any time of the year. For the author, the gorge provides an almost unblemished view of wild North Carolina and never fails to evoke a sense of awe.

A sense of awe can also come in very small sizes. Some Rufous Hummingbirds, weighing one-tenth of an ounce, travel from the mountains of the Pacific Northwest and Canada to spend the *winter* in North Carolina and at other East Coast locations. That's one tough little bird!

The first time you see a Venus Flytrap in a Longleaf Pine savannah, it is hard not to agree with Charles Darwin: North Carolina's most identifiable plant is "one of the most wonderful plants in the world."

tion we feel, and "stewardship" is the human response to protect things and places that cannot be replaced. Stewardship was (eventually) our national response to the wonders of Yellowstone and Yosemite. Stewardship is why we have the Great Smoky Mountains National Park and Pocosin Lakes National Wildlife Refuge. Stewardship is why North Carolina has set aside over three dozen state parks, and why two dozen local land trusts have sprung up across the state.

The words and actions of good stewards have changed law and governmental policy to reflect enlightened land-management practices—practices that have improved the quality of life for all of us. When the late Hugh Morton, owner of Grandfather Mountain, argued that large multiunit buildings on mountaintops and high ridges spoil the view for all of us, the North Carolina General Assembly acted (Mountain Ridge Protection Act of 1983) and prohibited such buildings on ridgetops. When Senators Sam Erwin and Jesse Helms, a Democrat and a Republican, appeared together in Washington, D.C., to oppose the damming of the New River, they did so because of its unique biological diversity and geological age. They spoke for the generations of families who lived in the ancient New River valley in northwestern North Carolina that would have been flooded by a power project with marginal benefits. We could have built on mountaintops, and we could have controlled another river valley because we had the power and engineering skills. Yet stewards stepped forward to speak for places

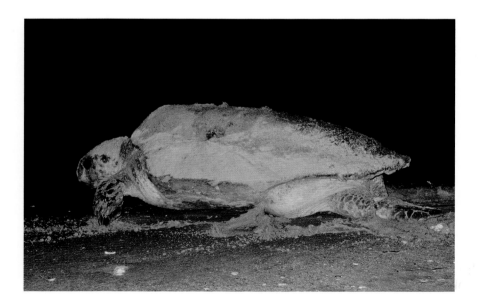

For those willing to stay up on an early summer night during the full moon, a fortunate few will be rewarded with one of the most unforgettable experiences the North Carolina coast has to offer. As they have for millions of years, several species of sea turtles, like this giant Loggerhead, come ashore to lay their eggs. (Photo by Walker Golder)

that were unique and worthy of protection for future generations. Building in the mountains is necessary for growth, and dams are important for power production and flood control. These spirited discussions relating to ridgetops and the New River also proved that sound public policy and good stewardship often coalesce.

Why we care about, and act on behalf of, unique places and "lesser" living things has no easy explanation, but it is touched on in law, ethics, theology, psychology, and biology. I believe we are inclined to protect the things that evoke awe in us. Perhaps my favorite explanation of why we are moved by nature comes from Harvard entomologist and naturalist E. O. Wilson. In the early 1980s, Wilson coined the term "biophilia" (in a book with that title), defining it as humans' innate love and affinity for other living things. His controversial theory is that as humans evolved, we continued to have a strong attachment to the natural world because we are still part of it. But Wilson explains it best in *Biophilia*:

> I have argued in this book that we are human in good part because of the particular way we affiliate with other organisms. They are the matrix in which the human mind originated and is permanently rooted. . . . To the extent that each person can feel like a naturalist, the old excitement of the untrammeled world will be regained. I offer this as a formula of reenchantment to invigorate poetry and myth: mysterious and little-known organisms live within walking distance of where you sit. Splendor awaits in minute proportions.

No Awe, No Connection, No Stewards

I believe that without awe, there will be fewer stewards. Children and adults detached from the land and its life forms have less desire to protect and care for the natural world than those who know it well. As more wild and rural lands have been developed, there are far fewer opportunities to be awed. It should not be news to anyone that even as our population grows, we are producing fewer stewards of the land. Many people in my generation have feared for a decade or more that children of the twenty-first century would become detached from nature. We have all heard anecdotal stories about children, not just from the inner city but from every socioeconomic background, who possess only minimal environmental literacy. Finally, in 2005 Richard Louv put all the anecdotal evidence and soccer-field-sideline conversations into a book titled *Last Child in the Woods*. Louv sounded the trumpet for a generation of children stunted intellectually and emotionally from lack of contact with wild places in much the same way that Rachel Carson had jolted the emerging environmental movement with her 1962 classic, *Silent Spring* (documenting the impact of chemical compounds on birds and ecosystems). Louv confirmed with compelling facts and observations that our suspicions were true that children had become detached from nature. He coined the phrase "nature-deficit disorder," a chilling and accurate diagnosis for the first American generation alienated from the natural world.

The fact that opportunities for encounters with nature have diminished is alarming, but what is more alarming is that it happened on our watch. In this brave new world of twenty-four-hour news, Amber Alerts (missing children announcements), and campus-wide lockdowns, the world seems less safe. As a nation, we have allowed concerns relating to terrorism and flu pandemics in faraway places to spill over into once-safe communities. The "woods" are now off-limits. The protective response of communities, schools, and parents is manifested in many ways. Gated communities used to be the province of the very rich, but now fences and locked gates can be found protecting the most modest homes and apartments. Seldom does a day pass that each of us does not hear a security alarm wailing in a nearby home or in a car parking lot, usually tripped by someone leaning on a car or a large dog walking near a motion detector. As a nation, we are no longer awed by wilderness. Instead, we fear it. Perhaps the most absurd response denoting the modern fear of parks—once deemed wild, safe places—has come from several state legislatures (including North Carolina's). Based on their passage of legislation allowing people with concealed-weapons permits to carry loaded guns in state parks, legislators with fertile imaginations apparently believe that thugs and predators are lurking in the Dogwoods.

We are also apparently afraid of *the dark*. Cities, streets, parks, and our own yards are illuminated to protect us from the evils awaiting in the darkness. Much of planet Earth now has a self-inflicted "cataract" of light-polluted skies. The combination of urban haze (particulates in the air) and too much night light have put most of Europe and the United States, including North Carolina, under light-polluted skies. When was the last time you saw the Milky Way standing out amid a dark sky filled with a thousand stars, or a really great meteor shower like the Leonids of November or the Perseids of August? It is now estimated that two-thirds of the population of the United States cannot see the Milky Way—another great reason to maintain wild places and dark skies. Darkness is part of many natural processes and a condition required by countless creatures. For most of human time, there has also been awe in dark places.

As a parent, I know that all of us have an instinctual desire to protect children from danger—real and perceived. We demand protection in our schools, daycares, and camps. Permission forms and waivers are now required for all but the most routine group activities. Although most of us don't think twice about signing reams of paperwork, the result is that as we protect our children from harm and our institutions from liability, we further isolate the next generation from the world around us. We gave our children smart phones for their safety and our peace of mind, only to worry if they will be found by predators on social networks such as Twitter and Facebook.

The same fears that are reflected in our lighted, gated lives and permission forms are also manifested in the actions of teachers, youth leaders, and caregivers. Several years ago, videographer Joe Albea and I drove to one of our favorite state parks in western North Carolina to film a segment for *Exploring North Carolina*. The ranger who greeted us was still shaking his head over a recent school-group visit to his park.

A yellow-orange bus bearing the name of a county school system had pulled into the parking lot filled with fifth graders. As the ranger stepped up to greet the visitors, a teacher emerged from the bus and in an official voice began a well-rehearsed warning that went something like this: "Please line up beside the bus! Remember what I told you: there are things here that can kill you! There are poisonous snakes, including rattlesnakes, copperheads, and water moccasins. Do not get off the path or touch anything. These woods are full of poison oak and ivy, and ticks that can give you deadly Lyme disease and Rocky Mountain spotted fever. And don't get near any mammal because they can carry rabies!"

According to the ranger, such ill-advised, fear-filled warnings are not uncommon: he had heard similar speeches to young visitors with warnings relating to spiders, bears, and falling rocks. The park ranger concluded: "When the teacher finished addressing the petrified fifth graders, I was ready to apply for hazardous-duty pay because I didn't realize my workplace was so dangerous. There was no joy in nature for those boys and girls!"

Sadly, too many children have never seen a snake in the wild, much less a fox, a bobcat, or a bear. Yet they fear them all. The real killers, however, are sugary drinks, fatty-salty diets, driving while texting, and lack of exercise. The twenty-first century has given us too many ways to be entertained, alerted, tweeted, and "friended." In a twenty-four-hour news cycle, it is hard to differentiate between child abduction in New York, Miami, or Los Angeles from one in Goldsboro or Asheville. The problems of drug addiction and spousal abuse on *Dr. Phil* seem all too local. There is always something or someone to fear—somewhere.

We are all drawn to things with which we are familiar, especially when they make us feel wanted and included. In producing an episode of *Exploring North Carolina* several years ago, I became fascinated by the number of marketing symbols—logos and slogans—that every adult and child has learned like a second language. No matter what age we are, most of us can immediately identify the product or recall the logo for Starbucks, Apple, Facebook, Nike, Volkswagen, Ford, Blackberry, McDonald's, Patagonia, British Petroleum, Viagra, Pepsi, and Honda. In addition to the logos, we also remember the songs and marketing slogans for product groups, whether autos, clothing, fast foods, drugs, or computer software.

Because fewer children have grown up on farms and most others have far less exposure to nature than previous generations, it should come as no surprise that only a small percentage of young people can identify more than a handful of native birds, and even fewer have any proficiency in identifying trees and wildflowers. Also absent are connections to the sounds of nature and any concept of which creatures produce them. To put it in modern lingo, nature needs a better marketing campaign. Corporate ad campaigns are winning the war for the hearts, minds, and time of our children. The first generation of the twenty-first century needs better exposure to "nature's logos"—leaves, shells, seeds, feathers, shapes, and barks—and the sounds of water, birds, frogs, and insects.

Please, don't misunderstand me: social networking, world events, and evolving knowledge of new technologies are important to our growth as individuals and our economic strength as a state and nation. But as parents, educators, and community leaders, we must give our children better, easier access to the natural world. To this end, I agree with E. O. Wilson that there is a need within each of us to affiliate with other organisms—a biophilia. Richard Louv is also correct: when our children are cut off from nature, they suffer physically, emotionally, and intellectually.

YOGI—Yards of Great Interest

As I write these words, I am heartened that many parents, grandparents, and mentors are beginning to wake up to the fact that important needs of children can best be met in a natural setting. In North Carolina, state and city parks, greenway systems, and federal lands (parks, forests, and wild-life refuges) offer wilderness opportunities within a few miles of home. Programs like Take a Child Outside (TACO), sponsored by the North Carolina Museum of Natural Sciences and its affiliates, and Muddy Sneakers, an award-winning initiative for fifth graders in some western North Carolina counties, have demonstrated that tech-savvy kids learn much more than natural science when they are taken outside. Unique ecosystems and dramatic vistas found in parks are not easily accessible to all children on a regular basis, but daily contact with nature in their own yards or at nearby greenways is available to most.

A small yard can be a place of awe, interest, and complexity. I am not talking about swing sets and basketball goals, although anything that takes kids outside is good. To be interesting, a yard must contain things of interest! Are there frogs and salamanders in the creek in your neighborhood or subdivision? Do you have a few caterpillars chewing on your plants, and some interesting beetles? When was the last time you saw grasshoppers and katydids in your yard? In the warm months, are butterflies of eight to ten shapes and sizes common in your yard and neighborhood? Do patches of Purple Violets, Buttercups, and Dandelions with their tiny parachutes—no child can resist blowing on them—appear during the first flush of green? Is there Spotted Jewelweed (also called Touch-Me-Not) with seed pods that spring open when touched by a tiny hand? Is there White Clover in your yard that gives your child a chance at getting lucky? Discovering a four-leaf clover with a small child is better than winning the lottery. My wife and I are still discovering pressed four-leaf clovers in books around the house, discovered in our yard many years ago by our children. We also remember that those patches of clover provided hours of free babysitting.

Do you have a climbing tree, or a tree limb capable of holding a knotted climbing rope? Forget the Bradford Pear and many of the fast-growing exotics in which limbs break easily. Most of our native oaks and maples will do fine, but may I suggest an American Beech, American Sycamore, Red Maple, or Basswood, each of which have excellent limb structure for climbing. They also make great shade trees. Plant a native tree in honor of each of your children when they are born or when you move into a new house. Even if you move away before the trees are mature, you will have done a great service for the next family to occupy your house by leaving a shade tree (that can reduce air-conditioning costs), a climbing tree, and *native* trees that will be home to countless birds and insects.

In the fall of the year, is your yard interesting enough to reveal birds' nests

There should be wild things in a child's yard, or in nearby parks, to excite and entertain them. Children are thrilled to discover a caterpillar munching on a leaf—like this handsome Hickory Horned Devil, the caterpillar of the Royal Walnut Moth (left)—or to uncover a four-leaf clover. (Caterpillar photo by Mike Dunn)

in trees and bushes? Are there lightning bugs in the summer, and mushrooms of different shapes and colors that pop up after a wet spell? In a dark, shady corner, do you have a couple of rotten logs or a stump on which some lovely fungus will grow and that will serve as home to any number of glossy beetles or even a salamander? And if you are really lucky, perhaps you have a "fairy ring" of mushrooms, which appears in ever widening circles in late summer?

Am I an expert on yard design? Absolutely—not. But my wife and I did spend a lot of time outside with our children, and we remember what excited them and what excited us at the same age. I have listened to teachers and educators describe the simple, natural pleasures that an interesting yard, a park, or a greenway can provide. When a yard contains many of the things listed above, they attain what I call "YOGI" status—Yards of Great Interest.

If you ask families if they want a truly child-friendly yard, a YOGI yard, all of them will answer in the affirmative. Yet many American yards have been hijacked by the belief that good yards are sterile and blemish free. As we have acquired more-perfect yards, we have at the same time eliminated the many important and stimulating places in which to raise our children. On what other piece of land will your children spend more time? The perfect kid lawn is not a bug-free, perfectly green parcel with ideally shaped trees.

YOGIs (Yards of Great Interest) have rotting leaves and stumps. Here, your child may find a Giant Stag Beetle (left) or a Marbled Salamander (right). Does your yard meet the test? (Photos by Mike Dunn)

It does not have brick-red mulch, uniform bushes, and an automatic sprinkler system. The perfect kid lawn is not visited quarterly and sprayed by men in white suits wearing respirators. More important, no "perfect," sterile lawn can hold enough exciting things to become a YOGI yard.

If your present yard is not child friendly, you can easily make a few changes. Add a bird feeder and start a compost heap of leaves (a dependable place to find earthworms). A small (think four feet by seven feet) butterfly garden with a mix of *native* wildflowers can provide excitement year-round. Plant it with your kids, and let them water it. Let the flowers go to seed. A butterfly garden can be even more interesting in the fall, as Goldfinches and sparrows feed on the seeds of coneflowers and milkweed. Check the dried stalks carefully for camouflaged cocoons that will provide butterflies next spring. In yards and gardens, bigger is not always better. E. O. Wilson got it right when he wrote: "Splendor awaits in minute proportions."

Unexpected Awe

Trips to mountain vistas, a hike in a pine savannah, and the spray from a mighty waterfall are almost guaranteed to evoke awe in any human. With your children or by yourself, you should be open to those special moments in nature—unexpected awe—that take in many forms. On a recent June morning, my wife and I were in a small boat near Beaufort, on one of those rare just-the-two-of-us trips, when she noticed a large dark form moving just under the surface. Being certain that it was a large ray, I maneuvered the boat within twenty-five feet for a better look. With no fanfare and no other boats nearby, a Leatherback Turtle, perhaps seven feet long and weighing close to 1,000 pounds, surfaced next to us. To our delight, it swam near the surface along a sound-side beach for another fifteen minutes, where we watched it surface four more times. Finally, the great animal turned slowly in front of us in calm, clear water. Its front flippers were enormous, making it look as wide as it was long. The creature's ridged, glossy carapace (no bony shell as with most turtles) was mostly black and accented with small, light, counter-shading spots. A string of Cobia, fish weighing as much as forty pounds, dutifully followed their reptilian leader. My wife, clearly moved by the experience, commented that the magnificent turtle and its "groupies" constituted a living, mobile ecosystem. The experience also provided a private, shared moment of awe that we still talk about.

Experiences with rare wild creatures may be uncommon, but visitors to the natural world must be prepared to rejoice in the moment when nature offers a show-and-tell. I remember pulling off of a rural road with my son one evening immediately after seeing a single meteor streak across the night sky. Within a few minutes, several more "shooting stars" were offered as a reward for our patience. On my daughter's twelfth birthday in early November, we went for a hike near a waterfall when an early-season burst of snow provided a more memorable show than the waterfall. Nature is generous with such moments if we pay attention and savor them.

One final example: it doesn't take an endangered giant, a heavenly fireworks display, or a waterfall to elicit awe. The section of Highway 70 that runs between Kinston and Goldsboro is flat, and during July and August, it's always very hot. If you are driving back from the beach along this stretch, the last thing you want to do is stop—but think again. In July and August, almost every fence post and telephone pole has a garland of green and orange or red-orange. It is the time for the Trumpet Vine (also called Trumpet Creeper). This lovely native seems to flourish in sandy soil or hard clay, even in the driest weather. There are few hardier plants in North Carolina.

A couple of years ago, during the last week of July, the temperature was still in triple digits at 5:00 P.M. Everything along Highway 70 looked wilted and scorched—except the Trumpet Vine. Perhaps because these vines and their flowers were the only survivors in the torrid heat, I decided to take a closer look. I turned off the four-lane road and stopped less than 100 feet

Even nonbirders can't help but be moved by the majesty of a Ruby-Throated Hummingbird sipping from a common Trumpet Vine.

from an intersection west of Kinston. On a half dozen fence posts were several hundred orange trumpets. From inside my car, I could see honeybees and bumblebees—some *very large* bumblebees that were making a distinctive humming sound. In between the noises of the passing cars, I realized that the sound was not coming from bees at all. As I refocused, I was looking at a half dozen Ruby-Throated Hummingbirds in one small area. They were looping and diving, often plunging neck deep in the Trumpet Vine blooms. I turned off my car's engine, leaned against the hood, and watched the show. At times, more hummers appeared, and I was uncertain whether to call the aerial assemblage a covey, gaggle, flock, or murder (the term for a group of crows).

The only time I've seen more Ruby-Throated Hummingbirds in one place was on Hugh Morton's porch at Grandfather Mountain. Their iridescent emerald-green bodies would have been enough, but a few of the mature males also had brilliant red-orange throats that were about the same color as the Trumpet Vine. My friend Susan Campbell, who has banded over 4,000 hummers in North Carolina, confirms that the same birds can make five or even six annual round-trips between their East Coast summer home and their wintering grounds in Central and South America. Susan always reminds me that eight to ten adult hummingbirds together weigh about *one ounce*. With wings fluttering at seventy beats per second over gorgeous Trumpet Vine blooms, this annual summer occurrence should evoke a sense of awe in anyone with a pulse. And "unexpected awe" may be the best of all!

■ Make nature a family affair. Encourage your children to try to learn a new leaf or bird for every commercial logo they can identify. Regardless of the size of your yard, make it a Yard of Great Interest, an outdoor laboratory with the daily possibility of an awe-inspiring discovery. Leave the smart phone, the Xbox, and the iPad at home and rent a canoe at a nearby park. Plan a special discovery trip *every month* to a new park or location (no need to drive more than fifty miles). Let your kids, your grandchildren, and your nieces and nephews go online and pick the park and location that interests them the most.

If you and your family can't find the time in your workweek or weekend to commune with nature, you may have to ask for an occasional "excused leave of absence." If you are part of a faith community, ask your minister, priest, imam, or rabbi for a day off to visit a special wild place. I hope you encounter your own Roy Bradford who asks some tough questions, especially this one: "Are you awed by the natural world around you?" Wise people know that time in the wilderness is never wasted. People who are given the chance to be awed by wild places and things will become the next generation of stewards. And Lord knows, we need more good stewards.

Amen, Preacher Bradford!

■ Every young life needs mentors and muses to introduce them to wild places. Muses open doors, inspire, cajole, and entice us out of our comfort zones. Mentors need only offer a steady hand and a dollop of advice. It is in the preteen years that nature's learning window is wide open—when spiders are not scary, fish are not slimy, and beetles are cool, not creepy.

10

MUSES, MENTORS, AND SLOW BOATS

I believe in muses. Every year, they compete for my time and loyalty. In mid-February, they beckon me to look for Tiger Salamanders in ephemeral ponds in the Longleaf Pine forests near Rockingham. That is the time that these large, striped amphibians are most active. By mid-March, the river muses call me to the Roanoke and Tar Rivers to greet the annual spring migration of Hickory Shad and Blueback Herring. In April, the wildflower muses invite me to see spring's best floral offerings, especially the seldom-seen ones. By May, the muses representing birds and butterflies are most active. I met each of these muses in my childhood and still hear from them each year. Sometimes they use human intermediaries.

I had met the owner of Grandfather Mountain, Hugh Morton, on several occasions and had long admired his photography, especially his photos of endangered wildflowers. I saw Morton in early March 2004 at the Grandfather Mountain sandwich shop, and I asked him where a person might see Gray's Lily and the even-rarer Oconee Bell *in the wild*. Morton didn't know me that well, so it was no surprise that his directions and advice were vague. A couple of weeks later, however, I got a call from Grandfather Mountain naturalist Jesse Pope, who worked with Morton. Pope told me that Morton wanted to let me know where the Oconee Bell would be blooming toward the end of March. After swearing an oath of secrecy on the phone, I was given the location and the approximate time of the bloom.

A few weeks later, I left Raleigh on a Sunday morning to drive to the secret location. Even if tortured, I will not give it up! All I will reveal is that Morton's trove of Oconee Bell (also called Shortia) was located next to a creek above 2,000 feet and within the triangle formed by Black Mountain, Grandfather Mountain, and Morganton (about four counties). What I haven't told you is that this was the "lost flower" first identified and collected around 1790 by the French naturalist/botanist André Michaux. They would not be seen again in the wild until 1877, when a teenage boy from Statesville sent a sample to the greatest botanist of the time, Asa Gray of Harvard. Even today, Oconee Bell is found only in a handful of places in the southern Appalachians.

After parking my car and walking a quarter mile through a field, I turned right and followed a faint footpath next to a small creek. Along the trail were mature Catawba Rhododendron extending up the hill. Several hundred feet later, in a rocky opening next to the creek, the Rhododendron thinned, allowing partial sunlight on the moist banks. Any other time, I would have thought I was looking at a patch of Galax with its waxy, shiny leaves mixed in with some white Canada Violets. But at age sixty, for the first time in my life, I was looking at a glorious 100-foot-long patch of Oconee Bell at the peak of its bloom. I stayed there for three hours, observing, taking pictures, testing the pH of the soil, and reveling in the moment. I had seen the flower in botanical garden plantings, but never in the wild. Why had the rare plant survived here and in only a few other places? What other plants occurred with it, and how much sun did it require? For me, it was a most special moment; I owed it to Mr. Morton and the wildflower muses. To this day, I am certain that the muses must have intervened with Hugh Morton and vouched for me.

Finding Muses and Mentors Early

The natural world has an extraordinary power to reach out, enlighten, and educate each of us at any age. Its power is found in remote mountains, desert landscapes, coastal wetlands, and the smallest stream. Nature is liberating, and it is free of cost. There is just one hitch: to get the full measure of benefit from nature's offerings, children must be introduced to the "muses" at an early age. I do not mean anthropomorphized animals (like Bambi or Smoky Bear), wood nymphs, or trolls. Because nature speaks to us through a thousand voices—wind, water, shapes, and colors—I choose to call these forces muses.

I didn't fully appreciate my muses at the time, but my early world was filled with them and their cousins: mentors. In Greek mythology, both muses and mentors rated a capital *M*. The Muses provided inspiration for artists, musicians, and poets, while Mentor—the wise old friend of Odysseus—offered sound advice and a steady hand. I believe in "lower-case" mentors and muses, which come in the form of moms and dads, grandparents, older siblings, and good neighbors. As in Greek mythology, the role of muse can also be played by the natural world around us as it inspires and invites us to explore and make connections.

Every young life deserves to have his/her own personal muses and mentors. Before the ages of twelve or thirteen, children aren't as self-conscious, inhibited, and fearful as they become after puberty and as young adults. In our first dozen years, when our brains are more plastic, we can learn a second or third language more easily. During this time, we begin to form lasting associations and allegiances. Many of us still root for the team that first attracted our loyalty before we turned twelve—perhaps the Tar Heels, Yankees, Dodgers, or Wolf Pack. In those critical years, most of us learn to ride a bike, swim, fish, and pick up critters—frogs, worms, and salamanders—without fear. While this easy-learning window is open, spiders are not scary, fish are not slimy, and beetles are cool, not creepy. Wildflowers are magical, and in our preteen years, it's okay to violate occasionally the "look-but-don't-touch" rule. Forests and swamps are places of opportunity and adventure. Never again in our lives are we more open to new experiences.

Great teachers in math, science, and the humanities can come later. In the early years, kids don't need experts—they need introductions. Muses open doors, inspire, cajole, invite, welcome, and entice us out of our comfort zones. Mentors need only offer a steady hand and a dollop of advice. Comfort in and acceptance of wild things and places after these tender ages is, of course, possible, but it will be more of an uphill battle.

There is a new mantra in this country and in most of the developing world: "connect and empower." We all want every child to have access to a computer and, where possible, access to high-speed Internet service. Here in North Carolina, there appears to be unusual unanimity among government, university, and business leaders that technical literacy is critical if we are going to compete in a knowledge-based global economy. Unfortunately, in our progression from an economy based on agriculture, then manufacturing, then knowledge and technology—a transition we should all support—important connections with the natural world have become frayed. As we surge forward in a world connected by fiber optics and satellites, the role of mentor has been institutionalized: law firms have mentor programs for new associates, and businesses assign "mentors" for new hires. We often turn over the roles of muse and mentor to strangers—coaches and instructors in everything from soccer, baseball, basketball, and football to dance, music, painting, and cooking. Some of us even have what are called "life coaches." Even more troubling, the time once given to muses and mentors has been surrendered to "apps" and "friends" on tiny flat screens.

Sometimes the roles of mentor and muse are wrapped up in a single person, but more often, two or more individuals perform each distinct and important role. Aside from having several human muses and mentors, I was introduced to nature's muses in my earliest years. There were muses in tiny creeks, in mountain forests, in trout streams, in tidal pools, in the backyard oak, and, most especially, in wetlands and marshes. I have discovered that once you are introduced to a muse in nature at an early age, you can always return to it, continue to learn, be inspired, and make connections without interruption. The same muses that had led me to the Oconee Bell had shown me Painted Trillium, Dutchman's Breeches, and Ginseng on Bearwallow Mountain fifty years earlier.

The Muse in the Marsh

In the winter and spring of 1973, my father was in and out of Baptist Hospital in Winston-Salem with a cancer that had sapped his strength for almost a year. On weekends and some weekday nights, I would drive from Raleigh to visit him, and my mother and brothers also converged on the hospital from their homes. In May at the end of a visit of several hours, Dad surprised me by saying: "I love having you visit, but how long has it been since you've been fishing in the mountains or at the coast? We're going to run out of things to talk about if you don't do something interesting. Go *somewhere* next weekend, and then tell me about it. You have a lot of places from which to choose."

I protested and said I would be back in Winston-Salem the following weekend, but my father insisted. I asked for his suggestions because we had fished in so many places—on the Outer Banks, in coastal rivers, in Piedmont reservoirs, and in the TVA lakes of North Carolina and Tennessee. Each place had special meaning and its own muse. Since all waters and wild places "speak" and entice in different ways, I wanted my father to help me choose my destination. At first, we discussed Hazel Creek (a remote stream on the "wild side" of Fontana Lake) and Dad's favorite mountain reservoir, Lake Nantahala. We discussed the limestone outcrops at Kure Beach, the only rocky (and, at the time, largely undeveloped) coastline in North Carolina. He then mentioned Cape Lookout and the salt marsh we had visited the previous October. On that fall trip, we had spent an entire weekend in the marsh behind Whitehurst Island fishing a little and observing a lot.

The following Friday, still feeling guilty for not traveling to Baptist Hospital, I left my job in Raleigh and headed for Whitehurst Island, located about a mile to the east of Harkers Island behind Core Banks. At that time, Core Banks and its marshes were not yet part of Cape Lookout National Seashore. The first thing that you should know is that Whitehurst is not an island at all, but a changing, irregular patch of marsh about the size of two football fields behind Core Banks. Salt marshes never look the same twice. From Maine to central Florida and along the Gulf Coast, there are several species of cord grass, or marsh grass; but one of them, commonly referred to as Spartina (from its scientific name *Spartina alterniflora*), holds them all together. In October, it had been the color of golden wheat, but in late spring, it was a vibrant new green—almost a chartreuse.

On the east end of Whitehurst was a deep slough draining a large mudflat. At low tide, the flat looked like a barren extension of the island, but

This is Whitehurst Island, which is really a patch of Spartina marsh that is flooded at high tide. It doesn't look like much is going on until you get closer and it reveals its secrets.

at high tide, it became a magical shallow lake. At first glance, a salt marsh and its surrounding shallows are just grass and mud, but even the most cursory examination reveals they are alive with crabs, snails, mussels, clams, worms, forage fish, and different birds in each season. Because salt marshes occupy the tenuous space between land and sea, my father and I had long regarded coastal salt marshes as the "edge of life." Dad could have picked other marshes from our past, but Whitehurst was representative of every marsh.

As I approached Whitehurst in a small skiff near the full moon in May 1973, a colony of Laughing Gulls began rising from the grass to protest my presence. Some even bombarded me and my boat with bird guano: I had arrived at the peak of nesting season. Every few feet, there was a nest with dark-olive, speckled eggs—clearly not a good time to walk on the marsh island. Nearby there were egrets, herons, and other wading birds. On another small island of the Whitehurst complex was a raucous colony of Forster's Terns. Just a few months earlier, the same marsh and mudflats had been home to ducks—Redheads, Black Ducks, and Buffleheads. Two birds were missing: Brown Pelicans and Ospreys, now common on the Outer Banks, were not at all common in the early 1970s.

Around Whitehurst, I had dug clams, caught fish, and hunted ducks with my father, but I never ventured far back into the marsh. That day, though, the tide kept rising. Because of the full moon, I had arrived during a "spring tide," when tide levels can be a foot or more above normal at that location. The skiff was pushed by my father's old five-horsepower Johnson outboard. With the motor off, I maneuvered easily with the twelve-foot ash "shoving pole" we had gotten in Currituck Sound several years earlier. That day, the muse of the marsh guided my trip. The incoming tide allowed me to slide effortlessly over water less than two feet deep. I poled next to an oyster bar, where I saw Sheep's Head hanging in the current with their wide black-and-white stripes. The water was clear, revealing hundreds of living oysters with shells slightly agape. I knew that oysters filtered their food out the nutrient-rich water of the salt marsh—as much as fifty gallons per day, per oyster.

Over the next hour, the muse and the surging tide pushed me another quarter mile across the huge flat between Whitehurst Island and Core Banks. In the Eel Grass, the primary vegetation on the flats, there were Bay Scallops, Banded Tulips, and two kinds of whelk (Knobbed and Lightning). Several species of ray flushed under my boat, including a large Southern Stingray, the species that would impale me with its barb and send me to the hospital twenty-five years later. Blue Crabs floated in the current, and an occasional shrimp or Stone Crab revealed its position in the Eel Grass. Then the fish appeared—Pinfish, Sea Robins, Striped Mullet, and Lizardfish. As motionless as driftwood came a Giant Needle Fish, a two-foot-long gar-like species from the Age of Dinosaurs with a toothy snout and eyes the size of a nickel. Finally, in a depression a foot deeper than the surrounding waters, I saw a school of Redfish, also known in North Carolina as Channel Bass or Red Drum, that would later become our Official State Salt Water Fish. Depending on the light, drum can appear silver or gold. The most distinctive features of drum, however, are the black and copper spots on their tails, which resemble eyes. In the marsh and on mudflats, drum will eat almost anything, including shrimp, minnows, crabs, and even sand dollars.

I wanted to catch something so that I could tell about it on the next visit to Winston-Salem. While trying to grab a fishing rod armed with a gold spoon, I made noise and sent ripples in every direction. By the time I secured the rod, all the Redfish had quietly slipped away. It would be years before I became semiskilled at stalking Redfish on the flats. Fishing extremely shallow water requires more stealth and technique than does fishing for the same species in deeper waters nearby.

Two hours into my drift across the flat, the surging tide began to slow;

Between Whitehurst Island and Core Banks, a *quiet* visitor can sometimes observe one of the real treasures of the marsh: a Diamondback Terrapin. (Photo by Walker Golder)

I was almost to the backside of Core Banks. It was there, on the line where Eel Grass and Spartina meet, that I saw one of the great treasures of the marsh: a Diamondback Terrapin. It is a magnificent small turtle less than a foot in length, including the head and tail. They can survive in the high-salt environment of seawater (34 parts per thousand, or ppt) like the water of Whitehurst Marsh and in the brackish waters of mainland bays and sounds, where the salt content is 5 to 25 ppt. They are distinguished by their beautiful shells, which have designs that are almost geometric in proportion and seemingly drawn with pen and ink. I had seen Diamondback Terrapins behind Ocracoke and at Portsmouth Island, but never at Cape Lookout. Little more than a century ago, the little turtle was abundant in marshes along the East Coast, but by 1973 it had almost vanished—into the nets and stew pots of coastal settlers. I couldn't wait to tell my father.

For me, the best was yet to come, and it wasn't the Speckled Trout (Spotted Weakfish) or the aggressive Bluefish that I caught later that day. In a thicket of Red Cedar, young Live Oak, and Cat Briar on a small hummock (a patch of higher ground) on the backside of Core Banks, a dazzling bird with bright green, red-orange, and blue plumage appeared. It was at most six inches long, but it was more colorful than anything I had ever seen in North Carolina. I got out of the skiff and walked closer to the hummock as Fiddler Crabs scurried to their burrows. The bird, which departed and

(top) On a very high tide, the waters between Whitehurst Island and Core Banks reach far back into the marsh to the hummocks of Cat Briar, Live Oak, and Red Cedar in the distance.

(bottom) Before 1973, the author had never seen a bird such as the Painted Bunting in North Carolina. The multiple tags help scientists follow the bird's nesting and migratory patterns. Couldn't you also mistake this creature for a parakeet? (Photo by Walker Golder)

reappeared several times over the next twenty minutes, looked tropical and parakeet-like in every way, except for one thing: it had a short, straight beak like a sparrow or wren, not the curved beak of a parakeet. It was not until late that evening, after I had described the bird to several people on Harkers Island, that I was told it was a male Painted Bunting.

After a half hour on the backside of Core Banks, I noticed that the tide was beginning to ebb—my cue to quickly depart the shallows. Even with limited experience in the marsh, I had learned years earlier that a falling tide can leave you stranded in the mud in the smallest of boats. The muse in the marsh had shown me a spectacular day and had lured me deeper into the Spartina maze than I had ever gone. I had seen more creatures than ever before because I had been slow and deliberate while poling and drifting. At that time, I was in my late twenties and had just spent a combined seven years in college and law school and several more years attached to the desks of my first jobs. Now, almost forty years later, even if a decade has passed since my last visit, these places and their muses remain welcoming and familiar. Every few years since 1973, the muse in Whitehurst Island marsh has shown me more secrets—large sharks, giant Loggerheads, some five-foot Cobia, enormous dragonflies, and even a family of otters. I have continued to respect the silence necessary to see the best of the marsh by poling a light, shallow-draft boat in the Spartina and over the flats.

As the years have gone by and my boats have grown larger and faster, I have tried to remember that *slow boats* are best. In slow boats—skiffs, canoes, and kayaks—you can observe and talk with friends, and especially your children. Many of the best conversations with my father and friends have occurred on slow boats over a few miles. I tried to remember that important lesson when, years later, my wife and I took our children to Cape Lookout and into the marsh.

Making Time for Muses and Mentors

All of us have a favorite teacher, and if we are lucky, we have a long line of them over many years. They are women and men who took the time to make a difference in our lives. They can come at any time and at any age. We generally think of teachers in the formal settings of kindergarten through twelfth grade or at the college/university level. Because of the importance of good teachers, we want our children to attend schools where those teachers are most likely to be found—strong public schools, magnet schools, charter schools, private schools, or schools with a specialty (math, science, drama, languages, or music). We have started our children earlier than any other generations in public and private preschool programs, sports programs, language immersion, and other accelerated instruction. Because we have come to believe that good teachers and excellent schools are necessary for our children's success, we are quick to allocate blame to those same teachers and schools when children are less than successful.

If I sound cynical, it is because I have come to believe that we live in a world with too much information and not enough inspiration. Don't get me wrong: we can never have enough great teachers in our schools, nor can the best teachers be overpaid. Too often, though, we have equated good teaching with end-of-year results on standardized tests. Perhaps because we have required educators at every level to "teach to the test," they have been given less time and opportunity for inspiring curiosity and creative thinking. To our credit, we have extended high-speed Internet to most school systems and have made computers available to students in every demographic. But in our quest to "leave no child behind" by utilizing the latest technology and standardized tests, we have missed the mark with a growing number of students.

All of our efforts have been for the noble purpose of helping our children and nation remain competitive, but the results have not been good. For at least a decade, we have seen a stream of depressing test data in which American elementary and high school students rank behind those of twenty-five or more countries (in Europe and Asia) in math and science and rarely higher than fifteenth in reading. Perhaps more disturbing is that observers have also charted a decline in creativity in children across the United States. "Creativity" is problem solving with fresh ideas and not a search for the "right answer." For many years, the Torrance Test of Creative Thinking (TTCT), designed by Professor Paul Torrance of the University of Minnesota and later the University of Georgia, has been used to test creativity, or "out-of-the-box" thinking. The TTCT is not intended to measure IQ (intelligence quotients) or the ability of a child to find the correct answer. Instead, in the TTCT, points are scored for unique approaches and nonconformity to determine a CQ (creative quotient).

While IQ scores have been stable or have risen slightly in the United States (a good thing), Torrance scores measuring creativity have *decreased* steadily. What should concern us is that more than a high IQ, a high TTCT score is often considered more predictive of success in later life in the creative endeavors of business, science, engineering, music, and writing.

After watching our own children and their friends, my wife and I are certain that you don't have to hire a coach or a tutor to help your children be more creative. Take them outside *at an early age* and on a regular basis. Give them interesting places to play, with or without their friends. The natural world is full of problems and problem solvers. Adaptation by plants and animals is problem solving—creativity—on the most basic level.

Think about it: the moth with the best camouflage and the most erratic flight pattern survives predation by birds and bats. Most species of flounder, and other flatfish in our coastal waters, cover themselves with sand to hide from enemies and to get closer to their own prey. The lovely Carolina Anole, known to many children as the "Chameleon Lizard," can change from emerald green on new vegetation to dusty brown on a rock outcrop as it blends in to its surroundings. Spiders spin their webs in just the right places to catch dinner. Trees that develop leaves with a glossy, waxy finish lose less water to evaporation and survive better during dry spells. The thick bark of the Longleaf Pine enables it to survive repeated forest fires. An owl is successful as a hunter because the "soft edges" on its wing feathers enable it to fly silently, even when flapping its wings. The teeth of beavers, very hard on one side and softer on the other, are self-sharpening and continue to grow throughout the life of the animal.

Where is the creativity in these things, you ask? In nature, form follows function. Plants and animals of all kinds compete to fill the niches in every ecosystem. Life forms that adapt and evolve are the ones that thrive. Connections and problem solving in the natural world are revealed to human visitors, especially the young ones. Are such things better learned in a classroom or by personal observation? Can you write or speak about things you have witnessed, touched, and smelled better than something only described by others?

While preparing an episode of *Exploring North Carolina* titled "Nature's Classroom," I learned about an outreach program in western North Carolina called "Muddy Sneakers." Its mission was simple: take fifth graders and their teachers out of their school buildings for ten or more days of a school year for day-long sessions at nearby forests, parks, and public lands (as many as five days each in the spring and fall). With the help of adult counselors experienced in wilderness and outdoor activities, students and their teachers are broken into small groups of eight to ten. Required science, math, and English curricula are covered utilizing plants, creatures, and experiences in the outdoors. The concept, known for many years as "experiential learning," allows students to absorb important lessons utilizing all of their senses. By being involved in the experience firsthand, students are able to reflect, analyze, and draw their own conclusions. To be sure, there are many kinds of experiential learning, including travel to other cultures and entry-level jobs that require interaction with people, but few experiences in life are as important as direct contact with the natural world.

Both students and teachers—justifiably skeptical about giving up school time—reported excitement, energy, and academic success as a result of their experiences with Muddy Sneakers. Some students reported holding and studying a variety of creatures (caterpillars, grasshoppers, salamanders, etc.), closely examining plants, and observing changing weather while spending hours in public parks or forests for the *first time*! Observations of positive results were not just anecdotal; over a period of several years, students who had been to nature's classroom scored higher on year-end tests than their peers who had not had the advantage of Muddy Sneakers.

I had the opportunity to talk with several children, both girls and boys, who had participated in the program; each claimed to remember what they had seen, touched, and smelled on Muddy Sneakers days better because it was his/her own experience and not that of someone else. Connections with nature make science at school more interesting, writing more textured and descriptive, and reading more enjoyable. Although experience in nature can never fully replace the formal learning opportunities available to students from kindergarten to college, it does provide context and greater depth to the things they learn from others. Time outside in those early years is critical for children, and it benefits the teachers charged with their education in all disciplines.

When I watched the kids in the Muddy Sneakers program discovering wild places near their homes for the first time, I thought about the men and women who gave their time to become mentors and muses for strangers. I also realized how fortunate I had been as a child. The people in my life who had inspired my creativity had offered me the most precious of all commodities: time. Time on the water, in the forest, and under a starstrewn sky was the best gift I received from my parents and friends.

My mother, not particularly outdoorsy and knowing little about science, was the perfect muse. She would often take me, without complaint, to faraway fields or trout streams—leaving as early as 5:00 A.M. Her only requirement was a cup of coffee and a good novel. One of my earliest mother-son trips was to a freshly plowed field in Davidson County in search of "arrowheads." She read while I searched. When I was twelve, she once drove me to the North Mills River in the hour before sunrise, some thirty-five miles from our cabin in Hickory Nut Gorge. By 8:00 A.M., I was back at the car with the largest trout I had ever caught: a twenty-inch Rainbow. By the end of the day, I had shown the fish to anyone who could stand the smell. Though to my knowledge she never fished a day in her life, Mom was more excited than I was, or at least she convinced me that she was. The perfect muse, she made it easy for the mentors and teachers to come.

My mother also supplied me with books corresponding to my "interest of the month." I still have many of the books she gave me on wildflowers, rocks and minerals, snakes, insects, and, of course, fish. In later years, however, she often gave me books disguised with an outdoor theme, such as Anne Morrow Lindbergh's *Gift from the Sea*. It was about shells—the Channel Whelk, the Moon Snail, the Double-Sunrise, and even the lowly oyster— but it was far more about love and relationships. My mother knew how to hide timely advice in discreet forms. I gave the same "seashell book" to my daughter, Rachel, when she turned sixteen.

There was nothing subtle about my father, who straddled the line between mentor and muse. No one was more content on the water. He loved to fish and introduced me to every fish he knew—in mountain streams, farm ponds, TVA lakes, the surf of the Outer Banks, and the Florida Keys. He held no fish in higher esteem than any other. To him, a fat Bluegill was as exciting as a Brown Trout, and a skinny Spotted Weakfish from the rock jetty at Cape Lookout was no less appreciated than a Sailfish from the Gulf Stream. On those adventures, I was introduced to the world of Arthropods, including aquatic insects—mayflies, caddis, and dragonflies. I soon learned that the same phylum, *Arthropoda*, also held all the shrimp, crabs, and other crustaceans of a salt marsh. Dad showed me how to turn over rocks quietly and catch the slipperiest of salamanders or pick up a Blue Crab without getting pinched. On land, trees were his thing, and he could identify most with or without leaves and in any season. He often told me that a tree's common name frequently tells us how to identify it—think Longleaf Pine, Bigleaf Magnolia, and his favorite tree name, Shagbark Hickory. Any conversation about forests usually ended with Dad saying, "Trees make the best neighbors."

Even as a child, I knew my father was not a great angler, nor a trained entomologist or botanist. In that way, we are much alike, but it made no difference. He took the time to share with me the world that he knew. He also had an uncanny sense of timing: he knew the right time to plan a fishing trip, usually when my life was getting "too cluttered with things." Few of the trips produced lots of fish, but all were filled with the opportunity to observe and

The author's father, Irwin Earnhardt, loved to point out the characteristics of his favorite trees. The Bigleaf Magnolia (above), which has among the largest leaves and flowers in North America, was easy to identify. And few trees have more distinctive bark than our native Shagbark Hickory (left). (Photo of Shagbark Hickory by Mike Dunn)

learn. It was on those trips that I met the muses and mentors in wild places that would sustain me long after my father and mother were gone.

■ In late June 1973, less than a month after my visit to Whitehurst Island, my father died. A year and a half later, my mother was diagnosed with another kind of cancer. I got to tell them both about the visit to Whitehurst Island and what the muses had shown me. In the fall of 1974, my mother surprised me by asking to see the same magical piece of land. In all the years before, she had never gone on a fishing trip with my father and me, and it was the first time she had ever ridden in my skiff. Over two days around White-hurst and at the Cape Lookout Jetty, another four miles to the south, we talked while traveling on a very slow boat. She was clearly awed by the land that would become Cape Lookout National Seashore. My mother saw the wet fields of Spartina, rays, turtles, jellyfish, crabs, and raucous shore birds, though no Painted Buntings. Most important, she met my muses.

Along with a good education and a means to make a living, my parents had given my two brothers and me time to explore, discover, succeed, and fail in the classroom of the natural world. As I write this book, both brothers, one a history professor and the other a pediatrician, are retired and living back on the upper end of Hickory Nut Gorge—a place still rich in fauna, flora, and the muses they had met before they were teenagers.

Retirement is not yet an option for my wife and me since we have two kids still in school. We cannot help them as we once did, and like most parents, we wince when they do not seek our advice. We feel a mixture of satisfaction and anxiety as we watch them make choices regarding their education and careers. As a family, we still have times and places that we will always share together; but more satisfying is the knowledge that each of our children has a full menu of personal muses in the natural world, along with trusted mentors, on which they can rely. And yes, they both appreciate slow boats.

■ Few people start out as naturalists, and even fewer work as full-time professionals. Naturalists—wearing many hats—can also be scientists, farmers, fishermen, barbers, engineers, ministers, teachers, park rangers, musicians, artists, moms and dads, grandmothers, and . . . even lawyers. For generations, North Carolina's magical wetlands, mountain crags, and tiny wonders have inspired a tradition of accomplished naturalists.

11

"NOTANOLOGISTS," SCIENTISTS, AND NATURALISTS

Several years after *Exploring North Carolina* had begun airing on public television (UNC-TV), I was stopped in a supermarket aisle by a viewer. After several complimentary remarks about the series, she asked: "My husband and I have wondered since the show began whether you are a geologist or biologist?"

I was flattered by the question. After thanking her for her interest in the series and the kind words, I responded, "I hate to disappoint you, but I am not an 'ologist.'"

The woman looked puzzled and then asked, "What do *they* study?"

After an awkward pause, I realized that I had run words together, creating a new category of scientist—the "notanologist."

We both began to laugh when I enunciated more carefully. "I am not an 'ologist' in any field of science, though I am delighted when people mistake me for a biologist, a geologist, a paleontologist, or an entomologist."

Although I am the writer and host of a natural science television series, I have no professional credentials in the animal-vegetable-mineral world. The only title I can claim linking me to the world of science and natural history is that of "naturalist," a catchall moniker that bestows a little extra credibility on certain scientists and others of us with degrees in history, art, religion, and law.

Law School had been my goal. It was what I had wanted in high school and during four years at Davidson College in the mid-1960s. My law degree from UNC–Chapel Hill was the prize that opened up career opportunities in the courtroom, government, and classroom. It was also a ticket to the corporate world. My law degree introduced me to countless friends, enabled me to travel, and supported me for over three decades.

Before, during, and after law school, however, it was no secret to friends and family that my chosen vocation and my passion were not one in the same. I enjoy the study of law, but it is the natural world that energizes me. Like others before me, I feel guilty that I live two charmed lives—one in a professional world defined by libraries, conference rooms, and button-down shirts, and another in a world punctuated by rivers, rugged mountains, and muddy boots.

The Role of Naturalists

It has always been easier to explain how one becomes a lawyer that to describe the fuzzy pathway to becoming a naturalist. First, not all scientists—not even those with advanced degrees in the study of birds, fish, forests, insects, or the Earth's crust—can be called naturalists. Few people start out as naturalists, and even fewer are full-time naturalists. Many start out in other jobs and professions and wear two hats. Naturalists can also be scientists, farmers, fishermen, engineers, ministers, teachers, park rangers, musicians, artists, grandmothers, and yes—even lawyers. Among the most important naturalists are the moms and dads who take the time to introduce their children and friends to the natural world. Often the most influential naturalists have no degrees and little formal science education.

Three traits are shared by most naturalists: (1) they are keen observers and listeners; (2) they act as interpreters and communicators; and (3) they log "time in the field." I first learned the difference between an observer and a "looker" over fifty years ago from my father. Dad would say, "Looking can be a waste of time unless you know what you are looking for. Most of us just look at a tree, but an observer with experience can *see* the whole tree, along with the squirrel, the owl, and the mistletoe hidden away in its branches. Learning to observe, to see, takes time."

Over many fishing trips, he taught me how to observe fish in a stream, along a tide line, or at a rocky point in a lake. Seldom did I see the whole fish in clear relief; usually, it was a fin, a shadow, a flash, or a "dimple" on the water. Dad also explained how fish habitats changed in different seasons, temperatures, and wind conditions. Slowly, my observation skills got better, and I became more successful at "seeing" fish in streams, lakes, and the ocean. Over the years, I have watched anglers, birders, amateur geologists, and wildflower experts teaching others how to look, or when and where to look. All good naturalists, whatever their interest in nature, are keen observers who have learned from others and who continue to learn.

In their role as communicators and interpreters, naturalists serve as liaisons, links, and "pollinators" while interacting with others. Naturalists are lifelong students who frequently serve as connective tissue between the world of science and the everyday world in which we live and raise our children. Some have knowledge of the ecosystems where they live, while others deal with complex regional and national topics, such as air pollution, climate change, and barrier-island migration. Most naturalists interact and communicate with small audiences—family, friends, or clients—while some communicate an understanding of the natural world to a state, a country, or even an audience of nations.

All naturalists are passionate about spending *time in the field*. Some naturalists are weekend warriors or pursue their outdoor interests only seasonally. Whether time in nature is measured in hours or weeks in the field each year, it is always a priority for naturalists. Books, museums, classrooms, the Internet, and high-definition television can promote interest in the natural world. I submit, however, that "remote experience" can never take the place of, or be as inspirational as, standing in a marsh, wading a river, or ascending a rocky peak—with the accompanying chill of a north wind, the chorus of unseen cicadas, the scrapes of Catbrier, the smell of evergreen, and the inconvenience of wet socks. Good naturalists, even those with considerable expertise in the literature of their passion, always have firsthand experience in their preferred natural resource.

Since many naturalists lead dual lives, some are uniquely positioned to comment on choices—matters of conscience and ethics—involving the frequent clashes between the desires of government and industry and the preservation of important natural resources. From time to time, naturalists have come along to help society "sort out" important issues of their generation. No topic in my generation has generated more spirited exchanges and sharper contrasts than discussions regarding climate change and global warming. With these topics, hard science often collides with politics and the economic practices of large industries. Geologists Dr. Stanley Riggs of East Carolina University and Dr. Orrin Pilkey of Duke University are both internationally known experts on coastal geology and barrier-island migration. As scientists and naturalists, they work with geologists, climatologists, and the public at large on the issues of climate change and sea-level rise. Although these men are trained geologists, those who have worked with them know they also have an impressive knowledge of coastal ecology and the ability to communicate effectively. Each has offered strategies and public-policy options to diverse, and sometimes hostile, audiences.

Lawrence Earley, a writer-photographer and the former editor of *Wildlife in North Carolina*, is, by any measure, a highly regarded naturalist. *Looking for Longleaf*, Earley's 2004 book on the history and future of the Longleaf Pine, is important for its scholarship, but it is equally important for its examination of ethical issues regarding past and present forestry practices. No one has written more eloquently about, and in support of, our remaining Longleaf Pine ecosystems than Lawrence Earley.

Who better knows an area of land than the people who live on it? In the first years of the twenty-first century, two women, Jennifer Alligood and Doris Morris, became the voices and conscience of the Albemarle Peninsula during the U.S. Navy's attempt to locate a 30,000-acre Outlying Landing Field in Washington County and surrounding environs. As you may recall from chapter 8, the same lands also happened to be the last, best southeastern habitat for Tundra Swans, Snow Geese, and other migratory waterfowl. As farmers and as women with a passionate attachment to the natural ecosystems around them, Alligood and Morris spoke on behalf of these birds and the people of the Albemarle low country, knocking on doors in Raleigh and Washington, D.C., writing to navy admirals, and enlisting the support of numerous individuals and organizations. Without Jennifer Alligood and Doris Morris, the navy likely would not have relented, and more jets than birds would today occupy the skies of Washington County.

When I think about the courage and tenacity of such individuals—Riggs, Pilkey, Earley, Alligood, and Morris—I am reminded of Rachel Carson, who, in her 1962 book *Silent Spring*, sounded the alarm about the deadly side effects of commonly used pesticides and faced withering criticism from much of the nation's political and corporate community. The life of those who speak most eloquently and effectively for natural resources, even in a free society such as ours, is not for the thin-skinned or timid.

You have probably noticed that I have still not fully answered the question, "How does a person become a naturalist?" Perhaps the best way to explain the road to becoming a naturalist is to put members of the naturalist community, past and present, into loose categories. I know that categorization can be restrictive or too simplistic, but examples often provide clarity.

In the paragraphs below, I have listed four categories of naturalists, complete with examples of men and women who best represent each niche. Is there a group with which you can identify?

Classical Naturalists

Most of us have heard of some of the "classical naturalists" who help us to understand the natural world as it was in centuries past. In North Carolina and the Southeast, a number of classical naturalists left us records and insights that serve as baselines to understanding how resources have changed, or how they have remained the same. Thomas Harriot, an Oxford-educated mathematician-astronomer-writer, visited Roanoke Island in 1585–86 with the Raleigh Expeditions. In his 1588 publication *A Briefe and True Report of the New Found Land of Virginia,* Harriot was among the first Europeans to write about the diversity of plants, birds, fish, and mammals in the land that would become North Carolina. More important, his descriptions of Native Americans are invaluable. Almost prophetically, he wrote of the effects of "invisible bullets" on the Native inhabitants—pathogens carried by European explorers and settlers that decimated Native populations.

Equally important to our understanding of the early natural resources and Native people of Roanoke Island and the Albemarle Sound are the paintings and drawings of John White, who was also with the Raleigh Expedition of 1585–86. White's paintings, the originals of which are now housed in the British Museum in London, offer one of the earliest and most important visual accounts of North Carolina and the New World.

In 1701 John Lawson, an adventurer and collector of plant and animal specimens, left Charleston on a historic journey into the heart of the Carolinas. His route, which generally followed Native American trading paths, took him through the location of present-day Charlotte, then east to the land that would become Hillsborough and Raleigh, and finally across the Coastal Plain to the site of North Carolina's first town, Bath. Along the way, Lawson observed and later described in detail things that are different or missing from today's Carolina landscape. From Lawson, we know about vast grasslands ("Piedmont prairies") that stretched for miles through North Carolina's interior. He also described Passenger Pigeons (now extinct) so numerous that they darkened the sky over forests in the places we now know as Concord and Kannapolis. John Lawson's observations can be found in his extraordinary book, *A New Voyage to Carolina,* first published in 1709. There is no better description of the land and Native people from

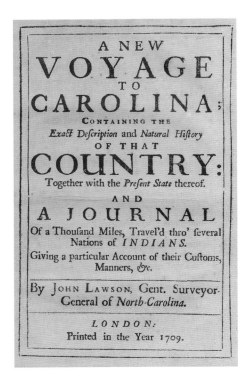

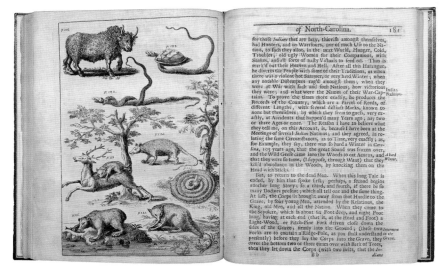

There have been many naturalists who were also writers, but no person has captured the totality of the natural landscape of North Carolina better than John Lawson during the first decade of the eighteenth century. Lawson's *A New Voyage to Carolina* definitely should be added to your reading list. (Photos courtesy of the North Carolina Collection, UNC–Chapel Hill)

the colonial period in North Carolina. The book was so popular that it was widely plagiarized by later writers. For me, it tops the required-reading list for anyone interested in the early natural history of North Carolina.

A decade after Lawson's death in 1711, another classical naturalist, Mark Catesby, began painting an invaluable collection of birds, fish, mammals, and reptiles found in Florida, Virginia, and the Carolinas. In his work, we can recognize native plants and animals that still live among us, as well as some that are lost forever, including the Ivory-Billed Woodpecker, the Carolina Parakeet, and the previously mentioned Passenger Pigeon. It would be a hundred years before another artist-naturalist of Mark Catesby's caliber would paint the fauna and flora of the southeastern American landscape. His name was John James Audubon. (It should be noted that although both artists traveled extensively in what would become the southeastern United States, neither is known for his time in North Carolina.)

No two American naturalists are better known or more important for their work than the father-son duo of John and William Bartram from Pennsylvania. Together, their lives and work spanned almost the entire eighteenth century. John Bartram is often called the "Father of American

One of the most talented naturalists to study the fauna and flora of the Southeast was also a great artist. The work of Mark Catesby, done in the first part of the eighteenth century, shows us plants and animals still with us today, like this magnificent Painted Bunting (top). Catesby's work is also important for showing us animals that we have lost, such as the Ivory-Billed Woodpecker (bottom). (Photos courtesy of the North Carolina Collection, UNC–Chapel Hill)

Botany." He traveled widely across eastern America, including in North Carolina (see *Journey through the Carolinas, Georgia, and Florida*). Bartram supplied numerous North American plants and their descriptions to Carl Linnaeus (creator of the modern system of taxonomy) in Sweden, to collector Peter Collinson in England, and to the great universities at Oxford and Edinburgh. Although John Bartram did not discover nor name our most celebrated plant, the Venus Flytrap (declared North Carolina's Official State Carnivorous Plant in 2005), it was largely through his cultivation and distribution of them that the world learned about the plant with the "iron spring fox trap." So influential was the elder Bartram that in 1765, a decade before the American Revolution, he was named the King's Botanist in North America.

It is rare that a father and a son in the same field are equally famous. William Bartram, John's son, traveled with his father and helped him run the family plant business in Philadelphia. Over time, he also became known as one of the eighteenth century's best writers about and observers of the natural world. His work and that of his father inspired not only other scientists of their day but also writers, poets, and travelers.

Perhaps the only thing that William Bartram was not good at was coming up with book titles. The complete title of his only book, published in 1791, was, in its entirety: *Travels through North and South Carolina, Georgia, East and West Florida, the Cherokee Country, the Extensive Territories of the Muscogulges or Creek Confederacy, and the Country of the Chactaws. Containing an Account of the Soil and Natural Productions of Those Regions; Together with Observations on the Manners of the Indians.* Whew!

Individually and together, the Bartram legacy is powerful and still has many admirers. An important reminder of their contributions to the natural world is the Bartram Trail, which traverses some of the most rugged and beautiful lands in the Southeast, including eighty miles across the Nantahala National Forest of Macon and Swain Counties.

There were other classical naturalists, but none more gregarious than the French botanist and explorer André Michaux. After arriving in America in 1785, he probably saw more of the North American continent than anyone else. Often traveling alone, he crisscrossed eastern America from the Bahamas to Canada. During his travels, Michaux collected thousands of plant specimens and kept meticulous records. He visited North Carolina seven times, and no place excited him more than the peak we now know as Grandfather Mountain, which he climbed in August 1794. Michaux believed

Almost a century later, John James Audubon, perhaps our best-known naturalist and artist, recorded the creatures of the New World in astonishing detail. He is well known for his birds, such as his haunting painting of the extinct Carolina Parakeet (left), but his other animals were equally remarkable, including these grinning Opossums (above). (Images courtesy of the North Carolina Collection, UNC–Chapel Hill)

it to be the highest mountain in North America and in the center of one of the largest concentrations of diverse flora found anywhere. (Michaux's work is also discussed in chapter 6.) Among the many plants across this state that now bear his name is the Carolina Lily, also know as Michaux's Lily, North Carolina's Official State Wildflower.

The naturalists mentioned above collected, wrote, and painted for many reasons, including fame and profit. Some sold their discoveries to plant and animal collectors in England and on the Continent, while others were supported by wealthy patrons. It can be argued that the conclusions of most early naturalists—almost all of whom were men—regarding Indigenous people, the role of women, and the conquest of land were frequently shaped more by loyalties to a foreign crown and religious dogma than to science and discovery. However, though their motives may not have been pure, these naturalists were all keen observers and intrepid adventurers with a firsthand knowledge of the early American landscape. Through their collections, writing, and art, they communicated a treasure trove of information about the natural wonders of new lands to their patrons and employers and to future generations.

Scientist-Naturalists

As I have already stated, not all scientists are naturalists. The work of many scientists, especially those involved in research, is by necessity focused and highly technical. Fortunately for the rest of us, some scientists from the various "ologies" also have the inclination and ability to communicate with a broader audience: they serve as bridge builders between the world of Latin names and chemical formulas and the general public. These individuals qualify as my scientist-naturalists. They usually come from the natural sciences, which include such disciplines as ornithology, entomology, botany, marine biology, geology, paleontology, climatology, and even astronomy.

Certainly the most famous, and the most controversial, person in this category is Charles Darwin, the English scientist educated at the University of Edinburgh and Cambridge University. During his travels on the HMS *Beagle* beginning in 1831, Darwin, then in his midtwenties, collected and studied fossils and the distribution of wildlife at various locations along the east and west coasts of South America and the southern Pacific. From his observations of change—transmutations in species—Darwin developed his theory of natural selection. His 1859 book, *On the Origin of Species*, became the basis of evolutionary biology that best explains variations and diversification in nature. Charles Darwin is by any standard one of the most influential scientists and naturalists of any century. His conclusions are still not universally accepted, however, even in the twenty-first century, because they conflict with the literal creation story as told in some world religions.

Although *On the Origin of Species* may have been written for scientists and presents difficult reading in places, it is also a wonderfully written text that is frequently used by nonscientists and theologians looking at the ecosystems that surround us. Darwin was clearly in awe of all life forms, no matter how humble their function. Illustrative of such writing is the first sentence of the last paragraph of his epic tome: "It is interesting to contemplate an entangled bank, clothed with many plants of many kinds, with birds singing on the bushes, with various insects flitting about, and with worms crawling through the damp earth, and to reflect that these elaborately constructed forms, so different from each other, and so dependent on each other in so complex a manner, have all been produced by the laws acting around us."

One of the best-known scientist-naturalists of the twentieth century is Rachel Carson. As a marine biologist with a graduate degree from Johns Hopkins University, Carson observed and understood life in the ocean. Some of her important fieldwork was done on barrier islands across from Beaufort, North Carolina; two of these islands, Carrot Island and Horse Island, are now part of a sanctuary that bears her name.

In her 1951 book, *The Sea around Us*, Carson eloquently communicated the grandeur and life-sustaining power of oceans to a lay audience hungry for information. Her most lasting legacy, however, is as one of the great messengers of the environmental movement. Her 1962 classic, *Silent Spring*, laid bare the environmental dangers of many commonly used pesticides. Few other scientists or naturalists have had a greater impact on public attitudes, governmental policy, and environmental ethics than Rachel Carson. Even today, she is often referred to as the "Mother of the Environmental Movement."

Another giant from the world of science and the naturalist community is Harvard biologist, E. O. Wilson. He is an acknowledged expert on ant species and their societies (myrmecology). More than any other scientist, however, Wilson has understood the power of myth and story, and the human need for a grand sense of place. To Wilson, the greatest story comes from history and science in the form of the "evolutionary epic." His writing skills, and his ability to connect with a worldwide audience far beyond his

Harvard classroom in the last quarter of the twentieth century, is evidenced by his two Pulitzer Prizes.

Fortunately, North Carolina and the Southeast have had no shortage of scientist-naturalists, men and women at the top of their games in various science disciplines who also communicate easily with a wide audience. Few had a greater impact on our understanding of natural resources than H. H. Brimley (1861–1946), a self-taught naturalist and zoologist who headed the North Carolina Museum of Natural Sciences for over four decades. His taxidermy, exhibits, and photographs (often done with the help of his brother C. S. Brimley), many of which were prepared for expositions in other states and nations, helped publicize this state's natural diversity. A contemporary of the Brimley brothers and one of the most influential botanists and ecologists of his time was Dr. B. W. Wells, who headed the Botany Department at North Carolina State University for thirty years beginning in 1919. His book, *Natural Gardens of North Carolina* (1932), promoted the preservation and understanding of natural communities (habitats and their vegetation). Wells's message is just as important today as it was when his book was published eighty years ago, during the heart of the Great Depression.

Each of us can probably name a few of these women and men, naturalists who can be found on almost every college campus and in laboratories across this region. Examples from my own experience include Dr. Alvin Braswell at the North Carolina Museum of Natural Sciences. Highly regarded in the herpetology community, Braswell is equally well known by nonscientists through his writing and advocacy about the importance of reptiles and amphibians in the Southeast and the threats facing them. Dr. Ritchie Bell (professor emeritus) and Dr. Peter White, both botanists at UNC–Chapel Hill, have made this state's diverse plant communities exciting to their students and to the thousands of visitors to the North Carolina Botanical Garden in Chapel Hill, which each man has directed.

In explaining North Carolina's coastal ecosystems and dynamic coastal geology, few have done it better than the late Dr. Dirk Frankenberg, a professor of marine sciences at UNC–Chapel Hill. In his speaking and writing, Frankenberg connected with everyone. His books—*The Nature of the Outer Banks* (1995) and its sequel, *The Nature of North Carolina's Southern Coast* (1997)—are a unique combination of coastal geology, climatology, and ecology. He pulled no punches in discussing development and environmental issues.

Finally, Dr. Betsy Bennett of the North Carolina Museum of Natural Sciences has done as much as anyone to make science and the natural world "cool" to all children of North Carolina—and to the rest of us. Many know her as a scientist and an accomplished administrator, but no naturalist is more at home on the Outer Banks, in a mountain forest, or on a farm pond than Betsy Bennett. At the museum, she is surrounded by an unmatched staff of scientists and communicators in the natural sciences. Dr. Meg Lowman (director of the museum's Nature Research Center) is a world-renowned expert in tree canopy biology. Her work has led to the discovery of a myriad of new species in treetops around the globe. Paleontologist Dr. Mary Schweitzer, on the staff of the museum and a faculty member at North Carolina State University, has in recent years rocked the scientific community with the discovery of soft tissue from bone matrix made of collagen from a sixty-five-million-year-old femur of a female *Tyrannosaurus rex*. Schweitzer's discoveries have opened up new avenues of study in evolutionary biology and excited a new generation of dinosaur lovers. Access to women scientist-naturalists like Bennett, Lowman, and Schweitzer through the North Carolina Museum of Natural Sciences is especially exciting to a new generation of aspiring women scientists and naturalists, a phenomenon that I have witnessed personally through the experiences of my daughter.

Again, the names above are not intended to be a listing, but rather some examples from my own experience. Think about similar individuals that you have met or who have inspired your interest in the natural world. The work of these scientists and communicators is not always easy: almost all experienced pushback and rejection from their peers or from policy makers at one time or another. When such men and women from the past and present ask hard questions, challenge conventional wisdom, and communicate their findings to the lay community, we are all the beneficiaries.

Naturalists by Occupation

By far the largest class of naturalists is that of "naturalist by occupation." These are the men and women who live and work outdoors and whose very livelihoods are tied to natural cycles. Farmers, commercial fishermen, fishing guides, foresters, and park rangers fall into this category. To such people, understanding weather patterns, soil conditions, and the presence (or absence) of certain insects are not just matters of curiosity but of personal and economic survival. Some of the people in this category have university degrees in agriculture, forestry, or wildlife management; however, it is the time they spend in the outdoors that makes them different from the rest of us.

I have had a number of epiphanies in the outdoors, and many have come while in the company of naturalists by occupation. Captain Donald Gray Willis left Harkers Island School after finishing the tenth grade and never worked in a laboratory, but I am certain that he possessed more practical information about the ocean and its edges than anyone I have ever known. During most of his ninety years, Donald lived on Harkers Island behind Cape Lookout. Even when he was away from the island, he was on the water with the Coast Guard or the Army Corps of Engineers. Like other water-men—no matter their country of origin—Donald's lifetime on the water made him a weather forecaster, a fisheries biologist, and an astronomer. A quick glance at the Sun or Moon, or at trees moving in the wind, gave Donald volumes of information.

One a June morning in the early 1990s, I approached Donald Willis as he worked on his clamming skiff. "Yesterday afternoon, I had my best day ever finding Puppy Drum (young Channel Bass) on the flats," I told him. "The fishing is best on an incoming tide about two hours before sunset. I'm coming back next weekend for sure."

Without pause, Donald replied: "You'll be wasting your time, Tom. Next week will be the *exact opposite conditions*—an outgoing afternoon tide and no fish! By now you should know the lunar calendar is twenty-eight days and that tide conditions repeat twice a month. For another incoming after-noon tide, you have to wait *two* weeks."

Donald's response regarding tides was instant and almost instinctual. Acquired over a lifetime, such knowledge of the outdoors is common among naturalists who become part of the resource in which they live.

At the western end of North Carolina, I knew another group of naturalists with heightened instincts about weather and natural cycles: beekeepers. In Hickory Nut Gorge, above Bat Cave, there were many families that had tended bees for several generations with such last names as Barnwell, Oats, Freeman, Lyda, and Pryor. In the same way shepherds protect sheep, bee-keepers watch over and protect their hives from predators and from bad weather. Over many summers, I observed men and women moving their hives every couple of weeks to keep up with the bloom of Sourwood Trees. The trees bloomed in July at lower altitudes around Lake Lure, but it would often be well into August before peak blooms occurred 2,000 feet higher up on the mountains. Earl Pryor, a stonemason and beekeeper from Bat Cave, once told me, "When its Sourwood season, you know when the bloom is right and when its time to move the hives. Watch the bees: they'll tell you everything you need to know."

Think about the North Carolinians you know whose work and safety requires them to observe the weather and live in the natural world every day. No university can teach this experience, and there is no substitute for "being there" for naturalists by occupation.

Naturalists by Preference

My fourth category, "naturalists by preference," is the most diverse group of all. These are men and women from every profession imaginable who are drawn to nature. Given a preference, they choose activities oriented around wild places and things. Some even consider themselves to be "nature addicts." These are weekday mechanics, schoolteachers, preachers, accountants, and members of the armed forces who on weekends morph into world-class birders, fly fishermen, butterfly lovers, mushroom hunters, river watchers, rock hounds, and wildflower experts. Some lead environmental organizations, give lectures, paint scenes from the natural world, photograph the seasons, and write extraordinary books. These are people who often lead two lives. As you have probably surmised, this is my category.

All of us know men and women who are very good at their day job but are prone to get excited (sometimes even goofy) when talking about their outdoor lives. In this group I think of Curtis Smalling, who for many years was the general manager of *Horn in the West*, an outdoor drama in Boone. Those who really know Curtis are aware that he is one of the Southeast's premier authorities on migratory warblers, which includes the Golden-Winged Warbler, the Cerulean Warbler, the Chestnut Warbler, and nearly two dozen other species. He knows when they arrive, their sounds, the habitats to which they are attracted, their diet, their Central American wintering grounds, and the weather patterns that affect their movement. Curtis is a remarkable naturalist drawn to warblers (his passion), and he works with other talented birders, especially through Audubon North Carolina.

One of the Southeast's leading environmental lawyers, Derb Carter of the Southern Environmental Law Center in Chapel Hill, is also a birder of equal renown. Knowing that the best birding times are often morning and late afternoon, Derb also has a midday obsession when the weather is warm and the sun is high in the sky: butterflies. The same binoculars enable him and the few others like him to fill an entire day almost anywhere in North Carolina, observing birds and butterflies. With a combined 450 resident and transient avian species found in our state, birding can be a busy and fulfilling activity. And our approximately 175 species of butterfly are just half of the viewing opportunities, since for each butterfly, there is also an equally interesting caterpillar. It almost goes without saying that to find specific birds, naturalists have to know their habits and habitat; and to locate butterflies and caterpillars, they must know nectar plants and host plants. Derb Cater combines all of these skills.

The natural wonders of the mid-Atlantic and the Southeast have long inspired naturalists who are also great writers. Bland Simpson of UNC–Chapel Hill is an English professor, a playwright, a musician, and a naturalist by addiction. Bland grew up in northeastern corner of North Carolina on the Albemarle Sound, and fortunately for the rest of us, he keeps returning to and writing about the land of his youth. Simpson has given voice to the history and natural wonders of forgotten islands in North Carolina's sounds and the great hardwood bottomlands of the Roanoke River in a series of books, which include *Great Dismal: A Carolinian's Swamp Memoir* (1990), *Into the Sound Country* (1997), and *The Inner Islands: A Carolinian's Sound Country Chronicle* (2006).

Jan DeBlieu, who at the time of this writing is the Cape Hatteras Coast-keeper for the North Carolina Coastal Federation, is one of the most distinguished writers in the naturalist community today and a winner of the John Burroughs Medal (usually considered the top award for writing in the natural history genre) for *Wind* (1998). Her first book, *Hatteras Journal* (1987), offers the reader searing insights in the geology and life on America's best-known barrier islands. Another prominent southeastern writer in the naturalist tradition is Janet Lembke. Like the others in this category, Lembke is not a trained scientist but a skilled translator of Greek classics—think Aristotle, Virgil, and Aeschylus. Her immersion in the natural world shines through in elegant literary metaphors. Even her book titles make readers think; they include *Looking for Eagles* (1990), *Skinny Dipping* (1994), and *Despicable Species: On Cowbirds, Kudzu, Hornworms, and Other Scourges* (1999).

No discussion of naturalists by preference in North Carolina would be complete without mentioning the work of Hugh Morton. Morton was the owner of Grandfather Mountain, a successful businessman, and a renowned photographer; yet no one was a more passionate observer of the natural world. Morton knew the arrival time of every migratory bird and the bloom time of each wildflower on Grandfather and in the surrounding mountains. From the end of World War II until his death in 2006, Morton documented the changes in the highlands of North Carolina, including the effects of acid rain on spruce/fir forests and mountaintop construction

There is one more category of "naturalist" who would cringe at having this label attached to them. They are not traditional naturalists at all but people who, by their very words and actions, profess to loathe the natural world, with all of its dirt, inconvenience, and things that go bump in the night. Ironically, the bloviators who trash the natural environment the most often have much to teach the rest of us. North Carolina has had some first-rate antinaturalists.

The most famous name on my antinaturalist list is William Byrd II. Classically educated in England and a member of the prestigious Royal Society, Byrd was heir to large tracts of Virginia land. After failing in his bid to become the governor of Virginia, he was selected to direct the survey between North Carolina and Virginia in 1728. Although some argue that much of his writing is satirical—a way to employ his wit and sarcasm—it is clear that he held many things in low esteem, including women, American Indians, North Carolinians ("lazy and ignorant!"), and alien landscapes. Although he knew a great deal about the plants and animals of his region, he still wrote with disgust about lands and places he disliked, such as the Great Dismal Swamp on the North Carolina–Virginia border. Rather than seeing it as a place of mystery and diversity, he described the Dismal as a "filthy quagmire." He wrote that "this vast body of Mire and Nastiness infect[s] the Air for many Miles around." Within such diatribes, Byrd gives us valuable descriptions of the landscape, plants, and animals of his day.

Although Byrd's pompous pronouncements should make him the winner in the antinaturalist category, my choice for the top award goes to Frances Anne Kemble. In *The Journal of a Residence on a Georgia Plantation*, she wrote about travels through the "poorest State in the Union" in December 1838. On her journey from Philadelphia to Georgia, Kemble had the misfortune of passing through eastern North Carolina from Roanoke Rapids to Wilmington via railroad and stagecoach. Her opinion of the Tar Heel State is one of utter distain, but she left us one of the finest descriptions of virgin swamp forests and longleaf pine savannahs ever written. Her depressing writing about North Carolina swamp forests is sheer poetry.

> To describe to you the tract of country through which we now passed would be impossible, so forlorn a region it never entered my imagination to conceive. Dismal by nature, indeed, as well as by name, is that vast swamp, of which we now skirted the northern edge, looking into its endless pools of black water, where the melancholy cypress and juniper trees alone overshadowed the thick-looking surface, their roots all globular, like huge bulbous plants, and their dark branches woven together with the hideous matting of giant creepers, which clung around their stems, and hung about the forest like a drapery of withered snakes.

Kemble's description of the Longleaf Pine forests that once covered almost all dry lands from the Virginia border south across the Coastal Plain is equally disapproving—and stunning.

> After passing this place [endless swamps], we entered a country little more cheerful in its aspect, apparently endless tracts of pine forest, well called by the natives, Pine Barrens. The soil is pure sand; and, though the holly, with its coal berries, and the wild myrtle, grow in considerable abundance, mingled with the pines, the preponderate, and the whole land presents one wearisome extent of arid soil and gloomy vegeta-

tion. . . . [W]e set forth again through the eternal pinelands, on and on, the tall stems rising all round us for miles and miles in dreary monotony, like a spell-land of dismal enchantment, to which there seemed no end.

It is important to remember that, whether Byrd's and Kemble's writings were satirical or represented their true feelings, they were both good writers and very knowledgeable about the natural world around them. They knew the names of plants, animals, and habitats and how to describe them in remarkable (and sometimes depressing) detail. Even though their writing does not always take us to a "happy place," we can learn much from environmental curmudgeons who knew their stuff.

projects that marred vistas. With his camera and an obsession for unblemished mountain ecosystems, Morton changed laws and attitudes.

Given a little time off from their day jobs, the naturalists by preference spend time in the field and frequently volunteer for work with conservation organizations and local land trusts. These are men and women who are drawn to the world outside and know its importance to economic growth and quality of life. Most people in this category, like me, are not experts but passionate amateurs in the naturalist tradition.

■ It should come as no surprise that, in today's world, being called a naturalist is not always an accolade or compliment. As already mentioned, naturalists sometimes kick the hornet's nest of powerful economic interests. Within the naturalist community, there is rarely total agreement on any issue, and that is the way it should be.

To those who are quick to label naturalists as antibusiness, as people standing in the way of progress, jobs, and technology, I remind them that scientist-naturalist Rachel Carson sounded the alarm about the effects of pesticides in the food chain. I mention photographer-naturalist Hugh Morton, who alerted us to the effects of acid rain on mountain ecosystems and our own health. I tell them about Stan Riggs and Orrin Pilkey, who have the clearest understanding of sea-level rise of any citizens in North Carolina and tell us how dynamic change on our coasts can be of benefit to our economy. I remind them of the work of Betsy Bennett, who has made science education exciting and accessible to a new generation of North Carolinians. I recount the efforts of farmer-naturalists Jennifer Alligood and Doris Morris, who, against incredible odds, helped save the winter home of tens of thousands of migratory waterfowl and saved the navy from its own poor planning. Just as sports fans and movie buffs have their stars and heroes, we naturalists also have ours. The message of our heroes is that if we ignore indicators and warnings in important ecosystems, we do so at our peril.

There is no better place in the world to put on your boots, pick up a pair of binoculars, carry a wildflower book, or grab a fly rod than North Carolina. It is easy being a naturalist here. There is also joy in knowing that the woman next to you in the supermarket, your child's math teacher, the new lawyer across the courtroom, and the mechanic at the corner garage are likely to be as passionate as you are about the outdoors. No matter what category in which we fit or the route we followed, the label "naturalist" is a badge of honor.

So now you know why I was flattered by the viewer of *Exploring North Carolina* who inquired about my knowledge and background in North Carolina's natural resources. Simply being part of the community of naturalists is reward enough for the opportunity to observe and study wild things, communicate with children and friends, and spend time in places that inspire. And let's not forget the other benefits of being a naturalist: there are no admission fees, no age limits, and no "ology" degree is required.

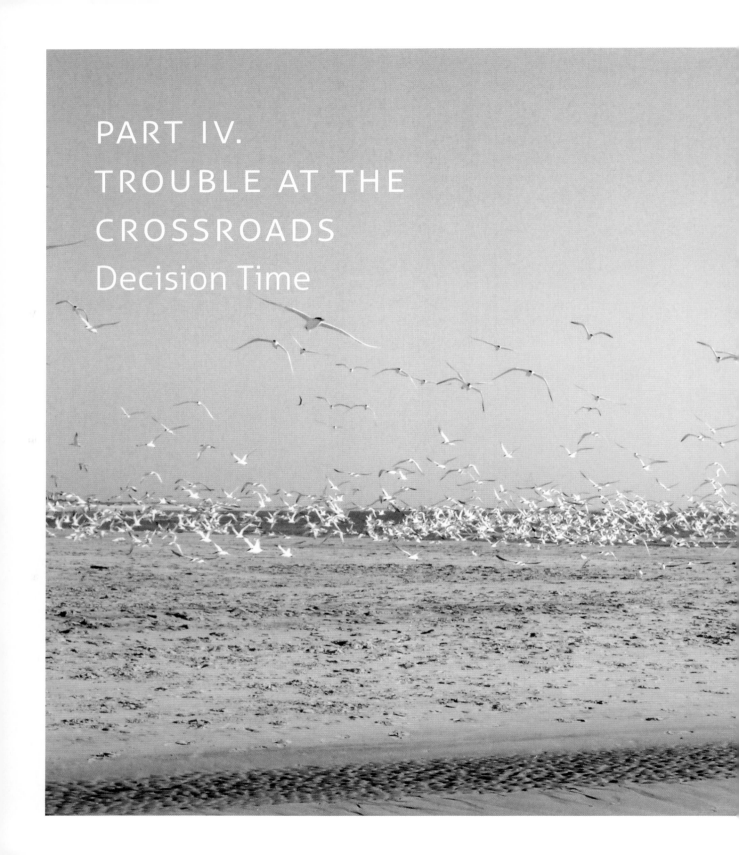

PART IV.
TROUBLE AT THE
CROSSROADS
Decision Time

■ The Southeast has been home to introduced fauna and flora since the arrival of the first humans. We all know about Kudzu, the mile-a-minute vine, but other exotic species have had a far greater and more negative impact on our landscape and biodiversity. Some of our neighbors with feathers, fins, and lovely flowers are not friends; they have become unwanted invasives that strangle or displace native diversity.

12

ALIENS ON THE LAND

Most of us believe that the United States has thrived in part because it is a melting pot. We have been more generous and evenhanded than most other nations in welcoming religions, cultures, and races. From the sum of our eclectic parts, America has produced the Founding Fathers, the feminist movement, the Greatest Generation, the baby boomers, and Generation X. It is becoming more difficult to isolate what is quintessentially American. American architecture incorporates arches and columns from Greece and Rome, mansard roofs from France, the domes of the Middle East, the formality of Victorian England, and the earth tones of our own Southwest. Even "American cuisine" is a hodge-podge of foods that are stir-fried in a wok, wood fired, French fried, curried, and wrapped in a tortilla. The recent history of our southern border reminds us, however, that the process of assimilation is not always easy.

With each new wave of immigrants, supporters of the status quo have often bemoaned the arrival of more aliens on our shores—whether they were from Italy, Ireland, China, Egypt, Poland, India, Vietnam, or Mexico. In time, the most recent wave of immigrants always generates new ideas and creates new businesses, and their descendents become part of a "new status quo." It is through this difficult process of assimilation that the American fabric has been woven and strengthened. Unfortunately, the very process of mixing the foreign and exotic with existing populations, which has tempered us as a nation, may not have benefited America's natural ecosystems and landscape.

During the colonial period and our first two centuries as a nation, passenger ships and merchant vessels also brought *other* aliens to our shores. Although individuals and families generally arrived with more passion than possessions, even the poorest arrived with a few items from their native land—books, clothing, small items of furniture, and food. Some early arrivals also brought living organisms, which came as a "piece of the old country" in the form of seeds, flower bulbs, and dormant tree seedlings. In time, ships from every ocean introduced birds, fish, livestock, and even pets. It is part of human nature to carry vestiges that connect us to our past. Potential problems went largely unnoticed, probably because most of these living things were brought to this region with the very best of intentions. Today, we know that numerous exotic species of fauna and flora have quietly become indistinguishable parts of America's natural landscapes.

As a child, I learned about only a few plants and animals that had been "mistakes" during the settlement of this country. Some had been brought to North America on purpose, and others had arrived by accident or as "stowaways." In the fourth grade, I heard the story of the Brown Rat (originally from central Asia but frequently given the misnomer of Norwegian Rat). These cunning creatures had hidden in ships, crawled down mooring ropes, and subsequently occupied almost every barn, vacant lot, and sewer in America. I knew about the "blight" that had come from Asia with some imported trees and killed all of the American Chestnut trees, not only in North Carolina but also from Maine to Alabama. Every child in the Carolinas and Virginia knew the story of Kudzu, the escaped "vine that ate the South." Finally, many of us have been bitten—literally—by a mistake that entered the United States through the port of Mobile, Alabama, in the 1930s: the Fire Ant. The genus and species name of this pest, *Solenopsis invicta*, is most appropriate for this unwanted invasive. The literal meaning of *invicta* is "the unconquered," but unfortunately this species moniker could apply to a number of plant and animal invasives that have proved almost impossible to eradicate.

What my generation didn't know was that some of the common plants, fish, and birds in North Carolina and America—in our yards, rivers, and forests—are capable of doing irreparable damage to native ecosystems. I don't mean some obscure mussel, killer bees, alligator-eating pythons, or jumping killer carp that pop up from time to time in the supermarket tabloids; rather, I'm talking about everyday neighbors in your ecosystem.

You have already guessed that when alien organisms reproduce too rapidly, "get out of control," and begin to displace native plants and animals, we label them as "invasive." It is generally a good thing for plants and animals to replicate themselves, but replication without the normal checks and balances that occur in nature can be disastrous. Plants and animals labeled invasive are not bad in and of themselves; when placed in an environment with the right temperature and moisture and no competition, many plants and animals will become invasive. Although invasives have the potential to cause harm to agriculture, fisheries, and even to human health, it is their potential to have major adverse impacts on native flora and fauna—and ultimately on biodiversity—to which I will direct my comments.

Ignorance and Bliss

As immigrants and landowners in North America brought plants and animals from Europe and Asia, collectors in Europe also wanted to know more about the fauna and flora of the New World. They employed some of the early scientists and naturalists—including John Lawson, John and William Bartram, and André Michaux—to collect literally thousands of specimens from North Carolina and eastern America for their clients.(See the discussion of classical naturalists in Chapter 11.) They were good at what they did and often found new species in North Carolina's diverse ecosystems. Some plants still bear the name of early collectors. Certainly the best known of the new species discovered here is North Carolina's favorite Christmas tree, the Fraser Fir, named for Scotsman and botanist John Fraser. It is native only to the high mountains of North Carolina and a few locations in Virginia and Tennessee.

At the same time that magnolias, rhododendrons, azaleas, fir, and oaks from the New World were being sent to the gardens of Europe by the naturalists/collectors mentioned above, European and Asian plants, often introduced to America by the *same* individuals, began arriving and thriving. Crepe Myrtle and the Ginkgo Trees (both from Asia), now common in American yards and parks, arrived about 1790 and are usually attributed to Michaux, the French botanist and explorer. By the early 1800s, most elegant homes in Charleston, Philadelphia, and New York were landscaped with exotic trees and plants, including English Oak, European Beech, Mimosa, Princess Tree, English Ivy, English Boxwood, Oriental Wisteria, and Japanese Honeysuckle. Another early arrival, and still a favorite today, is the Deodar Cedar, native to the mountains of India, Pakistan, and Afghanistan. The most famous homes and gardens of the new nation, including George Washington's Mount Vernon and Thomas Jefferson's Monticello, had exotic

The Crepe Myrtle (top) and the Gingko (bottom) both arrived in the United States from Asia at about the time of the American Revolution. Like many alien trees, they are beautiful but overused at the expense of native species.

plants on display. As the years went by, exotics became popular at botanical gardens, on college campuses, and even at state and federal landmarks. In 1912 the Japanese government gave the United States over 3,000 Japanese Cherry Trees (the Yoshino cultivar), many of which were used to line the tidal basin in Washington, D.C. Here in North Carolina, slipped in among a variety of native trees, you can even find a large Chinese Gingko adorning the grounds of our legislative building.

Don't associate the introduction of exotic plants and animals with only the rich and powerful or grand buildings and gardens. The earliest settlers, travelers, city dwellers, and small farmers also brought in insects, birds, fish, and more. Among the prolific importers of exotic plants were state agencies dealing with agriculture and wildlife. It is accurate to say that for over 300 years, good intentions and ignorance have gone hand in hand.

I am one of the many North Carolinians who, long after I finished my formal education, was surprised to learn that some of the most common "wild" plants and animals in our landscape aren't actually native to the Carolinas. For example, some introduced flower species are so much a part of our landscape that we readily call them North Carolina wildflowers and can't imagine the state without them. Woolly Mullein (sometimes known as Lamb's Ear), Queen Anne's Lace, and the first flower many of us could recognize, the common Ox-Eye Daisy, were all introduced and are said to be "naturalized"—but this does not make them native. Some of us are even more surprised to find out that a number of familiar and often lovely plants and animals are exotics that have turned into monsters.

Friend or Foe?

It has been difficult for me to differentiate between friend and foe in nature. This is especially true in the animal world, where the lines between beneficial and harmful are often blurred. It is also hard to dislike a bird that sings in your yard, or a fish that you caught as a child. Here is a short list of exotic animals that may surprise you.

The common honeybee that we have all known since childhood is in reality the European Honeybee, which arrived in North America in the 1600s. Less appreciated is the copper-and-green Japanese Beetle, which is thought to have hitched a ride on nursery plants into America around 1915. Regarding these insects in our region with alien pedigrees, I have never found a person who does not love the benefits and services performed by honeybees or one who wants to keep plant-chewing Japanese Beetles around.

Other insects pose a far greater danger to southern forests than voracious beetles. For example, the Hemlock Wooly Adelgid (*Adelges tsugae*), thought to have been introduced with exotic hemlocks in the 1950s, has killed or is now threatening the remaining stands of Eastern and Carolina Hemlock. This creature is similar to the Balsam Woolly Adelgid (*Adelges piceae*) that has, in conjunction with acid rain, damaged or killed mature stands of Red Spruce and Fraser Fir in the southern Appalachians, leaving only bleached ghost remnants.

French settlers are thought to have introduced the lovely European Rock Dove, with its melodious "cooing" sound, to North America as early as the 1600s. The cooing soon turned to booing almost as soon as the birds escaped. They are now the "domestic pigeon" ("rats with wings," in the words of Woody Allen), inhabiting every city park and coating statues and buildings with their droppings. Two of North Carolina's most common songbirds—the House Sparrow, commonly known as the English Sparrow (*Passer domesticus*), and the House Finch (*Carpodacus mexicanus*)—are exotics. The House Sparrow, native to Europe and Asia, is thought to have been released in the Northeast in the 1850s; and the House Finch, native to the Southwest and Mexico, went from caged pets to wild birds along the East Coast in the 1940s. The House Sparrow is now one of the most widely distributed birds outside of its natural habitat in Europe. Because they prefer cavities of older trees for nesting, they have outcompeted and displaced native species such as the Bluebird. The House Finch, found at many North Carolina bird feeders, causes few problems, except for their numbers, which can adversely impact native birds as they compete for nests and food.

Perhaps the most common and certainly one of the most prolific birds in North Carolina and America is the European Starling, released into New York's Central Park in the 1890s by New York druggist Eugene Schieffelin simply because they were mentioned in plays by William Shakespeare. Alas, within a few decades of their release into Central Park, the birds from Shakespeare plays created both drama and tragedy as they multiplied all the way to California. Their extreme numbers have proved costly to American agriculture and make them a hazard for general aviation: a flock of starlings (often mixed with other birds, such as the Red-Winged Blackbird and Brown-Headed Cowbird) can create a dark, undulating cloud of birds up to a mile long. Because of their aggressive nature, Starlings also displace a variety of native North Carolina species by outcompeting them for food and nesting sites.

Larger birds like the graceful Mute Swan (the long-necked birds from the

The European Rock Dove—the pigeon on statues—the English Sparrow, the European Starling, and the lovely House Sparrow (shown here) were all introduced. Such birds compete with native species for food and nesting locations.

Both the Carolina Hemlock and the Eastern Hemlock are seriously threatened across North Carolina by the introduced Hemlock Woolly Adelgid. Could the hemlock suffer the same fate as the American Chestnut?

ballet *Swan Lake*), with their long curved necks, were brought to America from northern Europe at the end of the nineteenth century with all the best intentions. To keep such large birds from escaping, their wing feathers were clipped; but to no one's surprise, the feathers grew back. Even a beautiful swan can be an undesirable neighbor when it consumes and destroys large quantities of aquatic vegetation, makes ponds and rivers turbid, and damages habitat for migratory waterfowl, fish, and shellfish.

The introduction of alien plants and animals has been nothing short of a national lottery, with some winners and lots of losers. One of the few birds in the winner's circle is the Chinese Ringneck Pheasant, a tough upland game bird from China that was released by individuals, clubs, and government agencies in many parts of the country in the nineteenth and early twentieth centuries. The Ringneck is perfectly suited to the grain fields and hedgerows of the upper Midwest, and it is so popular that, even as an alien, it is the state bird of South Dakota. They have reproduced and thrived in many states, and they can be found in the wild on Core Banks on our own Cape Lookout National Seashore. On a number of occasions, I have had them literally explode from native grasses like Sea Oats at Cape Lookout near the old Coast Guard station—a totally unexpected sight when you're used to seeing gulls and terns within yards of the ocean.

Determining the relative merits of fish species has long been a problem. The Common Carp, a favorite food fish in Asia, made its way into the wild in New York in the 1840s. Within a few decades, it had migrated, or was introduced, into most river systems, including the rivers of the Carolinas. Because they have a severe impact on shallow-water vegetation and literally muddy the water, Carp have long ago worn out their welcome.

More recent introductions to our waters include Blue Catfish and Flathead Catfish, both capable of reaching weights of over 100 pounds. Because anglers were thought to prefer bigger fish, these giants were introduced to a few locations by the North Carolina Wildlife Resources Commission over four decades ago. Although both are native to waters of the Mississippi drainage, they were not native to any river east of the Appalachians. They have voracious appetites and consume tons of native catfish, perch, and sunfish—including the most popular fish of all, the Largemouth Bass. Because the Blue and Flathead Catfish have both supporters and detractors, determining whether they are "friend or foe" is difficult. If you value their size and sport potential, they are in the "friend" category, but if you are concerned about their impact on native fish populations and biodiversity, they are definitely "foe."

I could spend a long time on the relative merits of introduced-versus-native fish, since I have pursued most of them since childhood. One of the most difficult problems we have had in North Carolina is weighing the merits of the three trout found in mountain waters. The Rainbow Trout, a beautiful fish native to western rivers flowing into the Pacific, and the Brown Trout, a favorite fish in British Isles and Europe, were introduced to many eastern American river systems by the 1880s. Because they reproduce and have become truly "wild trout," providing phenomenal food and sport in many North Carolina streams, few if any anglers want them removed.

As with most introduced species, Rainbow and Brown Trout have caused problems. The only trout native to North Carolina is the Southern Appalachian Brook Trout, known locally as "Brookies" or "Specks." During my lifetime, I have watched prime Brook Trout "pocket water" streams at higher altitudes turn into Rainbow-only streams. By the last quarter of the twentieth century, our native Specks were relegated to a few tiny streams in Jackson and Transylvania Counties, a few streams along the Blue Ridge Parkway, and some isolated headwaters in the Great Smoky Mountains. The larger and more aggressive Rainbow Trout, and in some cases Brown Trout, simply outcompeted and eliminated Brook Trout and other fish from their native habitat.

In recent decades, state agencies like the North Carolina Wildlife Resources Commission and private conservation organizations like the well-known Trout Unlimited have developed a plan of action. Even the North Carolina General Assembly got in the act and declared the Southern Appalachian Brook Trout to be North Carolina's Official Freshwater Trout in 2005. In order to save the much-smaller but iconic native Brookie, Rainbows and Browns have been removed from many of the cold, clear headwaters of western North Carolina rivers, and wild strains of Southern Appalachian Brook Trout have been reestablished in streams with high water quality, mostly above elevations of 3,500 feet. The good news for anglers is that a large percentage of North Carolina's several thousand miles of coldwater streams and rivers will still hold plenty of stocked or stream-raised Rainbow and Brown Trout. Both of these fish, especially the Rainbow, are very hardy and can survive in temperatures not suitable to the Southern Appalachian Brook Trout. This story of North Carolina's native and alien trout is unique because everybody wins—both anglers and the fish.

Dealing with, or eliminating, an exotic or invasive animal is difficult because they are living, breathing things. Spraying fire ants or invasive beetles may not present an ethical problem, but controlling (killing) birds, fish, or

mammals to diminish their population is anathema to many people—even if not acting means that a number of native species will be squeezed out of their home range. At some point, we may have to choose between Piedmont and coastal rivers inhabited by multiple species of native sunfish, catfish, and perch and rivers inhabited by only a handful of giant alien predator catfish that were originally brought in to satisfy perceived angling needs.

Plant Blindness

Dealing with exotic or invasive plants poses different problems and fewer ethical dilemmas. For most of us, plants are not cuddly living things in the same way that swimming, singing, flying, and breathing animals are. As indicated above, many exotic and invasive plants have been with us for decades or centuries, so we see them as part of the North Carolina landscape. Thus, outside of a handful of professional botanists, experts with wildlife agencies, and a few watchdogs from conservation organizations, most of us do not even *see* invasive plants. I am one of the many who failed to detect significant shifts in the flora of our landscape. Other than recognizing patches of Kudzu, I saw "green as good."

Several years ago, two botanists from Louisiana State University, Elisabeth Schussler and Jim Wandersee, put a name on the problem: plant blindness. They believe that in today's society, there is an "inability to see or notice the plants in one's own environment, leading to the inability to recognize the importance of plants in the biosphere and in human affairs." This means that in a modern world where most of us spend our time in urban and suburban environments, we have not only lost the ability to recognize the plants around us but, more important, we cannot distinguish between good and bad plants.

Every plant category now includes exotic and invasive plants that are rapidly changing the floral landscape of North Carolina. I cannot eliminate plant blindness, but I can alert you to a number of the most common problem plants and where you will see them. The number and types of noxious trees, shrubs, and grasses in every eco-niche in North Carolina will surprise you. My purpose in helping to sharpen your "plant vision" is not to spoil your time outside by pointing out what's wrong but to help you become part of the solution to a serious problem.

A substantial percentage of the plants along our roadways, and especially our interstates, are invasive. Although the U.S. Department of Agriculture, the botany departments of major universities, and various state agencies have slapped the "invasive" label on the worst offenders, accepting that many plants of your childhood are villains is still not easy. Who among us wants to take an axe to a Mimosa with its pink, sweet-smelling powder-puff blooms; destroy a Princess Tree, with its delicate lavender blooms; or commit a cardinal sin by killing a Tree of Heaven? Is there a town in North Carolina where Privet hedges (plants from the genus *Ligustrum*), many neatly clipped, cannot be found? Some North Carolina roadsides would be naked were it not for the dark foliage of China Berry, Japanese Knotweed with its heart-shaped leaves, impenetrable thickets of Multi-Flora Rose, and introduced *Elaeagnus*, our "olives"—Russian-Olive, Autumn Olive, and Thorny-Olive. Take a close look: these trees and shrubs are among the most common plants in this state—and they are invasive.

Life in North Carolina is also intertwined with lovely, smothering invasive vines. Is there anything more "southern" than a porch or a tall pine covered with an Oriental Wisteria vine, with its purple, grape-cluster-shaped flowers? Is there any smell sweeter than the flowers of Japanese Honeysuckle, the vine that covered the trees along the pathway to my elementary school fifty years ago? The most striking berries of summer are produced by the Porcelain Berry vine—berries of mixed pastel-blue, purple, and white on the same vine. Equally beautiful in autumn are the berries of Oriental Asian Bittersweet—berries my mother loved to use in dried-flower arrangements and in holiday wreathes.

There is another familiar vine with which the adjective "stately" is fre-

The Princess Tree (top left), the Mimosa (top right), the Tree of Heaven (bottom left), and several species of *Elaeagnus* (bottom right) are all beautiful—and invasive. Combined, these plants occupy thousands of acres along our roadsides and in woodlands by outcompeting native species. Large flocks of Cedar Waxwings (such as the individual shown here) migrating through North Carolina will eat berries from many plants, including *Elaeagnus*.

Oriental Wisteria (left) and Porcelain Berry (right) add touches of beauty across the Southeast, but they can also smother native trees and out-compete equally beautiful native vines.

quently used. Perhaps because it is part of the walls of churches and the halls of academia, and also covers many stone-faced mansions, English Ivy gets a pass from us. But like the plants mentioned above, English Ivy is on everyone's invasive list. Look around in your town and I'll bet you'll see whole forests, the ground and trees alike, covered with a choking layer of stately English Ivy.

You would think that by now we should have learned that good intentions in the plant world often bring bad results. A relative newcomer to the list of bad North Carolina vines is Beach Vitex, which came from the Pacific Rim. Since its introduction on the South Carolina coast following Hurricane Hugo over twenty-five years ago, this part shrub and part vine has covered oceanfront sand dunes from Florida to Ocracoke Island, North Carolina. The "Kudzu of the Coast" not only chokes out native cover plants such as native Sea Oats, but it also inhibits nesting success of both sea turtles and shore birds.

I've saved the most famous invasive vine of the South for last—that vine from Hell, the winner and still champion: Kudzu. It is estimated that in the southeastern states alone, this vine introduced to the United States in 1876 covers over 7 million acres.

With the possible exception of Kudzu, some of the noxious vines mentioned above are still sold in garden centers. Before purchasing any non-native vine for your yard, think again: they may be silent stranglers of our native landscape.

There is another category of invasives that may be more harmful than all of the others. These are the exotic grasses, of which I will mention only three. One recent October, I was in Bakersville, a picturesque mountain community in Mitchell County near the Tennessee border. In the town's center are historic markers commemorating the area's plant diversity, discovered during visits by Harvard botanist Asa Gray and the great French explorer/naturalist André Michaux. The fall leaves were almost at their peak, and around many curves stood a lovely, tall grass with five-foot plumes swaying in the breeze. It was the same tall grass, topped by a silvery "flag," that I had seen the day before along Interstate 40 near Marion and Old Fort. It was growing in the same ditches and on the same banks where I had once seen Turk's-Cap-Lilies, several wild varieties of aster, Butterfly Weed, and Joe-Pye Weed. Suddenly, it dawned on me that I was looking at another common landscape plant that had gone rogue: Chinese Silver Grass. Silver Grass is another in a long line of nursery plants that have "escaped" and are now displacing the very plants that had once attracted the great botanists and naturalists of past centuries to North Carolina.

An even taller grass, Common Reed (or Phragmites), can be found on ever-increasing acreage in both brackish water and freshwater across the Southeast and in many parts of North America. Although there is a native strain, the invasive version of Phragmities probably came from the Middle East through Europe. I first got tuned into Phragmites during a visit to Phelps Lake. Along a shoreline once filled with Buttonbush and Common Cattail, there was a tall, stiff, eight-foot grass, which, like other invasives, had overwhelmed native plants. In the years since that first encounter, I have seen it outcompeting local plants in Currituck, Carteret, and other coastal counties.

For the last of my three invasive grasses, I could include several species of Asian bamboo found in many parts of the state, but there is one much smaller grass—Japanese Stiltgrass, also known by its genus name, *Microstegium*—that is to me worse than any of the others. As the story goes, it arrived in Tennessee in packing material in 1919 and now covers thousands of acres from North Carolina to New England. During the summer months, Japanese Stiltgrass literally blankets roadsides, stream banks, and every open patch of soil in partial sun or shade. If the adjective "smothering" was

Native grasses and wildflowers, essential to many birds and animals, are being displaced by aggressive invasive aliens, such as Japanese Stiltgrass (left) and Chinese Silver Grass (right).

ever appropriate when describing the effects of a plant, this is the plant to which it best applies. Umstead State Park is about seven miles from my house and is one of my favorite places to walk in any season—except summer. In recent years, small openings in the forest that once supported wildflowers next to Crabtree Creek are now covered by a thick mat of Stiltgrass. If you have ever wondered if invasive plants are really harmful and not just another topic for environmentalists to rant about, take a walk along one of the creekside trails in Umstead and know that many species of native plants have been ousted by this ubiquitous invasive.

I have left out numerous invasive plants, all of which meet the common criteria for these destructive members of North Carolina's plant community. Invasive plants have (1) fast growth rates; (2) seed production with a good "dispersal" system; and (3) the ability to spread quickly. It goes without saying that most invasives are exotic plants that have few, if any, natural enemies to keep them in check in their adopted habitat. There is another piece of the "invasive puzzle" that you may have missed—as did I, until an epiphanal moment several years ago with Dr. Peter White, director of the North Carolina Botanical Garden in Chapel Hill. Peter told me that the success of many invasives in our region involves more than a lack of competition and a good seed-dispersal mechanism. Many of the most infamous invasives come from temperate climates possessing many of the same climatological characteristics and lying near the same latitude as North Carolina.

A few days after my visit with Peter White, I spun an old globe in my den and saw what he had told me. Using a globe—better yet, look at "Google Earth" on your computer—you will see that Washington, D.C., and Beijing, China, are almost at the exact latitude, near 39° north. The 35th parallel that runs through the center of North Carolina (touching Morehead City, Charlotte, and Asheville) also crosses Japan (near Tokyo) and the southern part of the Korean peninsula. Jacksonville (Florida) and Shanghai (China) are both near the 31st parallel. Not only are we similarly situated on the globe, but much of the southeastern United States, Korea, Japan, and southeastern China have similar temperatures and comparable topography. Even our rainfall is the same: Osaka (Japan), Seoul (Korea), and Greenville (North Carolina) average around fifty inches of rain each year. Shanghai, Charlotte, and Raleigh all register about forty-four inches of precipitation per year. It should therefore come as no surprise that since many of the invasive plants mentioned on previous pages are native to Japan, China, and Korea, they should feel right at home in North Carolina and much of the Southeast.

It should be noted that introduced organisms are a problem around the globe. Plants and creatures indigenous to the southeastern United States have also become invasives in England and Europe, across islands of the Pacific, and in the same Asian locations where many of our problem fauna and flora originated. For example, our beloved American Bullfrog, after being introduced in the 1970s, ate its way across the southern British Isles, crowding out other frogs and creatures. Another Carolina favorite, the Eastern Gray Squirrel, introduced in 1876, has dramatically outcompeted England's own Red Squirrel and earned the labels of vermin and invasive. Finally, North Carolina's Catawba Rhododendron has interacted with local plants and become an invasive in England and Scotland. Other than the destruction of habitat and the potential for rapid landscape changes due to climate change, few things pose a more serious threat to biodiversity everywhere than invasive plants and animals. Simply stated, one person's favorite native is another's invasive.

Invasive by Overuse

In 2008 the Department of Environment and Natural Resources (DENR) released some projected growth figures for North Carolina that are cause for both celebration and sober reflection. By 2030 the population of this state is expected to increase from roughly 9 million to 12 million. Growth can be good for the economy, but hidden in all growth projections are also unintended consequences. The DENR release went on to say: "North Carolina leads the United States in lost farm and forests lands—more than 1 million acres in ten years. At least 383 acres per day are converted to new roads, shopping malls, and housing developments."

Unless we change the ways we manage new development, there is a growing risk that we will rapidly lose the diverse, native landscape that has helped us define what many writers have referred to as our "sense of place." As stated above, the Tar Heel landscape has already sacrificed thousands of acres to invasive plants, which are among the first to get established along new roads and in the buffer strips around shopping centers. Invasive plants are not the only problem, however; in every urban area in this state, a substantial percentage of all landscape vegetation being planted along our highways, around shopping centers, on corporate campuses, and in new subdivisions are exotics, or variations (cultivars or hybrids) of exotics. The majority of such exotics planted by homeowners and landscapers are not invasive and will not escape and propagate wildly. Simply because exotic plants do not rise to the level of invasive may in fact be a hollow distinction. Whether the diverse native flora in North Carolina's landscape is slowly nibbled away by the march of invasives or replaced with exotic plantings in our subdivisions one five-gallon pot at a time, the effect is the same. Either way, we are replacing and losing our natural diversity.

My concern today, especially during a time of rapid growth and alteration of the landscape, is not with the use of exotic plants but with their overuse. It is not as though nature gave us nothing to choose from: we live in a state with literally hundreds of native trees, shrubs, and flowers. This flora is part of our state's heritage and an essential link in plant and animal biodiversity. It makes no ecological sense for a substantial percentage of urban vegetation to be nonnative plants, whether it grows in our neighborhoods, in parks, or on rights-of-way. The simple truth is that this switch has occurred so quietly that it has gone largely unnoticed. Remember that most people—clerks in "big-box" home-improvement stores, landscapers for developers and municipalities, and consumers (you and me!)—do not know the differences between native and alien trees, and more important, they are unaware of the long-term consequences of changes to the floral landscape. "Plant blindness"—the inability to see plants in one's own environment and to recognize their importance in the biosphere—is epidemic.

I realize there are some legitimate reasons for using nonnative exotics.

Some planners don't want vegetation that produces foliage and seeds that attracts wildlife, whether mammals or birds, to roadways. Some exotic trees with small trunks are thought to be safer in medians and along roadsides in the event of a car crash. Trees such as Crepe Myrtle or Chinese Flame Tree, being small to medium in size, do not form an unforgiving barrier for out-of-control vehicles. Other trees are chosen for their ability to grow quickly in small spaces, or for their uniform shapes. Finally, I fully appreciate that some landscape designers are looking for specific colors and shapes, or a certain "look" that may be provided by an exotic.

Each of the reasons above has merit, but I am concerned that we have now arrived at a new status quo, a "default setting" for nonnative vegetation. All of our computers and personal electronic devices have default settings for language choice, font, and font size; *native* must be the default setting when we add or replace any tree, shrub, or flower in our yard. Landscape services and the jobs they provide will not be hurt if we begin to return to native plants as our default setting. Native grasses will still have to be mowed, native shrubs trimmed, and the leaves from native trees raked. If home buyers and city landscapers begin requesting (demanding) native plants, local nurseries will grow them. The home-and-garden business will respond if customers ask for certified native plants.

I am not advocating a return to a native-only wilderness tableau, only to a restoration of urban and suburban plant diversity utilizing native plants wherever possible. We have acquired our alien, urban landscapes over many decades, and we can return to higher plant diversity in our yards and neighborhoods by slowly, steadily reversing the process. Native plants are best adapted to this geography and climate; they evolved on this landscape over many millennia. Their root systems are in sync with our soil types and are accustomed to wind, ice storms, and occasional drought. Such change will require awareness on the part of consumers and purveyors of plants.

Changing bad habits will not be easy. Along our barrier islands and even further inland, developers insist on planting palm trees native to Florida or islands of the Pacific. Even more unsettling are the countless "Main Streets" now lined with overused trees that do not belong. I now live in Raleigh— "The City of Oaks." Yet like many other cities, it has lost its way when it comes to municipal plantings. On boulevards and downtown streets, you are likely to see long stretches lined with Crepe Myrtle, Saw Tooth Oak (an Asian exotic), Gingko, and Japanese Zelkova. Even the giant west-facing mural on the Raleigh Civic Center depicting the mighty oaks of Raleigh and Wake County is in stark contrast to the line of nonnative imposters lining

North Carolina's capital city is Raleigh, which has promoted itself as the City of Oaks. Yet Raleigh and every other major city in North Carolina have lined many streets with alien plants that contribute little value to local ecosystems.

McDowell Street below and other nearby streets. It is not just Raleigh; almost every new interchange and large thoroughfare servicing Tar Heel cities is landscaped with many of the same mystery plants. We are losing our identity one alien tree, flower, and shrub at time.

Let us not forget the reason why your neighborhood and town should be planted with native vegetation: the native insects, birds, fish, and mammals that evolved with local plants depend on them. In chapters 5, 6, and 7, I tried to make the case for preserving native biodiversity. In each food web, there are insects whose very existence depends on a specific plant or group of plants. For each insect, there are birds, fish, and even mammals whose very survival depends on them. And did I mention even larger creatures—foxes, raccoons, bobcats, bass, water snakes, and raptors—that evolved with, and are dependent upon, the fish and birds that ate the insects, that ate the native plants, that grew in North Carolina's diverse ecosystems?

The "Green C"

In my own yard and in the neighborhood around me, I have reverted to a habit with which anyone who has ever taught school can identify: I assign a grade. There was a time before grade inflation when a *C* meant satisfactory—an honorable passing grade. As a law professor for two decades, I used "bell curves" and sliding scales, but in the end, I believed students who made a *C* in my classes had a sufficient mastery necessary to move on in the study of law. I regarded such students as capable and able to assist future clients. If there was a percentage number that best illustrated a *C*, it was a 75. Maintaining a *C* average was never my goal, nor should it be the aspiration for anyone striving to excel in any subject. An honest *C*, though, should be considered acceptable as we move to break bad habits relating to the ecosystems under our control.

We can return to a time when exotic plants were used as the *garnish and accents* in our yards—not the main course. It has taken decades to develop societal bad habits of overusing alien plants, so I am under no illusion that most North Carolinians will be persuaded to revert to an all-native landscape. We can strive, however, for a respectable, passable "Green C" by making sure 75 percent of all yard, street, and highway plantings are done with native flora. Any garden center or landscaper who says that this is not possible simply does not know, or appreciate, the great variety of native vegetation available in North Carolina.

Should we seek to eliminate all exotics? Of course not! Scotland Neck should keep holding its annual Crepe Myrtle Festival, and Wilmington should continue celebrating its Azalea Festival. The Sandhills Camellia Festival should be observed in the Pinehurst area, and Castle Hayne should rejoice in its Wisteria Festival. All of us, however, should celebrate and maintain the hundreds of native plants, vines, and trees that define our unique biological and ecological address. As I drive across North Carolina, I still feel the professor in me as I unconsciously assign grades for native biodiversity in yards and city landscapes. Does your place deserve at least a Green C?

We live in a unique place with plants and ecosystems that attracted, and even astonished, the best botanists and collectors of their day. When, as predicted, North Carolina's human population jumps from 9 to 12 million by 2030—and 300-plus acres is cleared and replanted *each day* to make way for the new human arrivals—will Tar Heel biodiversity have survived? Will the new arrivals from other states and other continents, people who come to North Carolina for a new life and a better job, be wowed by the greatest biodiversity found in a temperate zone, or will they be greeted by a cookie-cutter landscape of alien plants devoid of the sounds of native birds, amphibians, and insects? The Tar Heel landscape of tomorrow—of 2030 and beyond—is being determined this very moment by your choices and mine.

■ Few locations have a brighter future regarding water supply than North Carolina and its seventeen river basins, each with more than forty inches of annual precipitation. The best water is found in basins with robust, forested buffers protecting creeks and rivers. As water becomes one of the region's most precious assets in the coming century, all landowners must make their property part of the buffer.

13

BUFFERS AND BASINS

If you grew up in North Carolina, chances are you took water for granted. Whether you got water from a tap, a well, a stream, or a spring, there was plenty of it. Compared to the southwestern United States and other parts of the world, our "droughts" are rarely noteworthy, falling more into the inconvenience category. With an abundant average annual rainfall across the state—Asheville, 38 inches; Boone, 51 inches; Charlotte, 43 inches; Raleigh, 42 inches; and Wilmington, 55 inches—there are no "Tar Heel deserts." In the state's far southwestern region, several ridges in Jackson and Transylvania Counties actually slip into the category of "temperate rain forests," with average precipitation approaching 100 inches per year.

With such a generous statewide allotment from nature, most of us don't have to think about water. Even my first two jobs involved unlimited water. While in junior high school in 1960, I had a water-dependent job: soda jerk. When school ended at 3:00 P.M., I would sprint six blocks to the Rexall Drug Store in Thomasville, wash and cut citrus fruit for the fountain drinks, load the cooler with ice, and put on a fresh pot of coffee. It was a classic 1950s drugstore, with a marble counter and little round tables in front of the immaculately clean fountain area. During my two-year career, I was only a soda jerk, never a *barista*. As a mixer of drinks, I displayed talent by making hand-crafted lemonades, orangeades, fountain Cokes (Coke syrup hand stirred in carbonated water), and root beer floats. Coffee was ten cents, and all fountain drinks with crushed ice cost nine or fifteen cents, depending on their size. Water of any size was free! The pharmacist who owned the store never instructed me to conserve or even think about the amount of water I used on the job.

In high school and during the first years of college, I was a summer lifeguard at a pool near Asheville. There was water in the pool, in the creek running beside the pool, and in the lake above the pool. Our drinking water came from a large spring on the mountain above. Even the atmosphere was saturated, with an average annual rainfall approaching sixty inches in Hickory Nut Gorge. The place was alive with water.

As we entered the twenty-first century, I was one of many North Carolinians who continued to use water as if it was free and without limit for showers, lawns, toilets, and car washes. Depending on the source of data, the average American currently uses between 100 and 175 gallons per day. With quality water available to almost everyone, something strange began to happen. As we grew more flush (pun intended) with discretionary income, bottlers and advertisers convinced us to buy "premium" drinking water—Perrier from France, San Pellegrino from Italy, or Fiji from the South Pacific. American "brands" of water from Coke (Dasani) and Pepsi (Aquafina) cost the same as, or more than, a soft drink or beer of the same size.

As consumers, we are conditioned to believe that these waters taste better, have the right minerals, and are safer because they contain no dangerous contaminants. Never mind that "designer" water is sold in expensive bottles, transported halfway around the world, and stored for long periods of time. We pay for brand-name water even though some bottlers grudgingly acknowledge their product is only tap water run through a filtration process. When we buy drinking water one sixteen-ounce bottle at a time—150 to 200 bottles per year—we are frequently paying more for water per gallon than we pay for gasoline. I'm not even going to mention the amount of energy necessary to produce a plastic bottle filled with water, the space in landfills occupied by water bottles, and the water bottles in our rivers and oceans.

For me, the bottled-water-is-better movement reached an all-time high—or low—in 2007 when the University of Central Florida opened a new publically financed 45,000-seat stadium with *no water fountains*. This lack of public drinking fountains was not an oversight: school officials explained at the time that building codes for the "state-of-the-art" stadium did not require water fountains, even in one of the hottest, most humid venues in the country. All of the hydration needs of football fans were to be met through the sale of bottled water at several dollars a pop from concession stands located all over the stadium.

I will not keep you in suspense. In the first game played in the stadium—pitting the University of Central Florida against the University of Texas on September 15, 2007, in front of 45,000 thirsty fans—vendors ran out of bottled water, resulting in eighteen hospitalizations and numerous heat-related illnesses. At the next home game, university officials had a plan: they offered a free bottle of water with each ticket—and public fountains were later added.

As far as I know, all stadiums in North Carolina have public fountains; however, there are two far more serious issues facing North Carolina than any stadium faux pas or the use of water in expensive, well-traveled bottles. If we are to continue to maintain clean, bountiful water statewide for the next 100 years, every resident and public official must understand two concepts: buffers and basins. First, all of our water sources, including lakes, rivers, and even the smallest streams, need adequate buffers of soil and vegetation to protect them from human activity and degradation. Second, every North Carolinian needs to understand that their most important address is not a city or county, but the river basin in which they live.

A Tale of Two Buffers

Ever wonder what kind of water comes from a watershed with only hints of civilization nearby? There is a close-to-perfect example right here in North Carolina: the Asheville watershed on the North Fork of the Swannanoa River. The 325-acre reservoir is located just north of the town of Black Mountain. Asheville began acquiring and protecting land on the North Fork watershed in the early 1900s. When the lake was built about 1950, it became Asheville's principle water supply, although the city has now acquired other less-pristine sources. Outside of a similar situation for the city of Waynesville (an 8,400-acre watershed protecting a fifty-acre reservoir on Allens Creek), few better examples exist of protected reservoirs in North Carolina and the Southeast. To protect the lake, which is more than 125 feet deep in places, Asheville acquired the entire watershed feeding the lake. This means that along with land for the lake itself, the city also acquired all headwaters of the North Fork of the Swannanoa, including forests and mountain coves protecting the streams that feed the lake.

The result is a "textbook" forested buffer encompassing 14,000 acres. Rain that falls within the watershed first hits the high canopy formed by the tops of a mature forest of hardwoods and conifers. Water then falls through the secondary canopy of Dogwood, Sweet Shrub, Viburnum, and Rhodo-

dendron before settling on a carpet of fern, mixed trilliums, and moss. The organic and mineral soils in Appalachian coves are protected by a layer of detritus—decaying leaves, limbs and stumps being digested by bacteria, beetle grubs, and wood-decaying fungi. Nature does not offer a more perfect sponge and filter than the floor of a mature deciduous forest. Before water ever reaches the Swannanoa's North Fork, it has been stored in an organic sponge and filtered through protected soil and rocks. In times of heavy rain or drought, the river and reservoir are almost always clear.

By design, there is no easy public access to Asheville's North Fork Reservoir and its feeder streams. My visits were supervised, and we traveled over totally permeable roads and trails. This is a magnificent forest! Outside of remote areas on the north shore of Fontana Lake (part of the Great Smoky Mountains National Park), I can think of few places in the east less traveled and more pristine. Even along a stretch of the Blue Ridge Parkway on the northwest edge of this watershed, stopping is discouraged. The North Fork and its feeder streams are loaded with fish (I have seen them), but alas, they are not open to fishing.

When lands for the buffer were being assembled, there were homes, farms, roads, and even a tavern within the North Fork watershed. Because of the foresight of early city leaders, who insisted that the *entire* buffer be protected, no one lives there today. Would I allow more public access to this wild place? Perhaps, because I do not think that some public access and use is necessarily harmful when robust buffers are in place. However, I salute the tenacity and foresight of Asheville's planners and today's stewards of the watershed. Their proof is in the—water! The "product" coming out of Asheville faucets is almost pristine and requires only the most minimal treatment. Enjoying such high-quality water now and for decades to come is the result of a near-perfect buffer.

When Buffers Are an Afterthought

Aware that hindsight is 20/20, I offer the tale of another water source, not to indict or criticize public officials of another generation but as examples from which we can learn. To set aside water supplies—streams, rivers, or reservoirs—without effective buffers on surrounding public and private lands is folly and, in the end, costly.

In June 2010 I was not surprised to see this headline in the *Raleigh News and Observer*: "Cleanup May Hit $1.5 Billion." This was the sobering estimate to remedy water pollution problems for Raleigh's major water supply, the

(opposite)

(top) Few cities anywhere have a more robust natural buffer protecting its major watershed than Asheville. All creeks and streams feeding the city's North Fork Reservoir, including the North Fork of the Swannanoa River (shown here), are included within a 14,000-acre buffer.

(bottom) Asheville's pristine buffer includes lands where farmlands and buildings once stood, as evidenced by this chimney from a long-ago tavern on the North Fork of the Swannanoa River.

Falls of the Neuse Reservoir (also called Falls Lake), over the next twenty-five years. Unfortunately, inadequate protection of watersheds, degraded water quality, and long-term cleanup efforts are not just problems facing Raleigh-Durham; the same issues affect water supplies across the nation. Such outcomes are predictable when the protection of water sources is an afterthought. Long-term cleanup obligations will not be born by those who created the problem; they will become a financial burden for our children.

I am frustrated by such headlines for several reasons. The effectiveness of watershed buffers was well known when Falls Lake was being built in the late 1970s and before its completion in 1981. The dam was built as a U.S. Army Corps of Engineers project, and the lake was planned for multiple uses, including flood control and recreation, and to be a major source of drinking water. The reservoir site—which includes portions of rural Wake, Granville, and Durham Counties—starts where the Flat, Little, and Eno Rivers converge to form the Neuse. There were meetings at which the need for more-robust buffers and reasonable restrictions on residential and commercial development within the watershed were discussed. Although rapid growth in the upper Neuse basin (north of Durham and Raleigh) was predicted, efforts to protect the watershed were too often secondary to development. To be fair, planning for Falls Lake presented more than the usual logistical problems: the lake covers 12,000 acres, and feeder waters of the watershed included thousands of additional acres. Planning efforts involved several towns, three counties, the state of North Carolina, and the Army Corps of Engineers. Buffers alone would not have eliminated all pollution entering the lake, but meaningful woody buffers throughout the watershed would have prevented many of the problems, and clean-up costs, facing us today.

Aside from the staggering clean-up expenses that must be met by future taxpayers when watersheds are not protected, there is another equally important reason to exercise great care, or fiduciary duty, when such lands are acquired. The acquisition of any large piece of land for a public purpose—a school, a reservoir, a highway, or an airport—requires the dislocation of farmers, home owners, churches, and even small communities. Whether the sale by owners is voluntary or involuntary, public officials have a solemn obligation to protect the sacrifice of those asked to vacate their property and disrupt their lives for the public good.

When public authorities acquire or condemn land for an interstate highway, tracts include additional land beside the roadway, both as a buffer between the roadway and adjoining landowners and to protect the highway from encroachment. In the case of municipal airports, we now insist

In both rural and urban America, public officials must wrestle with pollution from two sources. The first, point sources, are locations where pollutants enter a lake or stream from drainpipes or ditches; these include manufacturing sites, mining operations, animal-feed lots, and the outflow from waste-treatment facilities. Pursuant to the Clean Water Act of 1972, all discharges from point sources are regulated by a permit and must be treated to remove toxic substances before water can be returned to a watershed. Although the law may have fallen short of its goal to make all waters "fishable" and "swimmable" by 1983, few laws have done more for the health, safety, and recreation of Americans than the Clean Water Act of 1972.

The second category of water pollutants is non-point sources, cumulative contaminants from widespread surface areas, including yards, fields, parking lots, farms, highway construction zones, and golf courses. Pollutants can include sediments (mud), fertilizer runoff (nitrogen, phosphorous, etc.), fecal waste, and petroleum residues. Non-point sources of pollution are best controlled when natural, woody buffers are used to protect all waterways affected by runoff, from the smallest creek to the largest river. When this two-pronged approach—attacking pollution from point and non-point sources—is used to protect and restore waterways, the results are measurable and immediate.

on purchasing adjoining property for safety and as noise buffers. Ample buffers help protect the public investment around roadways and airports, an investment that should last for many decades. No less should be done for our watersheds. Yet, too often, officials skimp on adequate buffers for protecting water resources.

How Much Is Enough?

I know what you are thinking: few cities, especially today, have the financial resources to acquire an entire watershed to protect water supplies. True, but for all North Carolina cities, there is a middle ground between complete protection and the minimal restrictions for which we too often settle. Woody buffers of intact natural vegetation are far superior to any grass or sod buffers for protecting water supplies, but how much is enough? Unfortunately, across North Carolina you will find no minimum statewide requirement, although most land is covered by some buffer restriction. Many areas have adopted "basin-wide" buffer requirements to protect water quality. For example, the basins of the Catawba, Tar-Pamlico, Neuse, and Haw Rivers ("Jordan Lake Rules") are all subject to some form of 50-foot buffer. Even within those basins, cities and counties frequently have separate buffer requirements of 100, 50, or 30 feet, depending on the type of water source to be protected. Perennial water sources (rivers and streams with a continuous flow) and ephemeral streams (drainage areas and waterways that flow only after rainfall) often rate buffers of a different width. To further complicate matters, lands used for forestry and agriculture have long been given exemptions from many buffer regulations (although they are supposed to follow "best management practices").

What is an acceptable buffer width to protect streams, rivers, and lakes used for drinking water and recreation? A 50-foot woody buffer will remove most sediments and significantly reduce runoff. A 75- or 100-foot forested buffer will provide major protection for all water supplies. Just as in the Asheville watershed, a wide swath of mature forest vegetation will hold stream banks in place, slow down runoff, and filter out sediment and other pollutants. In the world of buffers, bigger is better.

I have heard the complaints and criticisms of wide buffers: (1) such buffers are too costly for landowners and developers; and (2) such restrictions will slow down growth and are bad for business. With regard to future water

Woody buffers of seventy-five feet or more can also be used as walking/biking trails, as shown by this trail along the Haw River near Burlington.

supplies and water quality, relaxed buffer restrictions offer short-term phantom savings to homeowners and municipalities. The cost of cleanup is always greater than providing adequate protection in the first place. Is a house or business more valuable with a manicured lawn running to the shore of a polluted lake or with a 75-foot natural buffer separating it from a clean body of water?

In making your decision, know that there are other ancillary benefits to having forests next to water resources. Woody buffers provide great wildlife corridors, allowing all fauna and flora—mammals, birds, reptiles, trees, and wildflowers—to move. Finally, woody buffers do not have to be untouched and unused. More and more towns are discovering the importance of greenways and walking/biking trails that allow us to enjoy the great outdoors in a 75-foot forest by the water.

Learning Your Basin Address

In addition to including meaningful buffers in all water-management decisions, there is a second water issue about which we should educate ourselves: our basin address. My education about basins started very early and quite by accident. Near my family's summer cabin at the upper end of Hickory Nut Gorge is a magic line alluded to earlier in the prologue to this book. The line cannot be seen, but it can be followed. It runs along ridges and peaks, crosses mountain gaps but not rivers, and passes over the tops of watersheds. The line begins in Pennsylvania just south of its border with New York. From there, it follows the spine of the Appalachians through Maryland, West Virginia, Virginia, North Carolina, South Carolina, and into Georgia. The mysterious line virtually divides Georgia into equal parts before it splits the state of Florida down the middle all the way to the Everglades.

As a child, I couldn't see the line, but there was a sign next to the road at the west end the Gorge which read "Eastern Continental Divide—Elevation 2,880 Feet." An updated version of the sign can still be seen on old (now "scenic") U.S. 74 at the crest of a slight grade on the Henderson-Buncombe County line. I think it was my dad who first told me that when water is poured directly on the Eastern Continental Divide, half will flow toward the Atlantic Ocean and the other half toward the Mississippi River and eventually into the Gulf of Mexico.

The concept of a continental divide or a landscape divided into "river basins" was very easy to understand for me and the other ten-year-old

Beside an earlier version of this road sign over fifty years ago, the author learned that liquid streamed directly under the sign will divide—half to the Gulf of Mexico and half to the Atlantic Ocean.

boys between Bat Cave and Upper Hickory Nut Gorge. How do I put this delicately? It occurred to each of us almost instantly that if we peed (boys don't urinate) on the Eastern Continental Divide, half the liquid would go the Atlantic and half to the Mississippi. On several occasions, my friends and I walked an extra half mile just to pee on the crest of the hill by the sign marking the Eastern Continental Divide. In thinking back to the times when I stopped to water the signpost, I like to think of those visits as "science experiments" demonstrating the effects of gravity. What better way for a young man in the mountains to test the underlying hypothesis of liquid dividing equally on unmarked basin lines than to become part of a science experiment? If Sir Isaac Newton could understand the Law of Gravity by observing apples falling from a tree, is it not plausible that mountain boys should understand the concept of "divides and basins" by watching liquid flow in opposite directions when poured (or peed) on a ridgeline?

The same force—gravity—that causes apples to fall from trees and the Moon to stay in orbit around the Earth also causes water to seek its own level. From the moment we arrive on Earth, gravity pulls and tugs at our bodies. Double chins and saggy buttocks are visible manifestations of this mysterious force. A carpenters' level, a siphon hose, and the plumbing in your house are all "powered" by gravity. For me, however, the best example of gravity at work is the flow of water in a stream, dancing slow or fast

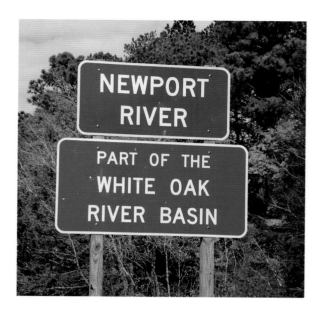

Signs across North Carolina tell us our "ecological address"— the river basin we are entering or leaving or the one in which we reside. All of our river basins provide water and recreation, but many are also home to endemic species found nowhere else.

from one level to the next. While seeking its own level, water always flows downhill so that it can reach that worldwide baseline known as "sea level."

Major rivers are separated from others by ridges and other elevated topography into drainage basins. In the most basic sense, basins are funnels or catchment areas that collect all waters and direct them to a single point. They should not be confused with "valleys" and "gorges," which generally comprise a considerably smaller land area. River basins are much more than a river fed by smaller rivers, streams, and creeks. Both visible water in springs, creeks, and lakes and unseen waters below the surface in wells and groundwater are part of each basin. Your toilet, kitchen drain, and the storm drain on your street are also part of basin "plumbing." River basins are frequently divided into several subbasins and watersheds, such as the one formed by the North Fork of the Swannanoa River previously mentioned. In the end, your basin includes all of the land—fields, forests, yards, and cities—drained by a river and its tributaries. Even if the river for which your basin draws its name is many miles from your home, it is still your natural or "ecological address." To help us understand the concept of basin address, and to tell us when we have crossed into another, North Carolina has placed signs on major highways at basin "divides."

Just as the Eastern Continental Divide apportions water to the Atlantic Ocean and the Gulf of Mexico, there are "basin divides"—subtle lines

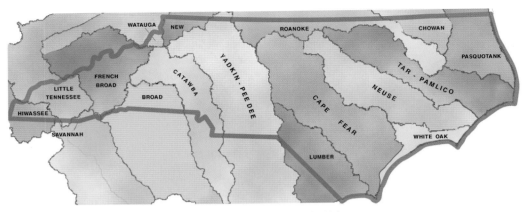

This map shows North Carolina's seventeen river basins, each of which averages more (some much more) than forty inches of rain a year. Such abundance contributes to our biodiversity and economic growth, but continuing growth will put new pressures on water resources. (Courtesy North Carolina Department of Environment and Natural Resources)

moving almost imperceptibly across hills and ridges—directing water to distant rivers. In our Coastal Plain, basin divides can occur at slight rises in elevation only a few feet above sea level, and in the mountains, divides can run along a 3,000-foot ridge line. As earlier indicated, North Carolina has seventeen river basins—or seventeen giant funnels!

The first thing you should note is that only four of our river basins—the Tar-Pamlico, Neuse, White Oak, and Cape Fear—lie entirely within North Carolina. The rest are shared with our sister states. In most cases, we are the situs of the headwaters of a river basin, including the Catawba, Broad, Savannah, French Broad, Little Tennessee, Watauga, Savannah, and New. Why? Most of these rivers begin on or near one of North Carolina's forty-three (or more, depending on who's counting) peaks over 6,000 feet, and water has to flow downhill. Of the basins originating in another state, the most notable is the Roanoke River basin, starting in Virginia's Blue Ridge Mountains and with watershed touching forty-two counties in North Carolina and Virginia, including over 2,000 miles of tributaries. By volume, it forms our largest river before flowing into the Albemarle Sound.

Sharing basins can present problems, because as you have probably guessed, political units within a river basin—states, counties, and cities—cannot always agree on fair use or allocation of water. Suffice it to say that there have been interstate basin squabbles in the past, most recently between North Carolina and Virginia over "inter-basin transfer" of water from the Roanoke basin to another river basin to supply the Norfolk–Virginia

Beach–Hampton Roads metro area. Past squabbles over sharing are nothing compared to what we will face in coming decades, as the population of the Southeast explodes and ever greater demands are made on the water basins originating in North Carolina.

Basins: A Tower of Babel?

While researching an episode of *Exploring North Carolina* for UNC-TV called "Basin Basics," I had the opportunity to talk with a number of experts, including a geologist, a regional planner/engineer, an ecologist/teacher, and a fisheries biologist. I asked each to define a river basin, and I was surprised at their differing responses. The geologist viewed river basins dispassionately as large drains: "It includes all the land drained by a major river and its tributaries." The planner viewed basins as a geopolitical boundary: "A basin includes the municipal planning units on a river from which their water is withdrawn, treated before and after use, and returned." My ecologist, who was also a teacher, gave the most holistic definition: "A river basin is an ecosystem in which all things, living and nonliving, are connected." Finally, the fisheries biologist gave the shortest, and most emphatic, definition of a river basin: "They are crucibles of evolution!"

For a time, I thought these definitions presented a problem. Very intelligent people had given four very different views of a river basin. Was this a modern version of the Tower of Babel, where people describing the same thing spoke multiple professional "languages" and couldn't communicate with each other? Ultimately, I decided they were all correct, because each definition encapsulated some of the demands on river basins in a complex urban society. Some river basins now include many dams that provide power and protect us from floods—but also impede the movement of living things, including migrating fish or sedentary mussels. There are basins in our state containing large metropolitan areas, thousands of acres of concrete and asphalt, and miles of suburban lawns. Other basins within North Carolina are still rural, or even wild. A few large metro areas, like the Research Triangle, even straddle several river basins (the Tar-Pamlico, Neuse, and Cape Fear).

Although rivers and their basins do a remarkable job of cleaning up after humans by filtering water through forests and wetlands and adding oxygen at waterfalls and riffles, there is a limit to nature's capacity to assimilate the entire human waste stream. We are all tied together—top to bottom—when cities like Hillsborough, Durham, Raleigh, Goldsboro, Kinston, New Bern, and Oriental share the same waters from the Neuse River basin. As the waters of the Neuse fall 700 feet toward the Atlantic along a 200-mile course, people use it to drink, bathe, farm, swim, fish, and baptize their children; the same is true for the Yadkin, Catawba, Cape Fear, New, and French Broad basins. The water from our basins hydrate, employ, entertain, exercise, feed, and assure spiritual well-being. What more can we ask of our water?

The experts were correct: a river basin is a big drain, an assemblage of municipal planning units, and an ecosystem where all living and nonliving things are connected. But what did the fisheries biologist mean when he said that river basins are "crucibles of evolution?" In other essays, I have emphasized the biodiversity found across North Carolina. We have large species numbers of Crayfish (45), freshwater fish (265), salamanders (60), mussels (63), and turtles (20). Some of these animals are found only in *one* basin, while others live only in a few rivers, making them "endemic" to a small location. The Neuse River Waterdog, a magnificent salamander reaching a foot in length, is found only in the Neuse basin and the nearby Tar-Pamlico basin. The Carolina Heelsplitter is an extremely rare mussel found only a few places on the border of North and South Carolina. There are endemic fish, such as the Cape Fear Shiner, found only in the upper Cape Fear.

Why are these creatures unique to specific river basins? They *evolved* there, making North Carolina's very old (and unglaciated) river basins "cru-

Virtually all of our river basins have endemic species, plants, and creatures found nowhere else. This Neuse River Waterdog is found only in the Neuse and Tar-Pamlico River basins. (Courtesy of North Carolina Wildlife Resources Commission)

cibles" in which unique animals and plants adapted over thousands, even millions, of years. Each endemic animal fills a niche in the basin and is directly tied to other plants and animals located there. To protect Carolina/Virginia river basins is to protect species found nowhere else. Think about our "crucibles of evolution" the next time you apply pesticide to your yard or see a plume of mud running off of a construction site into any North Carolina river.

Just a Little Mud

Many years ago, I worked with several conservation organizations to prepare an *amicus curiae* (friend of the court) brief in a case involving sediment pollution in a river caused by the removal of forest buffers. All of the attorneys involved knew water law well, but each of us came from different life experiences. During the proceedings, one lawyer remarked that we were working awfully hard on such a small problem: "It's just a little mud."

I quickly remembered the lessons learned while trout fishing across western North Carolina. Trout streams running through forests were always clearer compared to streams passing through developed areas. Streams shaded by a forest canopy stay cooler, and cool water holds more oxygen, making it a far better aquatic habitat.

If a sediment plume clouds a stream during the fall and winter (spawning season), it often covers and suffocates the trout eggs deposited in fine gravel—meaning no young trout the following season. Muddy water heats up much faster when exposed to the sun; think of the hot water inside a dark-colored garden hose that has been lying out in the summer sun. Clear, sediment-free water does not absorb heat as quickly. Warm, dirty water holds less dissolved oxygen, making it less suitable for aquatic insects (mayflies, caddis, and stoneflies), snails, small fish, and other sources of food for fish. Fewer snails, crayfish, mussels, and fish mean less food for birds, otters, and raccoons. Dirty water means a damaged food chain and ecosystem. My own observations and experience had taught me "just a little mud" is a very big problem.

By now I hope you understand that buffers and basins do not present issues handled only by the state and your municipality. Every owner of a house, a farm, a forest, or a business has the opportunity, and obligation, to maintain and create buffers. Shrink the yard you mow; plant less grass and more native plants, shrubs, and trees. Put less fertilizer on your lawn, and stay away from fertilizers loaded with pesticides and herbicides: much of

Every business and homeowner can be "part of the buffer." Rather than continuing to pave all parking lots and driveways, we should use permeable surfaces that allow rainwater to be absorbed rather than carry pollutants to nearby streams. This permeable driveway and parking lot is at the North Carolina Botanical Garden in Chapel Hill.

it will end up in your water. If you live on a stream or a lake, cut only a few trees to provide your water view and leave a wide swath of vegetation (not grass or sod) between you and the water. Use impermeable (nonporous) surfaces *only* when necessary. Rainwater falling on permeable (porous and absorbent) surfaces is absorbed and does not run quickly to nearby streams with a load of nitrogen, phosphorus, and petroleum residues. Permeable driveways and parking areas can actually be components of your buffer.

Whether you believe that buffers should be 30, 50, or 100 feet or cover the entire watershed, you should become part of the discussion. Learn the buffer rule for your region, and protect the "basin address" in which you live. As we look to the future, remember that few places on the planet have a more idyllic water situation than North Carolina—seventeen river basins with generous annual rainfall/moisture over each.

The options going forward are the same for both buffers and basins: we can protect them now or pay later. *Good stewardship requires all of us to be part of the buffer.* If we squander what we have been given, importing bottled water from France and Fiji may become a necessity, not a choice. Stewardship also requires knowing your ecological address and how basins work. If you should forget, take your young son(s) to a basin divide on a hill and explain the principles of gravity. Then, let the science experiment proceed as water divides and flows in two directions.

■ Parcels of land across North Carolina are not equal; in some places, real estate is essentially permanent, while in others it is moving, dynamic, and ever changing. The Outer Banks and other barrier islands of our coast have never stood still for long. Only recently have we tried to make these ribbons of sand permanent through policies and actions that alter their form, economic potential, and natural productivity.

14

LIVING WITH AN EPHEMERAL COASTLINE

I grew up in a BMP (Baptist, Methodist, and Presbyterian) household rife with schism. My mother was the daughter of a Baptist minister from Ohio, and my dad came from staunch Presbyterian parents in Charlotte. My parents compromised after marriage and became Methodists—"diluted Protestants," in the eyes of all grandparents. During my early years, with grandparents close at hand, Bible references in our house were common.

One passage that came up on a regular basis is from Matthew, chapter 7. You probably know the story, or at least the lesson it teaches, even if you are not a religious person. It goes something like this: the house of a wise person is built on a rock—a firm foundation—and it will stand even if the floods and winds come. A foolish person builds on shifting sands, and the house will fall to the power of wind and water.

This story can be read for its allegorical meaning, or, in the case of North Carolina's barrier islands, it can be read literally. It now appears that many folks have never heard this biblical story (or similar stories from other religious faiths), have forgotten it, or are willing to gamble with nature. If you have visited the Outer Banks of North Carolina in the last decade, or any other barrier island from New Jersey to Florida, you have stood on some of this planet's most dynamic and volatile lands. Miles of the ribbon-thin sandy strips are covered with wall-to-wall houses, condominiums, or hotels. Anyone with a house or business on a barrier island has placed a bet in the game of "hurricane roulette." From August to October, the heart of each hurricane season, we watch the weather. All Tar Heels know the names Hugo, Fran, Floyd, and Isabel. Some are even etched in lore, with Hazel being North Carolina's worst storm in history and Katrina, Andrew, and Sandy rating among the nation's worst weather nightmares.

Living or vacationing near the water is wonderful and worth the weather gamble for many North Carolinians. My family and I have a cottage on the coast, and we love it. It is not on the oceanfront, but on an island between the mainland and barrier islands. I knew when I bought it that living near the ocean involved risk, but I placed my bet. I am constantly reminded of this when I visit nearby Shackleford Banks, an uninhabited barrier island nine miles long that is now part of Cape Lookout National Seashore. At the end of the nineteenth century, this beautiful barrier island was the home of several thriving communities, the largest being Diamond City, a village of over 500 residents at the east end of Shackleford. The town had gardens, churches, and cemeteries just like any other North Carolina community. An adjoining community, known as Bell's Island, lay just to the west of Diamond City and was famous for its Persimmon Trees, according to local historians. What many people don't realize is that most of the homes in Diamond City, on Bell's Island, and in other nearby communities were not on the beachfront but on the sound side of Shackleford Banks. Separating the homes and gardens from the ocean was a long, high sand dune said to have been over 1,000 feet long and up to forty feet high.

The hardy residents of Shackleford eked out a living from gardens and the sea—including whaling in the early spring of the year—during two centuries of habitation before the hurricanes of 1896 and 1899. The storms were large and the destruction widespread (especially the storm of August 1899), causing the people of Shackleford's communities to rethink their futures and relocate, many to nearby Harkers Island. Shackleford Banks was essentially abandoned by the first decade of the twentieth century.

If Diamond City had just hung on until the last quarter of the twentieth century, there would have most likely been a causeway or bridge from the mainland, paved roads, fast food, and demands for "beach nourishment." Unlike the early residents who lived on the back side of the barrier island, modern vacation homes would have been built near the ocean, facing the beach. Following the hurricanes and tropical storms in recent decades, there would have been "overwash" on Shackleford, which would have most certainly covered or washed away sections of paved road. As with today's Topsail Island, South Nags Head, and Highway 12 below Oregon Inlet, any modern development on Shackleford Banks would require more sand and pavement to save the roads and the beachfront. So what is the difference between Shackleford Banks, inhabited for two centuries but now abandoned, and many of North Carolina's highly developed strands of sand? In short: not much.

Since the late 1960s, Shackleford Banks and Core Banks, both part of Cape Lookout National Seashore, have been my teachers. From my experience on the water and the barrier islands—but most of all, from listening to and observing local residents—I have learned that barrier islands are a buffer between the mainland and the full force of the ocean. I have also grown to understand that the two main components of our coastal ecosystem—barrier islands and shallow sounds—are ephemeral. Barrier islands, including the flats and channels behind them, constantly move and change in form and size, making them relatively short-lived.

A case in point: in the late 1960s, I used to climb up to the World War II gun mounts (a coastline-defense installation built in the 1940s) in the side of large sand dunes southwest of the point of Cape Lookout. To me, the massive concrete-and-steel structures looked permanent. By the mid-1970s, the dunes had been eaten away by waves, and the concrete relics of war lay on the beach. Now, forty years later, the concrete ruble is in the Atlantic beyond the surf line. During this same period, I have also watched channels in Core Sound and Back Sound fill in with sand and new ones form by shifting currents. This is unlike any other real estate in North Carolina. Where land and sea meet, the word "permanent" is seldom applicable.

This is not the case on the mainland. In my two decades as a law professor, one of my teaching areas was real property law. Most real estate law is based on the concepts of "permanence" and "possession." Under our system, the same piece of real property (land) can be passed on by deed, will, or intestate succession (inheritance where there is no will) through the ages. In England and across Europe are estates that have been in the same families for centuries. Even in North Carolina, it is not unusual, especially in the eastern part of the state, to find land held by members of the same family for seven or eight generations. Owners in "fee simple" have the right to convey land with no restrictions to family or strangers. Although owners may change, the land stays the same. The underlying assumption is that land does not move; it is permanent, like the Rock of Gibraltar. Because of land's permanence and stability, land ownership confers wealth and status.

Boundaries are generally accurate and unchanging, whether they are marked by natural features—ridge lines, identifiable rocks, or "witness

The foreshore, the beach below the mean high-water mark, belongs to everyone. The location of these public lands is constantly changing, especially on dynamic barrier islands.

trees"—or determined by a survey crew "measuring courses and distances" and placing iron stakes. Despite occasional boundary disputes, tracts of land measured in the North Carolina Mountain region, the Piedmont, or the Coastal Plain 100 years ago have the same boundaries today (although most have been broken into much smaller tracts). Because land has always meant wealth and control, precise boundaries are important. Measurement of real estate is equally important to cities and counties because land provides a tax base that pays for many services of local government.

As a former law professor and an observer of the natural world, it has long been clear to me that not all land is equal when it comes to permanence or longevity. Property on the oceanfront has always presented a problem: the ocean boundary moves. Law students and their teachers have wrestled with beachfront boundaries and ownership since the colonial days. As a student,

I wrote a piece for the *North Carolina Law Review* in 1971 dealing with the definition of navigable waters and "public trust" lands. The issues I dealt with then are just as important now.

At that time, major coastal development in the Carolinas was in its infancy. Today, a single beachfront lot or dwelling can cost hundreds of thousands of dollars or more. With the specter of sea-level rise bringing change to all coastal areas, the financial stakes have never been higher. It is understandable that coastal landowners and beachfront communities want to protect, fortify, and "nourish" beaches. Just as in 1971, the implications of ownership on the ocean's edge is a hot topic for students and professors alike.

A fact that every citizen and public official should remember is that the public has the right, under North Carolina statute and common law, to use ocean beaches and ocean inlets. The seaward or ocean boundary for all property is the "mean [average] high-water mark." The foreshore, the land below the high-water mark, belongs to all of us as "public trust lands." Everyone has the right to collect shells, sunbathe, fish, or stroll in the moonlight on any North Carolina ocean beach. Ownership and control can extend only to the mean high-water mark and not to the ocean's edge. The owner of an oceanfront house in our state cannot exclude other citizens from using the beach below that magic line. The problem for lawyers, landowners, and beachgoers is that the location of the "mean high water mark" is ever shifting—and ocean-front lots are constantly changing in size—due to erosion, storms, and rising seas.

A Change in Expectations

Ocean lots do not possess the primary attribute of mainland real estate: permanence. This should not make us fatalistic about building or living near ocean beaches; we must simply understand, individually and as a society, that the nature of these lands is impermanence, and we should act accordingly. The builders of early vacation homes understood this.

Coastal geologist and East Carolina professor Stanley Riggs likes to point out that in the early days of settlement on the northern Outer Banks, residents generally did not build on the beachfront but on higher ground away from the shore, or on the back side of the barrier islands (in the same way that the residents of Diamond City lived behind ocean dunes). The first vacation homes on the front of barrier islands in North Carolina and along the East and Gulf Coasts were usually built on long, narrow lots running perpendicular to the coastline. Early residents and vacationers knew that the beach was dynamic and moving. By having a long, narrow lot, vacation houses could be moved from time to time as the ocean advanced.

From the 1930s to the 1960s, when there were few large developments on North Carolina coast, it was not uncommon for vacation houses to be lost to a nor'easter or a hurricane. If the house and most of the lot remained, it was patched up or rebuilt. If the house and its oceanfront parcel were washed away, the beach and dunes were not rebuilt. Both local residents and early vacation home owners were aware of the risk in building on the oceanfront. You were in essence placing a bet, and the chance of losing that bet was understood.

Somewhere along the way, the understanding and expectations of owners changed. Fragile dunes, held together only by the roots of wispy Sea Oats, sprouted expensive homes and paved highways. By the 1990s, landscaping with exotic trees and rolled-out turf lawns with sprinkler systems made some beach neighborhoods look just like suburban developments in North Carolina's Piedmont—and also made them look permanent. The illusion of permanence was underscored by cheap federal flood insurance. Federal flood-insurance programs, starting in 1968, had the beneficial goal of nudging coastal landowners to comply with building ordinances that would reduce future damage. Unfortunately, flood insurance actually encouraged building on previously undeveloped flood-prone areas, such as barrier islands. Cheap flood insurance—far below what private insurers would charge—diminished the risk for beachfront home owners by eliminating much of the risk of financial loss. In addition to government subsidized insurance, the government nourished (rebuilt) eroding beaches, paved roads, and closed "breaches"—gaps created by storms in barrier islands—whenever a storm surge washed over barrier islands.

I am the first to admit that construction and development, and the jobs they create, are good for the economy, and that *some* subsidies are, in the end, cost-effective for all taxpayers. I also know that a strong tourist economy—in North Carolina and every other state—built around ocean beaches is good for all of us. However, when the risks are too costly and much of the infrastructure is no longer sustainable, it is time to reexamine state and federal programs that underscore the illusion of permanence. The longer we wait to implement changes to coastal building policies and to educate new generations about the dynamic nature of beachfront lands, the more financial obligations we will incur in years to come.

The Illusion of Permanence

What do you love most about the North Carolina coast? The wide sandy beaches or vast salt marshes? Fishing with your children? Fresh shrimp and oysters for a cookout, ducks circling your decoys, magnificent wading birds, or a house with a view? Above all else, are you willing to take the steps necessary to ensure that future generations will be able to enjoy these things? Whether you call it global warming or climate change is beside the point when it comes to the future of the North Carolina coast. Atmospheric temperatures and the sea are rising; beaches and barrier islands are moving west; and we are in a worldwide warming cycle, with seas that have been rising for almost 18,000 years (by over 400 feet).

Even if there was not a human fingerprint on the Earth's thermostat, the evidence is indisputable and there for all to see. Just as I saw the ocean engulf a concrete gun emplacement near Cape Lookout over a few decades, I have also stood in the breakers among large stumps from a maritime of Live Oak that had flourished behind oceanfront dunes a century ago. To reach barrier-island forests, the shoreline had to move westward and past the dune line, leaving the ghostly cemetery of stumps now visible near Corolla. Even more dramatic are aerial photographs on which we can measure and demonstrate the westward movement of barrier islands here in North Carolina.

If you need more convincing that our barrier islands are constantly changing, you need only look at the visual proof offered in maps. In my office, I have reproductions of perhaps two dozen early maps of North Carolina and the Southeast—most from the 1500s to the late 1800s. Some of them can be found in William Cumming's 1966 book, *North Carolina in Maps*. In many of the earliest maps, you'll see mountains placed almost as decorations on the mainland, where it is clear that explorers or mapmakers had no firsthand knowledge of the topography. As Professor Cumming correctly observed, much of what the early cartographers and pioneers placed on their maps was "often fantastically wrong." For example, some of the earliest visitors to the North Carolina coast believed that just beyond the sand strips that we know as the Outer Banks lay the Pacific Ocean and the long-sought "shortcut" to China. One such explorer, Giovanni da Verrazano (sent by the king of France), visited the North Carolina coast in 1524 and believed that only a very narrow isthmus separated him from the Pacific. Professor Cumming noted that "Verrazano's Sea" and the notion of a short-

This slow westward migration of ocean beaches is demonstrated in this aerial photograph of South Nags Head. In this photograph, you will note that between 1849 and 1998, the oceanfront moved approximately 1,000 feet. (Courtesy of Stanley R. Riggs and Dorothea V. Ames, Department of Geological Sciences, East Carolina University)

cut to India and China tantalized explorers and merchants until the middle of the sixteenth century.

For all of their flaws, maps prepared from the late seventeenth century onward were remarkably consistent—and even accurate when it came to locating, marking, and naming inlets. Early mariners in small sailing vessels could sail close enough to see the inlets and even explore them using longboats. For sailors far from home, inlets provided safe haven in the event of storms. What jumps out from map to map is that, within a few decades, inlets appear and then disappear up and down the Outer Banks, from Cape Lookout to the Virginia border. The *only* inlet of the Outer Banks that is present in all the maps since the 1500s is Ocracoke Inlet. All the rest are ephemeral. Four maps produced between 1733 and 1882 illustrate the fleeting nature of inlets on the North Carolina coast.

The Moseley Map of 1733 shows Currituck Inlet at the location of the North Carolina–Virginia border. To the south about fifteen miles, near present-day Corolla, is another inlet called New Inlet ("New Currituck Inlet" on later maps). East of Manteo, running through present-day Nags Head, is the famous Roanoke Inlet, the passage used by the Raleigh Expe-

(opposite) Outer Banks ocean beaches, like this one north of Corolla (top), sometimes display the stumps of maritime forests from the past. This "stump forest" once grew on the back of the barrier island and looked like a living maritime forest (bottom) located a few miles to the south. The ocean moved to the west, erasing beach and dunes before it reached the forest.

ditions in 1584 and 1587. Near the south end of Roanoke Island is Gun Inlet, and a few miles farther south is Chickinecommock Inlet. Between Cape Hatteras and Ocracoke Island is Hatteras Inlet. Three inlets are shown in Core Banks south of Ocracoke.

The Mouzon Map of 1775—prepared just four decades after the Moseley Map—shows no Currituck Inlet at the Virginia border; it had closed completely. Near present-day Corolla, however, you will see New Currituck Inlet, which, like the original Currituck Inlet to the north, kept Currituck Sound open to oceangoing vessels. In 1786, shortly after the American Revolution, the thriving Port of Currituck reported visits by 194 oceangoing schooners and forty-three sloops. By 1828 New Currituck Inlet had closed completely, cutting Currituck Sound off from the Atlantic. The salty oysters of Currituck Sound and the Port of Currituck disappeared, except as chapters in the rich history of the Outer Banks.

Mouzon's map still shows Roanoke Inlet and, to the south, Gant Inlet and Chickinecommock Inlet. Unlike on the Moseley Map of 1733, however, no Hatteras Inlet separates Cape Hatteras from Ocracoke. Fickle are the inlets of the Outer Banks!

In the MacRae-Brazier Map of 1833, you will find no inlets where the Port of Currituck had once flourished. Even the reliable Roanoke Inlet that had kept Albemarle Sound and Roanoke Island open to the Atlantic had filled in. In fact, the *only* inlet shown between the Virginia border and Ocracoke Inlet is New Inlet, near present-day Rodanthe. Below Ocracoke Inlet, only one passage is shown through Core Banks: Cedar Inlet.

Almost 150 years after the Moseley Map of 1733 and less than fifty years after MacRae-Brazier, the Kerr-Cain Map (1882) was published. Again, new inlets and change were the order of the day. On this map, Oregon Inlet, opened in 1847 and spanned today by the Bonner Bridge, appears just above Bodie Island. Below Bodie Island are two more inlets, the larger called Loggerhead Inlet. Between Cape Hatteras and the dependable Ocracoke Inlet, another inlet appears as Hatteras Inlet.

(opposite) All four of these maps—Moseley (top left), Mouzon (top right), MacRae-Brazier (bottom left), and Kerr-Cain (bottom right)—created between 1733 and 1882, include detailed renderings of North Carolina's Outer Banks. The same section of our coastline over 149 years reveals dramatic change in the opening and closing of inlets just decades apart. Until recently, all major openings in barrier islands were referred to as inlets—not "breaches," a term adopted by some public officials in recent decades. (Image of Moseley Map of 1733 courtesy of Special Collections, Joyner Library, East Carolina University; other images courtesy of the North Carolina State Archives)

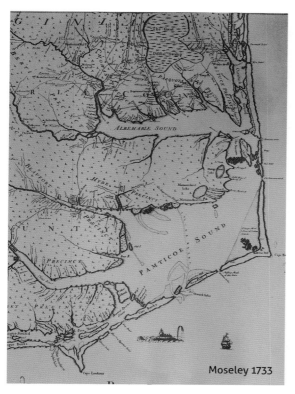

Moseley 1733

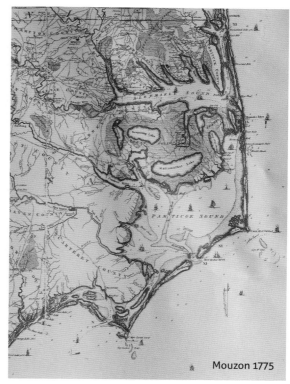

Mouzon 1775

MacRae-Brazier 1833

Kerr-Cain 1882

There are a number of other maps representing different decades before, during, and after the 149-year period described above. The fact is that along most of the ribbon of sand we know as the Outer Banks, dozens, or perhaps several hundred, inlets have existed over many centuries, many of them named but most nameless and forgotten. The maps don't lie. Why is it, beginning in the twentieth century, we came to be so surprised when one of our old inlets closed and a new one opened? Just as barrier islands have moved westward across the Continental Shelf as the great glaciers of the last Ice Age melted and retreated, the opening and closing of barrier-island inlets is part of the dynamic nature of these lands. They offer only the illusion of permanence.

Sisyphus at the Coast

There are two major options, with many possibilities for compromise in between. The first option will be the most costly and will, in the end, be a fool's errand. We can attempt to construct longer, stronger bridges and maintain existing roads on the Outer Banks and other barrier islands. We can also attempt to "nourish" beaches and dunes *in the same places* over and over again. All of this is the equivalent of leaving lawn furniture overnight on the beach and being surprised the next morning when the wind and tide have rearranged it.

We attempt these miracles of construction on the same frail ribbons of land that have seen multiple inlets—not "breaches"—come and go over the last 300 years, with new inlets attempting to punch through each decade. Development of or large "forever" houses, bridges, and roads a couple of feet above sea level on simple barrier islands is neither smart policy nor sustainable. This is a modern version of the Greek tragedy of the mythical Sisyphus, a king condemned for eternity to push a large rock up a steep hill but never succeeding in reaching the top.

Even if we triumph over nature in building bridges connecting permanent vacation enclaves encircled with stone and concrete, what will we have preserved? When seas rise only a few feet against seawalls, there will be no beaches and no protective marshes. Who is the winner if beach communities become fortresses? North Carolina will still have barrier islands, but they will have continued to move westward ahead of the advancing ocean. Like Sisyphus and his rock, is there any governor or member of the General Assembly who wants to haul sand and build seawalls for eternity?

The second option is to allow barrier islands to do what they have always

This dense maritime forest of Live Oak, Yaupon, Red Cedar, and even Cabbage Palm is located several hundred yards from the beachfront on Bald Head, much of which is a complex barrier island. Similar complex barrier islands (without the palms) can be found along the entire coast and include much of Bogue Banks, Ocracoke Village, Hatteras Village, and Nags Head Woods.

done: move, expand, contract, and protect the mainland. Some of North Carolina's most experienced coastal geologists and planners, including the previously mentioned Dr. Stanley Riggs of East Carolina University, Dr. Orrin Pilkey of Duke University, and Dr. Robert Young of Western Carolina University, have pointed out for years that our barrier islands are a mix of *simple* and *complex* islands. Both types move and change, but the complex barrier islands are far older and more stable, and they can support long-term human communities. Simple barrier islands are relatively short-lived and subject to rapid change. Through them, most inlets come and go.

Riggs has suggested that rather than trying to pave and bridge both complex and simple barrier islands, we should connect only the complex,

Where there is abundant sand, some of our barrier islands have grown high and wide. They have multiple ridges, high dunes, and, in some cases, old maritime forests. Because of their size and complexity, they are classified as "complex" barrier islands. A few examples include Nags Head Woods, parts of Ocracoke Island, sections of Bogue Banks, and much of Baldhead Island. These areas, being the most stable, have generally been settled the longest.

Although it may sound strange, sand is in short supply along many stretches of the Tar Heel coast. Where the supply of sand is limited, or "sand-poor," islands classified as "simple" barrier islands are invariably narrower, lower, and subject to rapid change. Surveys by the Department of Geological Sciences at East Carolina University classify almost three-quarters of our barrier islands as simple and only one-fourth as complex. Since the vast majority of our barrier islands are simple, you don't have to look far for examples. They include some famous stretches of Highway 12 south of Oregon Inlet, northern stretches of Ocracoke Island, much of Core Banks, and Topsail Island. Although rare forty years ago, development activity has exploded on many simple barrier islands.

The health and migration of simple barrier islands requires storms, overwash, and even inlets. As barrier islands absorb the pounding and energy of the Atlantic, dune lines are built up. During storm surges, overwash causes a barrier island to flatten out and widen. During major events, the formation of inlets is a natural process critical to the evolution and movement of the island. Where an inlet has punched through (remaining open from a few weeks to many years), a flood-tide delta forms and eventually creates a new platform for further barrier-island growth and migration.

long-lived islands by shallow-draft modern ferries. In some situations and locations, less-than-permanent movable bridges may also prove useful and cost-effective. As with fixed structures, other alternatives should have the same goal: providing safe, dependable transportation for both residents and visitors alike.

An equally important advantage in allowing our barrier islands to remain "unfortified" and dynamic—expanding and moving—is estuarine productivity. Active barrier islands mean healthy salt marshes, multiple deep channels, and flats covered with aquatic grasses—all integral to finfish/shellfish productivity. A paved highway, or a line of houses built on simple barrier islands, is an obstruction or dam hindering the movement of sand, the expansion of the island, and the growth of productive salt marshes.

There are many hard-working people and second-home owners at the ocean's edge whose homes and livelihoods will be impacted by any increase in sea level. They want our beaches and roads to stay in the same locations, and they desire the convenience and safety of bridges and roads that will always be there. They argue that unless we protect, nourish, and even fortify existing beachfronts and roads, tax bases will plummet and coastal economies will suffer.

In recent years, another group of citizens, equally concerned about the future of North Carolina's coast, has voiced its concern. Their message: protecting existing roads and structures is too costly and unsustainable, especially since road maintenance encourages development in high-risk areas. They argue that the time has passed when any of us can deny the certainty of a significant sea-level rise in the decades ahead and more westward movement in our barrier islands. They seek policies that will allow barrier islands to expand and change naturally, which they see as necessary to maintain the economic productivity of barrier-island economies. As much as I respect both views, I must stand with the latter.

■ Science is not perfect, but at its best it is honest, and the trends are clear. None of the choices being offered decision makers and coastal planners are easy and without risk. To be sure, we can differ on estimates of expected sea-level rise—whether the increase will be two feet or two meters by the year 2100. In all scenarios, though, the way we live, travel, and do business on the North Carolina coast will be altered dramatically. The *real* status quo on the Outer Banks, and the rest of our coast, is change; therefore, our policies dealing with permanent roads, bridges, and development must also change.

In the Outer Banks, from Oregon Inlet to Hatteras, Hatteras to Ocracoke, and Portsmouth to Cape Lookout, we have a national treasure of immense ecological and economic value. It will be necessary to maintain some permanent inlets and channels to a safe depth for commercial fishing fleets and public recreation, but the "hardening" of entire shorelines (jetties and seawalls) and maintaining an inflexible system of roads would be a serious mistake for the economy of North Carolina, for tourism on the coast, and for the future of productive ecosystems.

Public officials of North Carolina are getting excellent and timely advice from government and university scientists—climatologists, geologists, and coastal ecologists. Prolonged indecision will benefit no one, and there is room for innovation and compromise that will provide safe access through various forms of coastal transportation for all who want to live on, or visit, our treasured barrier islands.

Again, I ask you to list your favorite activities, sights, and experiences at the North Carolina coast. I'll bet most items on your list occur on a wide, wild beach or near a pristine marsh, both of which are products of a dynamic barrier-island system. Wouldn't it be a tragedy if future generations were not able to enjoy these things as you have?

■ North Carolina is now on almost everyone's A-list, with cities at or near the top of "Best Places" to live, do business, retire, and vacation. In virtually every high rating, writers applaud the state's green spaces and easy access to public land. With three dozen state parks; several national forests, parks, and wildlife refuges; and hundreds of miles of greenways and paddle trails, Tar Heels have long placed a high premium on open spaces and wild places.

15

NATURE AT THE CROSSROADS

In elementary school, one of the first and most awkward songs I learned was "The Old North State," the Official State Song of North Carolina. For students from kindergarten to the fifth grade, it is a terrible song: the melody drags, yes, but more important, the lyrics put on display for the world to see North Carolina's 200-year inferiority complex. The words were written in 1840 by William Gaston, twenty years before the American Civil War. It contains hints of pride—"Carolina! Carolina! Heaven's blessings attend her / We will cherish, protect, and defend her"—but for my two older brothers and me, the song was a real downer. In one demeaning line, the writer describes the state's young men: "Plain and artless her sons." We took it personally. Even more depressing were other lyrics that took us a long time to understand. Why would William Gaston have included the phrase, "Tho' the scorner may sneer at and witlings defame her"?

Who was "the scorner," and why would "witlings" say bad things about North Carolina? Several years later, I eventually learned that this fair land was widely known as the "valley of humility between two mountains of conceit"—Virginia and South Carolina. We were never good at following colonial rules: early settlers in the late seventeenth century and the first half of the eighteenth century, and especially those of the Albemarle region, were independent to a fault, both in their casual obedience to the Crown and their preference for religious tolerance. This line of thinking placed our forebearers at odds with our more-refined, and staunchly Anglican, neighbors. By 1840, as part of the antebellum South, North Carolina was still a land of small farms, budding industry on Piedmont rivers, and naval stores (tar and pitch)—a very different place from its richer sister states to the North and South. The perceived wealth and higher social status of neighboring states, along with the deepwater ports at Norfolk and Charleston, clearly gave William Gaston and several generations of North Carolinians much to fret about and envy.

Although there was a fleeting brush with wealth and fame during the "Carolina gold rush" from the 1820s to the 1850s, it was not until the twentieth century that success in tobacco, textiles, and furniture gave Tar Heels a kinder self-image. Yet compared to other states, we were still a "late bloomer." I like to think of North Carolina after World War II as the unsophisticated, gangly high-school kid with big ears (the shallow sounds and Outer Banks) and a big nose (Mt. Mitchell and other 6,000-foot peaks) who made it to the big time!

Both our topography and dearth of traditional natural wealth postponed success and a rise to the top. As a state, we were not cursed by quick wealth in the form of mountains of coal, huge deposits of copper and iron, oil and gas fields, or deepwater ports. All such resources brought more rapid industrialization to other parts of America. As a result, we have not suffered the indignity of mountaintop removal and strip-mining, as have some of our neighbors to the North and West. North Carolina's wealth came in the form of varied soils suited to forests of deciduous trees and evergreens, complex geology, and a generous allocation of water resources that should enable us to thrive in coming centuries. Our tall peaks, which were once barriers to development and travel, are now the envy of every state in eastern America. Instead of deepwater megaports like those in New York, Boston, Baltimore, Norfolk, and Charleston, fostering early, rapid growth, or the coastal oil fields of the Gulf Coast ringed with refineries, I believe nature dealt us a far better hand with two modest, strategically placed ports (Morehead City and Wilmington), exquisite beaches, and one of the largest and most productive estuarine systems in the temperate world.

Through the 1970s, 1980s, and 1990s, with the blossoming of Charlotte, the Triad, the Triangle, and a great university system, North Carolina—the late bloomer—was on everyone's A-list. We now have three of the nation's most progressive and desirable metropolitan areas (the Triangle, the Triad, and Charlotte) along the Interstate 85 corridor, and virtually every city in North Carolina—from Asheville in the mountains to Pinehurst in the Sandhills and Wilmington on the coast—is on someone's top-five list. We are frequently listed among America's best places to do business, best places to retire, and best places to live. In 2007 Asheville was on top of *MarketWatch*'s "Best Places to Live" list. Durham grabbed *Money* magazine's first place for "Best Places to Retire" in 2010 and placed first on the "Creativity Index" in 2012. In 2011 *Bloomberg Businessweek* rated America's "Best Cities," and when the points were counted, Raleigh was number one. In each selection process, numerous quality-of-life metrics are considered, including universities, restaurants, transportation, museums, sports teams, public schools, and employment. One metric, however, is almost always prominently mentioned when a North Carolina city is honored: parks and open spaces. For example, when *Businessweek* writers explained why Raleigh was atop its "Best Cities" list, they gushed about the "12,512 park acres, equal to several times the green space per capita in cities like New York and Los Angeles."

By growing slowly, and perhaps because of our agrarian roots, North Carolina cities and the state as a whole have valued open spaces and wild places. We are now being rewarded for it. Unfortunately and predictably, the public lands that have helped put us on top are, in the eyes of many, expendable. Our open spaces—an integral part of our state's "business model for success"—and our rich biodiversity are now under attack.

The Biodeficit

My wife and I have tried to provide our children with four things: unconditional love (including the freedom to explore ideas); the opportunity for first-rate education (books in the home, time in nature, travel, and good schools); a commitment to hard work and service to others; and as few financial burdens as possible (as they begin their own careers and families). So far, so good. There are two other things, however, over which we have far less control that will impact the lives of our children and yours. The first is a problem that has caused angst and anger for several generations: America's burgeoning national debt. Since the most recent economic downturn, this debt has loomed larger than ever, potentially stunting the American Dream for many. The second is barely noticed, little understood, and may be of far greater consequence to future generations. I am talking about an increasing "biodeficit."

Though I am concerned, I remain optimistic (is there another choice?) that our nation's financial woes will one day be solved, or at least better managed. My hope is that my generation will get its act together and be part of the solution. To fail is to leave a bitter national inheritance for our children and grandchildren.

The second problem—a looming biodeficit—is barely noticed, little understood, and perhaps far more intractable than mere financial burden. Both locally and nationally, we have strained ecosystems to the breaking point and diminished diversity in plant and animal communities, either unwittingly or through greed. For over two decades, I have been haunted by a prediction of E. O. Wilson—the kid from Alabama, blind in one eye, who became one of the great scientists and environmental ethicists of the last fifty years. I met him by chance many years ago near Boston and was taken by his measured, passionate plea for ecosystems under siege. In his 1984 book, *Biophilia*, Wilson wrote: "The one process now going on that will take millions of years to correct is the loss of genetic and species diversity by the destruction of natural habitats. *This is the folly our descendants are least likely to forgive us*" (emphasis added).

When I first read this, I was certain that Wilson, a Pulitzer Prize–winning writer, was referring mainly to the loss of rain forest habitat and the loss of biodiversity in tropical hot spots like the Amazon. Through my own travels and observations, I am now convinced that he was writing about the wild nature near all of us.

This is not another plea to save the world. There are problems with tropical corral reefs, rain forests being lost to megafarming and mining, a global thermostat stuck on "High," and a planet still working on the fundamentals of family planning. Because few of us have the clout to influence conduct in world arenas, I choose to concentrate my energies on the place I know best: North Carolina. We can continue to make North Carolina a model for living in concert with productive ecosystems into the next century by protecting freshwater resources; by allowing dynamic barriers islands to move and change; by protecting mountain vistas; and, most of all, by being stewards of native fauna and flora. This model for change begins in our yards, on our streets, and in our choices of elected officials. To be sure, there are elected officials who "get it" and work tirelessly to keep public lands and biodiversity integral to North Carolina's quality of life. They understand that the factors that currently rank us at the top in business and livability indices can be lost or degraded quickly. With 9 million citizens increasing to more than 12 million in the coming two decades, the way we build homes, businesses, and transportation infrastructure—while maintaining public lands and watershed buffers—will determine future ecological vitality. Keeping the natural world as a prominent component of North Carolina's ongoing "business plan" will continue to serve us well into the future.

To prevent diminished biodiversity—a biodeficit—the first requirement, just as it is in dealing with the national debt, is *understanding the problem*. A reduced appreciation and lack of connection with the natural world is not just a problem for young Americans; substantial numbers of my generation and of the body politic at all levels reflect a diminished environmental intelligence quotient. Even more troubling, as a nation, we have had an on-and-off love affair with science, technology, and conservation. How quickly we forget that, in the second half of the twentieth century, perhaps prodded by our race to the Moon with the Soviets, we *embraced* science, technology, a new conservation ethic (with clean air and water legislation), and intellectual curiosity in our homes and corporations. We invested in schools at all levels and built research campuses, like North Carolina's own Research Triangle Park, that brought together the best from the entrepreneurial and academic worlds. As we got closer to the twenty-first century, America's fickle relationship with science and technology again showed signs of strain, as some of our neighbors, including public officials, began to pander to antiscience interests.

Too often, when solid science conflicts with short-term gain, or the pendulum swings within political parties, we have devalued science and scientists. We love science when it saves our lives, identifies and controls old enemies like cancer, or produces next-generation antibiotics that cure once-deadly infections. Almost inexplicably, we won't listen to the *same doctors* who cured us when they also tell us that using life-saving antibiotics in healthy chickens, cattle, and hogs for weight-gain purposes is rendering antibiotics ineffective by allowing deadly pathogens to mutate into drug-resistant strains. The doctors and scientists who save lives with heart stents are endowed with genius—until they write articles telling us to cut back on sugary drinks, salt, and fatty/fried foods in schools. Remember the decades-long war over the dangers of tobacco, which was long touted as a "freedom of choice" issue and not a public-health issue? Change is difficult: tobacco-producing states and industries were resistant, and in some cases hostile, to any change to their business models because of demonstrated dangers to health. When science is convenient and helpful, we embrace it, yet regrettably, it is in our nature to fight it when the status quo is challenged.

The anger and frustration of individuals in business and government who feel threatened by findings relating to a changing climate and rising sea is now focused on geologists, climatologists, and ecologists. Naysayers have even included presidential candidates, members of Congress, state legislators, and school-board members across America. The welcome mat has been pulled for scientists who suggest that human activity has accelerated the warming of the atmosphere; such information would require adaptation and change—change in the way we build our houses, in the way we power our cars and factories, in the way we eat, and in the way we build near the seashore. When scientists from universities, governments, and the private sector began to reach consensus on the implications and probable ranges of temperature and sea-level rise, we heard suggestions of "conspiracy among scientists" from the naysayers. Just as in the tobacco controversy two decades ago, when results were not what we wanted to hear, it was time to question the science.

This preserve-the-status-quo mentality is all the more remarkable because, of all well-educated professionals, few are more disciplined, principled, and even competitive than those from the sciences. There is even spirited competition between major research universities, with published findings almost always scrutinized through a peer-review process; in the science research community, there is little room for shoddy work. In short, science communities are among the least likely places for conspiracies to evolve.

Much of the official brush-off of science is very subtle. For the last couple of decades, especially since the mid-1990s, winter storms and hurricanes have changed the face of North Carolina's Outer Banks, just as they have for centuries. During this same time, a new "climatological/geological vocabulary" has evolved at press conferences held by political leaders and emergency-management personnel (both state and federal). We have been told that storms caused "major overwash," "breaches in the barrier island," "gaps in the Banks," and "long-term disruption of traffic on Highway 12." In other centuries, *all* of these colorful phrases would have described *inlets*. Politically, it is much easier to close a gap, overwash, or a breach than an inlet. Such euphemisms also allow politicians to ignore the warnings of climate scientists and coastal geologists who have repeatedly told us that man-enhanced "thinning" of barrier islands would result in more storm-created inlets—oops, breaches! These were the same scientists praised by government and the media for providing increasingly accurate hurricane forecasts, tracking models, and storm-surge predictions. Go figure.

With satellites to view the entire planet Earth, sensors to measure the slightest change in temperature, telescopes to see into deep space, the ability to analyze the entire human genome (or that of any other living creature or plant), and computers to crunch unimaginable amounts of data, we are in the first generations of human history to be able to look back in time and perhaps into the future. We no longer have to guess as to whether whale populations are too low, whether we have removed too many trees, whether levels of carbon dioxide in the atmosphere are rising, or whether sea levels will rise noticeably during the lives of our children and grandchildren. Yet with all of our abilities and scientific knowledge, we don't want to see—or be reminded of—stressed fisheries, dwindling biodiversity, and melting ice.

Rather than conspiracies and cover-ups by science and scientists, collectively we suffer from ossification in planning and thinking—a crippling inflexibility and unwillingness to deal with change. Because of the *selective* embrace of the work and findings of the scientific community by some in authority, we have too often gotten short-sighted decisions regarding public lands, plant and animal diversity, and coastal resources. Adaptation is not always comfortable.

Cathedral Thinking

We have reached the point when we need to resort to an old remedy: "cathedral thinking," an elegant term to describe long-term planning. The concept dates to the Middle Ages in Europe and has been cited in various forums by scholars and planners. I first heard the term in a college history course when the professor explained the commitment required by religious leaders, architects, and workers to start a building that they would never see completed. The great cathedrals of Europe—Notre Dame, Salisbury, Cologne, Winchester, and Chartres—many of which were built between the twelfth and fifteenth centuries, were monumental undertakings in both engineering and art. The span of time from design—foundations, walls, spires, statuary, and stained-glass windows—to completion often took more than a century. It was not uncommon for two or three generations of workers to spend their lives on one cathedral. The professor reminded us that it takes courage to make decisions, especially when there is little short-term gratification.

Several years ago, the chairman and CEO of Duke Energy, Jim Rogers, gave a speech at the Massachusetts Institute of Technology in which he likened the building of a national "green energy" policy to cathedral thinking. He posited that we are producing too much carbon dioxide as individuals, through our companies, and as a nation, and that the ultimate energy solutions may found long after we are gone. Rogers, with the unenviable job of pleasing shareholders, regulators, and politicians, knows that green energy and its long-term benefits will not just miraculously appear one day; action is required. As with the cathedral builders, nothing will happen unless plans are made and risks are taken.

Fortunately, many state and federal leaders from the past had both vision and the ability to act when they left us natural-resource foundations on which to build. North Carolina has an unmatched trove of diversity in temperate America—the Great Smoky Mountains National Park, three dozen state parks, national forests (including the old growth of Joyce Kilmer), the Appalachian Trail and other major trails, national wildlife refuges, the longest portion of the Blue Ridge Parkway, state forests, and two national seashores. These public lands and resources help define us in the eyes of the world. These places are also where much of our biodiversity is studied and protected. Author Wallace Stegner wrote that parks were America's "best idea"—a sentiment that North Carolinians have embraced and run with for almost 100 years.

In recent years, I have had several knee surgeries, and part of my physical therapy has been walking. Umstead State Park, with a variety of trails, is less than fifteen minutes from my house, making it my physical-therapy destination of choice. On weekdays, and especially on weekends, I have noted that many families, couples, and groups hiking in the park are speaking another language—German, French, Spanish, Japanese, Arabic, or Chinese. Park trails often sound like a European café, or as one park ranger put it: "Close your eyes and you are standing on the steps of the United Nations building with multiple languages all around you."

Like New Yorkers who have never visited the Statue of Liberty, there are native North Carolinians who take our system of parks, greenways, and open spaces for granted. In much of the world, where public land is in short supply, opportunities to walk for miles through forests and open spaces are a luxury. To have Umstead State Park practically in the middle of the Triangle, Hanging Rock State Park only minutes from Winston-Salem, drop–dead gorgeous Raven Rock State Park (near Lillington) just south of Raleigh, and Morrow Mountain and Crowder's Mountain State Parks so close to Char-

(opposite) When you walk among the ancient trees in Joyce Kilmer Forest (shown in these photos), Linville Gorge, or Shining Rock Wilderness, you know that the preservation of big trees is a small part of the story. Only in a few places can we find North Carolina and America the way they were just a couple of centuries ago. This is "baseline" wilderness, and we are only beginning to understand the totality of biodiversity and connections found there. (Photo of tall trees by Mike Dunn)

North Carolina has established three dozen state parks across the state, with many only a short drive from major urban areas. Hanging Rock State Park (above), near Winston-Salem, and Umstead State Park (opposite), in Research Triangle Park, provide the opportunity for a wilderness experience to all citizens and visitors.

lotte is a world-class luxury, a fact often missed when we view our public-land assets as commonplace rather than exceptional.

Regular visitors to North Carolina parks know that Wallace Stegner was right: parks—large public spaces—are American's best idea. Setting lands aside *before* demand occurs is "cathedral thinking" at its best. When Yellow-stone and Yosemite became National Parks, only a few people appreciated their grandeur. When the Great Smoky Mountain National Park was opened under Franklin Roosevelt seventy years ago, the Great Depression was rag-ing: automobiles were scarce, roads were bad, and few Americans had the

financial resources to travel significant distances. Today, Great Smoky is America's most visited park, with almost 10 million visitors annually.

When Governor Locke Craig and the North Carolina General Assembly designated Mount Mitchell as our first state park in 1915, it is doubtful that anyone envisioned a statewide system of parks from Jockey's Ridge to the Tennessee border, free to citizens and visitors. The fact that this marvelous gift to the people of North Carolina was started *long before* we became an urban destination for the world will someday be used by professors and executives as a case study of a successful long-term business plan—cathedral thinking. The question remains: will this generation, and its elected representatives, continue to appreciate and preserve these natural assets and secure additional public lands before population growth makes acquisition more difficult and costly, or will it squander this legacy, leaving a biodeficit?

Our wealth in public lands comes in various categories—state and national parks (where access and visitation of people is encouraged), wildlife refuges (where animal habitats come first), state/national forests (where there are mixed uses, including the sustainable harvesting of trees), game lands (where hunting is allowed in season), and wilderness areas (where access is limited and nature reigns supreme). Unfortunately, much of what was accessible to earlier generations is now gone, including the endless forests and uninhabited beaches of 100 years ago. Small farms with bass-and-bream-filled ponds, which ringed towns and cities two generations ago, have morphed into subdivisions. Even though all of North Carolina's oceanfront beaches are open to the public (below the mean high-water mark) thanks to the centuries-old Public Trust Doctrine, beach access is becoming a serious problem. Where miles of beachfront are developed with private homes and private parking areas, it is increasingly difficult for nonowners to access public beaches (known as the foreshore) without trespassing on private land. As we have grown and prospered, one of the very things that has fueled our prosperity—public lands and public beaches—may become imperiled if we are not vigilant.

Over the years, there have been attempts to make state parks and other public lands "commodities and attractions" for which access fees can be charged. During such attempts, the benefit analysis of parks and forests by public officials is too often *quantitative* in nature—how many will come and how much can we charge? The real focus on public lands should continue to be *qualitative*—how do they contribute to our quality of life, how are they integral to science education, and how will they continue to harbor

Public lands are integral to quality of life in North Carolina. Few places on earth offer
its citizens greater variety or more access to nature; this is a tradition worth preserving.
Cape Lookout National Seashore offers solitude and some of the most beautiful
beaches in America—and like other public natural treasures, it belongs to all of us.

URBAN PARKS AND GREENWAYS

From the standpoint of maintaining plant and animal diversity and avoiding a biodeficit, my emphasis has been on wild, public tracts of land. There is another class of public land still in its infancy in North Carolina: great urban parks, large open tracts in the middle of our growing cities. The most famous is Central Park in New York, that 1,100-acre masterpiece of planned wilderness and open spaces. It was carved out of rocky soil just before the Civil War by Frederick Law Olmsted, America's most celebrated landscape designer. With Central Park and Prospect Park in New York and numerous other urban park creations across America, Olmsted gave everyone, rich and poor alike, access to open fields and great forests. Try to think of any important city that does not have a great park, or even multiple parks. In addition to New York, Atlanta has downtown Piedmont Park at over 225 acres, Chicago has Grant Park at 320 acres, and Boston has its Emerald Necklace of parks (also designed by Olmsted). In every instance, these parks have added to the quality of city life and increased adjacent land values far in excess of the cost of the park.

Charlotte, Raleigh, Greensboro, Asheville, and other North Carolina cities have excellent park systems but currently have no large, central parks, although several cities are working on it. It is never easy to find and set aside large amounts of land in growth areas. The cities that do it—again, this is cathedral thinking—are always rewarded. Such parks may not be true wilderness, but they invariably become a defining feature of the city, home to a great diversity of fauna and flora, and a central site of outdoor activities for both city dwellers and visitors. North Carolina's cities may never be among the nation's largest, but creating large urban parks will ensure that they will forever be among the nation's best.

plant and animal diversity? To be sure, visitors to public lands should pay for special services (improved camping areas, canoe rentals, etc.), but as with public libraries, free access and use of public lands and beaches must continue to be a North Carolina priority.

■ Remember the unsophisticated state with the inferiority complex portrayed in our official song? North Carolina is all grown up now, and it is the toast of the nation. The children of this land are no longer "plain and artless." From modest beginnings, we developed great schools, great museums, transportation hubs, and research centers, and we became a vacation Mecca by offering unbroken mountain vistas and the most pristine coastal landscapes in America. Few places on Earth can offer such urban amenities and quality of life punctuated by public spaces, access to wild places, and protected diverse ecosystems. We know how to build forest buffers in our watersheds, to connect wild lands with greenways, and to maintain native species in our yards and public spaces. Access to forest cathedrals and wide beaches is a right of all who visit North Carolina or call it home. In the future, we cannot separate outdoor recreation, preservation of biodiversity, access to public lands, and economic prosperity: they are one.

Although they still reside in our state song, "The Old North State," we no longer have to worry about "the scorner" and "witlings." North Carolina and its towns and cities have been accorded many accolades, but praise can be fleeting. We must remember that the metrics for determining "best places" honors have never included praise for reduced funding for public universities, intolerance for those with different beliefs and preferences, inadequate water supplies, public beaches lost to seawalls, and reduced access and size of public parks. At the heart of the Tar Heel "business model" is protecting quality of life and the natural treasures with which we were blessed. Even if we continue to argue about how to solve the national debt, it is within our power to pass on this splendid sliver of land to the next generation without measurable biodeficit. By continuing to be a good steward of its wild places and things, North Carolina will remain at the crossroads of the natural world.

Epilogue

NEVER BUILD YOUR OUTHOUSE
OVER YOUR WELL

In the late summer of 1971, I got the long-awaited letter informing me that I had passed the North Carolina Bar Exam. My first job was as a staff attorney at the North Carolina Department of Justice. Although I was assigned to work with a senior attorney who gave advice to a number of state agencies, I was also asked by Attorney General Robert Morgan to spend "up to one-third of my time" in a new legal arena: environmental law.

When you are standing on the edge of great change, it is not always readily apparent. At that time, few law firms had environmental law sections, and the same was true with the North Carolina Department of Justice. A month after arriving at the attorney general's office, I had my first one-on-one meeting with Morgan. I was surprised when North Carolina's top lawyer confided that he knew very little about the new laws of the environment, and that what he knew had not been learned in law school but in rural Harnett County. With a twinkle in his eye, Morgan said: "There is one rule that every good farmer lives by, and I guess you could call it old-time environmental law. Never build your outhouse over your well."

We both laughed, but I suddenly realized that Robert Morgan knew that he had captured the essence of the complex new laws coming from federal and state government. Morgan was from the country, but he was no country lawyer. He was fully aware that the National Environmental Policy Act had become law in 1969, and that state/federal projects (highways, airports, power plants, etc.) could trigger an Environmental Impact Statement. He also knew about the amendments to the Clean Air Act of 1969 and the controversial Endangered Species Act of 1969. In 1972, within a few months of my arrival at the North Carolina Department of Justice, other pieces of landmark federal legislation became law, including the Clean Water Act, the Coastal Zone Management Act, and the Ocean Dumping Act. Metaphorically, and correctly, Robert Morgan viewed the new legislation protecting air and water as national prohibitions against the continuing degradation of the air, water, and soil on which we depend.

What events caused this spate of environmental legislation in such a short period of time? It is no secret that the United States had not taken care of its most critical resources. By the late 1960s, Lake Erie, unable to support fish or even leaches, was declared a "dead lake" by scientists. So bad was the water quality of the Cuyahoga River running into Erie through Cleveland, Ohio, that it caught fire (just one of several fires on this industrial river) in the summer of 1969. On August 1, 1969, *Time* magazine reported: "Some River! Chocolate-brown, oily, bubbling with subsurface gases, it oozes rather than flows."

The Cuyahoga became the poster child for badly degraded waterways, but every state had water problems. At about the same time that Cleveland's Cuyahoga was declared dead prior to the 1970s, researchers also found sections of North Carolina rivers, including the Haw River near Chapel Hill, to be in serious trouble. Although I was not aware at the time of the dangers of polluted water, I personally observed some rivers at their worst. As I have described, I loved to fish with my father in the 1950s and 1960s, but too often we encountered stretches of Tar Heel rivers from the mountains through the Coastal Plain—the French Broad, Pigeon, Yadkin, Dan, Haw, Cape Fear, Neuse, and Roanoke—that were little more than cesspools. I vividly remember waters in my teen years that were frothy, smelly, colored with textile dyes, or alive with floating debris—but it was not just rivers that that were being fouled. There were frequent reports from coastal states about beaches closed to swimming because of raw sewage and medical wastes dumped untreated into near shore waters. While I was in law school in 1969, a new threat to coastal waters also gained national attention: offshore rigs off Santa Barbara, California, leaked thousands of barrels of crude oil on California beaches and its economy. Oil-industry officials at the time assured Americans that such leaks would never happen again because of "foolproof" shut-off safety devices.

Across the nation, the flesh of fish, birds, and even mammals was often found to contain dangerous levels of heavy metals, especially mercury, and a variety of industrial chemicals. One of the first issues Attorney General Morgan asked me to research in 1971 related to the danger of mercury concentrations found in fish and raccoons in the Cape Fear basin. Coastal finfish and shellfish populations on both coasts suffered not only from the unregulated dumping of toxins, but also from the ditching, filling, and draining of critical wetlands, which were still regarded by many as "worthless." Even large, powerful birds of prey, such as the Bald Eagle and Osprey, were in rapid decline in many areas because of the effects of DDT. So serious was the problem that in the late 1960s, even the sighting of an Osprey, much less a Bald Eagle, was a rare event in North Carolina.

Air quality had become poor in such disparate places as Los Angeles in the West and the Blue Ridge Mountains in the East. In the 1950s and 1960s, pilots frequently reported that Los Angeles and other major cities were completely enveloped in a thick yellow haze called smog. Even in North Carolina, Hugh Morton of Grandfather Mountain documented a noticeable decline in visibility in North Carolina mountains over a few decades. Morton and others also found that the rain, snow, and fog enveloping the Appalachians along much of the East Coast had become so acidic—from chemical reactions of sulfur dioxide and nitrous dioxide introduced into the atmosphere from coal-burning power plants—that even remote forests and watersheds were in dire trouble from "acid rain." The primary culprits—lead in gasoline and particulates from coal-fired industries—not only reduced visibility but also caused serious health issues for thousands of Americans.

Across North America and the industrialized world, problem chemicals and industrial wastes that we had tried to dispose of through burial began to show up as "cancer clusters" and other health problems. Americans of my generation know the horror stories of New York's Love Canal, Times Beach in Missouri, and other examples of toxic waste dumping, both intentional and unintentional. Even our own state made national toxic-waste headlines in 1978. North Carolina became the focus of one of the most celebrated cases when over 30,000 gallons of polychlorinated biphenyl (PCB) waste oil, a suspected carcinogen, was intentionally dumped over many nights by an unmarked tanker truck along 240 miles of rural roadways. The cleanup and high cost of removing thousands of truckloads of contaminated roadside soil made news, but an even bigger story arose as state and federal officials struggled to find an acceptable landfill site to dispose of the toxic mess. The NIMBY problem—"Not in My Backyard"—occurred across the country as officials wrestled with nuclear, chemical, and solid-waste issues. Love Canal, Times Beach, and North Carolina's PCB problems made it clear that most Americans wanted some action by government to solve these problems.

An Unlikely Hero

Although it is clear that the United States had arrived at an environmental crossroads in the 1960s and 1970s, change in the form of government regulation for many industries was still widely opposed. The petroleum industry disputed the dangers of lead in gasoline, the cigarette industry stonewalled against smoking regulations, and the chemical industry went after the messenger when Rachel Carson, in her book *Silent Spring* (1962), sounded the alarm against the indiscriminate use of DDT and other pesticides. Between 1969 and 1973, an unlikely hero for the environment appeared. In a 1970 speech, this individual clearly framed the environmental dilemma facing the nation: "The great question of the seventies is, shall we surrender to our surroundings, or shall we make peace with nature and begin to make reparations for the damage we have done to our air, our land and our water? . . . Clean air, clean water, open spaces—these should once again be the birthright of every American. If we act now—they can be."

You may be surprised to learn that the person who spoke these words was President Richard M. Nixon, and the forum was his State of the Union Address to Congress on January 22, 1970. For most Americans, Nixon will never be lionized as a champion of wild things and places but will, fair or not, likely be remembered for his diplomatic breakthrough with mainland China, the last years of the Vietnam War, and the Watergate debacle that destroyed his presidency. What is often forgotten is that Nixon's first term was also shaken and shaped by some of the environmental low points mentioned above—the fire on Cleveland's Cuyahoga River, the Santa Barbara oil spill, and the effects of DDT and other chemicals on wildlife.

Many, if not most, of today's most effective land-use policies, endangered-species protection, clean-water initiatives, and even the "scrubbing" of dirty air came from legislation signed by Richard Nixon between 1969 and 1973. Today, when I cross a clean Haw River near Burlington, fish or kayak in the once-filthy Pigeon and French Broad Rivers, and watch my own son and daughter catch shad and striped bass in the Roanoke River, I thank Richard Nixon. When I see Longleaf Pine forests once again supporting growing populations of Red-Cockaded Woodpeckers (still an endangered species), and see Osprey and Bald Eagles thriving in North Carolina, Nixon deserves some of the credit. I also know that many of the tax incentives and credits that have been so skillfully used by the Nature Conservancy and other well-run regional "land trusts" across North Carolina had their origins in the Nixon years.

To this day, I still have no idea whether Nixon was an "environmentalist" or a "conservationist," and I do not know what motivated his actions. What I do know is that a Republican president and a *bipartisan* Congress rose to the occasion when our air, water, and land were at a crossroads. The remarkable body of legislation from the Nixon era—National Environmental Policy Act, the Clean Air Act, the Clean Water Act, and the Endangered Species Act—had champions and detractors from both sides of the aisle in Congress. To the credit of both Republicans and Democrats, they acknowledged threats to natural resources, looked to scientists for guidance, and worked together for solutions. So nonpartisan was the legislation establishing the National Environmental Policy Act that it passed on September 23, 1969, by a vote of 372 to 15 in the U.S. House of Representatives.

In North Carolina, members of both political parties also worked together on some of the most contentious environmental problems of the time. One of the most bruising environmental battles ever fought in North Carolina was a struggle during the 1970s to stop a dam from being built on the New River that would have flooded much of the New River valley in northwestern North Carolina. It had all the usual players—a big power company, federal agencies, land speculators, and a busload of lobbyists. In the end, an unusual alliance of North Carolina Republicans (Congressman Wilmer "Vinegar Bend" Mizell, Senator Jesse Helms, and Governor James E. Holshouser Jr.) and Democrats (Representative Roy Taylor and Senator Sam Ervin) worked together to oppose the dam and preserve the river.

Crossroads and Tipping Points

In the fifteen chapters of this book, I have tried to convey the magnitude of natural resources with which North Carolina has been blessed. We have not always been the best stewards, but when forestry and farming practices left eroded fields and hillsides in the 1930s, we responded. When we understood the threats to our water, air, land, fish/wildlife, and vistas, we responded again in the 1970s. Nature is resilient and will recover when given half a chance. Today, we are at another crossroads: population growth, jobs, and prosperity have come to North Carolina. The fact that high-tech industries from around the world can coexist with multibillion-dollar agricultural and tourist industries is no fluke. Tar Heel land is still wonderfully productive, and our rivers and coastal waters are now among the cleanest in the nation. Unfortunately, however, in the name of jobs, cheap energy, and lower taxes, much of the environmental protection legislation that helped restore our natural and economic landscape is now under attack in both Raleigh and Washington, D.C.

We know that meaningful, woody buffers protect rivers and watersheds, yet uniform statewide buffer requirements are consistently opposed as unwarranted restrictions on property owners. Many of the long-standing restrictions on "hardening" beaches on the North Carolina coast are being challenged and rescinded to protect the "status quo" on highly developed beachfronts where, prior to the 1960s, the status quo had been change. Departments charged with monitoring and protecting water and air quality have seen budgets and personnel slashed in recent years in both Raleigh and Washington.

Much governmental action at all levels flies in the face of science and common sense. The vast majority of scientists dealing with climate change from government and academia (including the National Academy of Sciences and the American Geophysical Union), along with North Carolina's own Intergovernmental Panel on Climate Change, have warned of the probability of rapidly rising sea levels in the next century. North Carolina's science experts urged that the state begin planning for a rise in sea level of approximately one meter (about thirty-nine inches) by the year 2100. In spite of these admonitions, some elected state officials and business leaders (especially from our twenty coastal counties, through an organization known as "NC-20") ignored science-based planning guidelines. Perhaps succumbing to fears that acknowledging an increased rise in sea level might deter future coastal development and cause insurance rates to rise, the North Carolina Senate, in June 2012, passed a bill that would restrict state and regional planners to the use of sea-level data *from the past*. Since ocean levels on the North Carolina coast rose about eight inches in the twentieth century, the bill would have handicapped planners by requiring them to use last century's data and ignore the research and warnings of our state's best coastal planners. Even though the bill passed by the North Carolina Senate never became law, the coastal-planning legislation that eventually passed our General Assembly in the same session was only marginally better. This sad episode is another example of good men and women grasping to maintain the status quo no matter how convincing the science.

Anticipating a greater rise in sea level in the next century may be uncomfortable and even costly for taxpayers and businesses. Designs for sewage-treatment plants and storm-water runoff must reflect the likelihood of a rising sea. Planning to elevate important coastal roads and airports should not be postponed. Contingency measures should also require us to look at the viability of coastal fishery locations and salt marshes in the event of a one-meter rise. Ignoring identifiable problems will not make them go away.

In addition to smart coastal planning, as a state we must anticipate other challenges. With growing populations, every city and citizen in North Carolina should plan for reduced water usage and energy conservation and a reduction of the waste stream going to our landfills. Sustainability and conservation of resources is not a United Nations plot nor part of any secret agenda restricting personal freedoms. Rather, sustainability and conservation of resources have long been practiced by every smart farmer, business owner, and home owner. History has shown us that failure to plan for that which is foreseeable invariably leads to a more costly and undesirable outcome.

If your doctor told you that your abdominal discomfort might be caused by a pulled muscle, but that the early tests pointed to a dangerous aneurism (a bulge or weakening in a blood vessel), you would want a thorough examination to deal with the possibility of the greater danger. Knowing that modern medicine—science—has additional tools and tests to detect the greater danger, you would not accept inaction on the part of your physician based on the mere possibility of a lesser problem. Why should we accept anything less from planners and elected officials dealing with our state's economic and natural vitality?

I am concerned that the most formidable environmental perils facing North Carolina and our nation today will not be sea-level rise, invasive species, "fracking," or shrinking habitats, but a severe lack of fair-minded examination and deliberation on the part of elected officials. The work of many of our best minds, the scientists and engineers on whom we all depend, is too often being ignored and replaced by lobbyist-supplied "talking points" in both Raleigh and Washington. I can forgive an industry for fighting for reduced and less-onerous regulation; as a CEO, I would do the same thing. What I cannot forgive is a failure of civility, common sense, and independent thinking on the part of those who are elected to serve. When faced with the dilemmas that will affect the North Carolina that our children and grandchildren inherit, the very least I expect is an honest consideration of the facts.

When confronted with burning rivers, oil on American beaches, smog-choked cities, and wildlife in precipitous decline, Richard Nixon and a bipartisan Congress deliberated and acted in the nation's best interest. When confronted with the potential loss of a scenic and natural treasure in the New River valley, North Carolinians with now-famous names—Holshouser, Mizell, Helms, Ervin, Taylor—shed their political affiliations and ideology and acted together for North Carolina's future. It is my guess that none of these individuals would have willingly adopted the moniker of "naturalist," and certainly not that of "environmentalist," yet we are all in their debt.

None of us likes regulation and burdensome restrictions on our personal conduct. We sometimes forget, however, that even before detailed environmental regulations, unwritten rules, dictated by common sense, were in place. Whenever I hear arguments against protecting and maintaining any critical natural resources of North Carolina—those that have sustained past generations and attracted new families and businesses—I do not think of the body of legislation from the Nixon era but of the rural wisdom I have come to regard as "Morgan's Law." It applies equally to government at every level and to the conduct of every landowner and family: Never build your outhouse over your well.

Our uncluttered beaches, mountain vistas, inland rivers, unpolluted air, rich and varied soil types, and unparalleled natural diversity are all "wells" from which we draw our prosperity and inspiration. Those of us who drink from the well must also care for it.

Acknowledgments

How does one thank a lifetime's worth of teachers and mentors who, together, kindled and nurtured my love for North Carolina's natural landscape? For me, it starts with family—a mother, father, and brothers, Gene and Jim, whose support and tolerance for my constantly changing collections (arrowheads, rocks, insects, etc.) and interests never wavered. Today, my wife, Dana, still gives me unconditional love and the freedom to explore and write. She is always my first reader and editor. Our children, Izaak and Rachel, reinforce for both of us the reasons why wild places and things are critical to growth and learning, and why our remaining resources are worth fighting for. I cannot fail to mention another member of my "family," Donald Willis. Donald and his wife, Hilda, were my Harkers Island family for more than thirty years. He must have thought I was beyond hope as he tried to teach me the night skies, the nuances of wind and tide, the history of Diamond City, and the safest way to hold a crab or shuck an oyster.

At Davidson College, President D. Grier Martin gave me the leeway to argue for change and, in the process, showed me the importance of civility. At the University of North Carolina School of Law, Dean J. Dickson Phillips (later a judge on the U.S. Fourth Circuit Court of Appeals) gave me an unsolicited copy of Aldo Leopold's *Sand County Almanac* during my second year, the year when most law students wonder if the pain of law school is worth the effort. When he presented me with the well-worn paperback, the dean commented that Leopold's land ethic held the seeds for new laws and the importance for stewardship in a developing world. Phillips is still a treasured friend, and Leopold's thinking is still a source of inspiration. Also at the school of law, I must acknowledge the influence of Professor Thomas Schoenbaum, an environmental scholar who chose me as his research assistant and challenged me "to be concise and get it right." (It is the "concise" part with which I still struggle.) I am also forever in the debt of my first employer after law school, North Carolina attorney general (and later U.S. senator) Robert Morgan, who provided me with the most succinct rationale behind most environmental regulations: "Never build your outhouse over your well." (You may read more about Robert Morgan in the epilogue.)

Over several decades, organizations at the state and national level provided me the opportunity to learn about coastal issues, land management, endangered species, and water quality. Most influential in shaping my conservation views are the Nature Conservancy, Trout Unlimited, Audubon North Carolina, the North Carolina Botanical Garden, and the North Carolina Museum of Natural Sciences. I had the privilege of serving on the boards of these organizations and had access to their talented scientists and staffs.

In my life, the most influential of all of these organizations has been the North Carolina Museum of Natural Sciences, on whose board I served almost continuously from 1996 to 2012. The museum, directed by friend and North Carolina natural science champion Betsy Bennett (perhaps the most creative and tenacious environmental educator this state has ever known), gave me access to collections, experts, and critical thinking related to this state's diverse natural resources. Many on the museum staff have become friends and mentors, and without them, this book would never have come to fruition. Fearful I will leave out important contributors at the museum, I must single out Chris Tacker, Vince Schneider, Dale Russell, and Trish Weaver for fielding my thousand questions on geology and paleontology. Alvin Braswell, Jesse Perry, Mike Dunn, Mary Ann Brittain, Bill Reynolds, and Liz Baird took me to the field and unselfishly shared their time and knowledge of North Carolina plants, animals, and ecosystems. During my time with the museum, no individual's support was more steadfast than that of Bill Ross, an environmental lawyer, friend of more than forty years, and former secretary of the North Carolina Department of Environmental and Natural Resources (home of the museum).

I owe a debt of gratitude to North Carolina archaeologists Billy Oliver (North Carolina Department of Cultural Resources), Steve Davis (UNC–Chapel Hill), Brett Riggs (UNC–Chapel Hill), Randy Daniels (East Carolina University), and David Moore (Warren Wilson College) for sharing field sites, artifacts, and their knowledge of North Carolina's first people. It was during my time with them that I came to the conclusion that the fine line between history (knowledge preserved by the written word) and prehistory is often arbitrary and misleading.

For extraordinary courage under fire, I have to single out the work of geologists and coastal scientists Stan Riggs and Steve Culver of East Carolina University, Orrin Pilkey of Duke University, and Rob Young of Western Carolina University. They have provided solid science and timely advice on climate change and sea-level rise, not only for policy makers but for all North Carolinians. I am especially indebted to Stan Riggs and Steve Culver, who have worked with me to understand the ephemeral, dynamic nature of North Carolina's barrier islands.

Although much of the photography in this book is mine, I was aware that key images were available from others. You will find extraordinary work by Mike Dunn of the North Carolina Museum of Natural Sciences, one of the most talented naturalists and photographers in North Carolina today; and photographs by Walker Golder, ornithologist, photographer, and deputy director of Audubon North Carolina. I am also deeply indebted to the talented and patient staffs at the North Carolina Collection at UNC–Chapel Hill, the North Carolina State Archives in Raleigh, and the Brimley Library at the North Carolina Museum of Natural Sciences.

Time in the field is essential to the life of all naturalists and students of the outdoors. Over the past eight years, I have been privileged to be in the company of Joe Albea, a great photographer and outdoorsman, and Mark Crews, an editing genius, as we traversed North Carolina multiple times and prepared material for the UNC-TV series *Exploring North Carolina*. On our journey, we have been treated to snow storms, gentle rain, seemingly endless flights of waterfowl, a thousand shades of green, and friends at every stop. These trips and the opportunities they afforded would have been much more difficult without the support of Don Thimsen, friend and president of DTS Software, and the advice and encouragement of the late president emeritus William Friday of the University of North Carolina, an inspiration to generations of North Carolinians.

No book reaches the shelf without the women and men who tie down deadlines, insist on rewrites, edit manuscripts, design covers, plan marketing campaigns, and provide psychological support over coffee for authors for months on end. The staff at the University of North Carolina Press has provided all of these services for me, and much more. Editor in Chief David Perry convinced me that *Crossroads of the Natural World* was his most important project, while simultaneously saying exactly the same about the books of a dozen other authors. Even knowing that he is a literary philanderer, I forgive him and will be forever grateful for his help throughout the project. The tone and text that survived into the final manuscript reflects changes, both subtle and substantive, gently suggested by my multitalented editor, Jay Mazzocchi. Along with David and Jay, the product you see before you required the time and talents of the many professionals at UNC Press, including Kim Bryant (cover and design), Beth Lassiter (catalog and cover copy), Susan Raines Garrett (marketing), Gina Mahalek (publicity), and Caitlin Bell-Butterfield (assistant to David Perry). Finally, UNC Press distributed portions of my early manuscript to several readers, including James Parnell (professor emeritus at UNC–Wilmington), Kevin Stewart (UNC–Chapel Hill), and Charles Rowe (former director of the North Carolina Natural Heritage Program). Their insights, criticisms, and suggested revisions were incorporated and will forever be appreciated by me. Any mistakes or oversights, however, are entirely my own.

Thanks to all whose patience, support, and good counsel are reflected in these essays.

Common and Scientific Names of North Carolina Plants and Animals

Most of us grew up learning the common names of birds, trees, flowers, and fish. Unlike scientific (binomial) names, the common names given to plants and creatures frequently differ from region to region and even from county to county. Throughout this book, I have used the common/regional/local names that I heard most often in my experiences, but I am aware that the reader may know the same living organism by another name. The following list includes the common names of species that appear in the text, accompanied by their scientific names. In the case of organisms with more than one well-known common name, I have added an "also known as" name in parentheses or listed the organism under its alternate common name and repeated the applicable binomial. The term "introduced" signifies organisms that were established in this region after European settlement.

A

American Alligator (*Alligator mississippiensis*)
American Beech (*Fagus grandifolia*)
American Buffalo (*Bison bison*)
American Chestnut (*Castanea dentata*)
American Holly (*Ilex opaca*)
American Lion (*Panthera atrox*)
American Shad (*Alosa sapidissima*)
American Sycamore (*Platanus occidentalis*)
American Wisteria (*Wisteria frutescens*)

Ancient Bison (*Bison antiquus*)
Appalachian Brook Trout (*Salvelinus fontinalis*)
Armadillo (*Dasypus novemcinctus*)
Atlantic Sturgeon (*Acipenser oxyrinchus*)
Autumn Olive (introduced) (*Elaeagnus umbellate*)

B

Bald Cypress (*Taxodium distichum*)
Balsam Woolly Adelgid (introduced) (*Adelges piceae*)

Banded Tulip (*Fasciolaria lilium*)

Banded Woolly Bear (*Pyrrharctia isabella*)

Barn Swallow (*Hirundo rustica*)

Basswood (*Tilia americana*)

Bay Scallop (*Aequipectin irradians*)

Beach Vitex (*Vitex rotundifolia*)

Bee Balm (*Monarda didyma*)

Bigleaf Magnolia (*Magnolia macrophylla*)

Black Bear (*Ursus americanus*)

Black Cherry (*Prunus serotina*)

Black Duck (*Anas rubripes*)

Black-Eyed Susan (*Rudbeckia hirta*)

Black Racer (*Coluber constrictor*)

Black Walnut (*Juglans nigra*)

Black Willow (*Salix nigra*)

Blazingstar (several species of this plant in the genus *Liatris*)

Blood Root (*Sanguinaria canadensis*)

Blue-Back Herring (*Alosa aestivalis*)

Blue Catfish (introduced from Mississippi drainage) (*Ictalurus furcatus*)

Blue Crab (*Callinectes sapidus*)

Bluefin Tuna (*Thunnus thynnus*)

Bluefish (*Pomatomus saltatrix*)

Bluegill (*Lepomis macrochirus*)

Blue Heron (*Ardea herodias*)

Blue Jay (*Cyanocitta cristata*)

Blue Ridge Goldenrod (*Solidago spithamaea*)

Bobwhite Quail (*Colinus virginianus*)

Bog Turtle (*Glyptemys muhlenbergii*)

Bowfin (a.k.a. Grindel and Mudfish) (*Amia calva*)

Bradford Pear (a Callery Pear cultivar; introduced) (*Pyrus calleryana*)

Broad-Winged Hawk (*Buteo platypterus*)

Brown-Headed Cowbird (*Molothrus ater*)

Brown Pelican (*Pelecanus occidentalis*)

Brown Rat (a.k.a. Norwegian Rat; introduced) (*Rattus norvegicus*)

Brown Trout (introduced) (*Salmo trutta*)

Bufflehead (*Bucephala albeola*)

Bullfrog (*Rana catesbeiana*)

Bull Thistle (introduced) (*Cirsium vulgare*)

Buttercup (introduced) (*Ranunculus bulbosus*)

Butterfly Weed (*Asclepias tuberose*)

Buttonbush (*Cephalanthus occidentalis*)

C

Cabbage Palm (*Sabal Palmetto*)

California Condor (*Gymnogyps californianus*)

Canada Violet (*Viola Canadensis*)

Canvasback Duck (*Aythya valisineria*)

Cape Fear Shiner (*Notropis mekistocholas*)

Cardinal Flower (*Lobelia cardinalis*)

Carolina Anole (*Anolis carolinensis*)

Carolina Heelsplitter (*Lasmigona decorate*)

Carolina Hemlock (*Tsuga caroliniana*)

Carolina Lily (*Lilium michauxii*)

Carolina Parakeet (*Conuropsis carolinensis*)

Carolina Silverbell (*Halesia Carolina*)

Carolina Wren (*Thryothorus ludovicianus*)

Catawba Rhododendron (*Rhododendron catawbiense*)

Cat Briar (a.k.a. Smilax and Greenbriar) (several N.C. species in the genus *Smilax*)

Catesby's Lily (*Lilium catesbaei*)

Cecropia Moth (*Hyalophora cecropia*)

Cedar Waxwings (*Bombycilla cedrorum*)

Cerulean Warbler (*Dendroica cerulean*)

Channel Bass (*Sciaenops ocellatus*)

Channeled Whelk (*Busycotypus canaliculatus*)

Chestnut Oak (*Quercus prinus*)

Chestnut Warbler (*Setophaga pensylvanica*)

Chimney Swift (*Chaetura pelagica*)

China Berry (*Melia azedarach*)

Chinese Privet (introduced) (*Ligustrum sinense*)

Chinese Silver Grass (introduced) (*Miscanthus sinensis*)

Christmas Fern (*Polystichum acrostichoides*)

Clear-Winged Hummingbird Moth (*Hemaris thysbe*)

Cobia (a.k.a. Crab Eater) (*Rachycentron canadum*)

Columbian Mammoth (*Mammuthus columbi*)

Columbine (*Aquilegia Canadensis*)

Common Buckeye Butterfly (*Junonia coenia*)

Common Carp (introduced) (*Cyprinus carpio*)

Common Cat-Tail (a.k.a. Bulrush) (*Typha latifolia*)

Common Cord Grass (*Spartina alterniflora*)

Common Milkweed (*Asclepias syriaca*)

Common Raven (*Corvus corax*)
Cooper's Hawk (*Accipiter cooperii*)
Coral Honeysuckle (*Lonicera sempervirens*)
Crape Myrtle (species in the genus *Lagerstroemia*)
Crested Iris (*Iris cristata*)

D

Dandelion (introduced) (*Taraxacum officinale*)
Death Camus (*Zigadenus leimanthoides*)
Deodar Cedar (*Cedrus deodara*)
Diamondback Rattlesnake (*Crotalus adamanteus*)
Diamondback Terrapin (*Malaclemys terrapin*)
Dire Wolf (*Canis dirus*)
Dobsonfly (*Corydalus cornutus*)
Dogwood (*Cornus florida*)
Double-Sunrise (*Tellina radiate*)
Dutchman's Breeches (*Dicentra cucullaria*)

E

Eastern Bluebird (*Sialia sialis*)
Eastern Box Turtle (*Terrapene carolina*)
Eastern Goldfinch (*Carduelis tristis*)
Eastern Gray Squirrel (*Sciurus carolinensis*)
Eastern Hemlock (*Tsuga canadensis*)
Eastern Prickly Pear Cactus (*Opuntia humifusa*)
Eastern Spartina (*Spartina alterniflora*)
Eel Grass (*Zostera marina*)
Elaeagnus (introduced) (invasive plants from the genus *Elaeagnus*)

English Boxwood (introduced) (*Buxus sempevirens 'Suffruticosa'*)
English Ivy (introduced) (*Hedera helix*)
English Oak (*Quercus robur*)
English Sparrow (introduced) (*Passer domesticus*)
European Beech (introduced) (*Fagus sylvatica*)
European Rock Dove (introduced) (*Columba livia*)
European Starling (introduced) (*Sturnus vulgaris*)

F

False Albacore (*Euthynnus alletteratus*)
Fiddler Crab (*Uca pugilator*)
Fire Ant (introduced) (*Solenopsis invicta*)
Fire Pink (*Silene virginica*)
Flame Azalea (*Rhododendron calendulaceum*)
Flathead Catfish (introduced) (*Pylodictis olivaris*)
Forster's Tern (*Sterna forsteri*)
Fox Squirrel (*Sciurus niger*)
Fraser Fir (*Abies fraseri*)
Fringe Tree (*Chionanthus virginicus*)

G

Galax (*Galax urceolata*)
Giant Ground Sloth (*Megalonyx jeffersonii*)
Giant Needle Fish (a.k.a. Houndfish) (*Tylosurus crocodilus*)
Giant Stag Beetle (*Lucanus elaphus*)
Ginkgo (introduced) (*Ginkgo biloba*)

Ginseng (*Panax quinquefolius*)
Glyptodont (*Glyptodon reticulates*)
Golden Silk Orbweaver (*Nephila clavipes*)
Golden-Winged Warbler (*Vermivora chrysoptera*)
Gray's Lily (*Lilium grayi*)
Green Drakes (*Litobrancha recurvata*)
Green Turtle (*Chelonia mydas*)

H

Heller's Blazing Star (*Liatris helleri*)
Hemlock Woolly Adelgid (introduced) (*Adelges tsugae*)
Hickory Horned Devil (caterpillar for Royal Walnut Moth) (*Citherconia regalis*)
Hickory Shad (*Alosa mediocris*)
Hognose Snake (*Heterodon platirhinos*)
Hooded Merganser Duck (*Lophodytes cucullatus*)
Hooded Warbler (*Setophaga citrina*)
House Finch (*Carpodacus mexicanus*)

I

Ironweed (*Vernonia altissima*)
Isabella Tiger Moth (*Pyrrharctia isabella*)
Ivory-Billed Woodpecker (*Campephilus principalis*)

J

Jack-in-the-Pulpit (*Arisaema triphyllum*)
Japanese Beetle (introduced) (*Popillia japonica*)
Japanese Cherry Trees (introduced) (the "Yoshino" cultivar of the genus *Prunus*)

Japanese Honeysuckle (introduced) (*Lonicera japonica*)

Japanese Privet (introduced) (*Ligustrum japonicum*)

Japanese Zelkova (introduced) (cultivars of *Zelkova serrata*)

Joe-Pye Weed (*Eutrochium purpureum*)

K

Knobbed Whelk (*Busycon carica*)

L

Largemouth Bass (*Micropterus salmoides*)

Leatherback Turtle (*Dermochelys coriacea*)

Leopard Frog (*Rana pipiens*)

Lightning Bug (a.k.a. Firefly) (bioluminescent beetles in *Lampyridae* family)

Lightning Whelk (*Busycon contrarium*)

Ligustrum (introduced) (invasive plants known as "Privet" from genus *Ligustrum*)

Little Tunny (*Euthynnus alletteratus*)

Live Oak (*Quercus virginiana*)

Lizardfish (*Synodus foetens*)

Loblolly Pine (*Pinus taeda*)

Loggerhead Turtle (*Caretta caretta*)

Long-Eared Sunfish (*Lepomis auritus*)

Longleaf Pine (*Pinus palustris*)

Lubber Grasshopper (*Romalea guttata*)

Luna Moth (*Actias luna*)

M

Marbled Salamander (*Ambystoma opacum*)

Mastodon (*Mammut americanum*)

Mayapple (*Podophyllum peltatum*)

Megalodon (*Carcharodon megalodon*)

Menhaden (*Brevoortia tyrannus*)

Michaux's Lily (*Lilium michauxii*)

Mimosa (*Albizia julibrissin*)

Monarch Butterfly (*Danaus plexippus*)

Moon Snail (a.k.a. Shark-Eye) (*Polinices duplicatus*)

Mountain Ashe (*Sorbus Americana*)

Mountain Laurel (*Kalmia latifolia*)

Mountain Lion (*Puma concolor couguar*)

Mountain Magnolia (a.k.a. Fraser Magnolia) (*Magnolia fraseri*)

Multi-Flora Rose (*Rosa multiflora*)

Muscadine Grapes (*Vitis rotundifolia*)

Muskellunge (*Esox masquinongy*)

Muskrat (*Ondatra zibethicus*)

Mute Swan (*Cygnus olor*)

N

Neanderthal (*Homo neanderthalensis*)

Neuse River Waterdog (*Necturus lewisi*)

Northern Flying Squirrel (*Glaucomys sabrinus*)

Northern Red Oak (*Quercus rubra*)

Northern Red Squirrel (*Tamiasciurus hudsonicus*)

O

Oconee Bell (*Shortia galacifolia*)

Opossum (*Didelphis virginiana*)

Orange Sulphur Butterfly (*Colias eurytheme*)

Oriental Asian Bittersweet (*Celastrus orbiculatus*)

Oriental Wisteria (*Wisteria sinensis*)

Osprey (*Pandion haliaetus*)

Ox-Eye Daisy (a.k.a. Common Daisy; introduced) (*Leucanthemum vulgare*)

P

Painted Bunting (*Passerina ciris*)

Painted Trillium (*Trillium undulatum*)

Palamedes Swallowtail (*Papilio palamedes*)

Passenger Pigeon (*Ectopistes migratorius*)

Passion Flower (a.k.a. Maypop) (*Passiflora incarnata*)

Pawpaw (*Asimina triloba*)

Pecan (*Carya illinoinensis*)

Phragmites (a.k.a. Common Reed) (*Phragmites australis*)

Phytosaurs (extinct archosaurs) (family Phytosauridae)

Pigmy Rattlesnake (*Sistrurus miliarius*)

Pileated Woodpeckers (*Dryocopus pileatus*)

Pine Lily (*Lilium catesbaei*)

Pinfish (*Lagodon rhomboids*)

Pink Lady Slipper (*Cypripedium acaule*)

Polyphemus Moth (*Antherea polyphemus*)

Pond Cypress (*Taxodium ascendens*)

Porcelain Berry (introduced) (*Ampelopsis brevipedunculata*)

Princess Tree (introduced) (*Paulownia tomentosa*)

Prothonotary Warbler (a.k.a. Swamp Canary) (*Protonotaria citrea*)

Pumpkinseed (*Lepomis gibbosus*)

Purple Coneflower (*Echinacea purpurea*)

Purple-Fringed Orchid (*Platanthera grandiflora* and *Platanthera psycodes*)

Purple Martin (*Progne subis*)

Purple Violet (*Viola sororia*)

Q

Queen Anne's Lace (introduced) (*Daucus carota*)

Question Mark Butterfly (*Polygonia interrogationis*)

R

Rainbow Trout (introduced) (*Oncorhynchus mykiss*)

Ramp (a.k.a. Mountain Onion) (*Allium tricoccum*)

Rauisuchians (Triassic archosaurs) (informal group Rauisuchia)

Red Bay (*Persea borbonia*)

Redbay Ambrosia Beetle (introduced) (*Xyleborus glabratus*)

Redbreast (Longear Sunfish) (*Lepomis auritus*)

Red Bud (*Cercis Canadensis*)

Red Cedar (*Juniperus virginiana*)

Red-Cockaded Woodpecker (*Picoides borealis*)

Red Drum (*Sciaenops ocellatus*)

Red-Eyed Vireo (*Vireo olivaceus*)

Redfish (*Sciaenops ocellatus*)

Redhead Duck (*Aythya americana*)

Red Maple (*Acer rubrum*)

Red Oak (*Quercus rubra*)

Red Raspberries (*Rubus strigosus*)

Red-Shouldered Hawk (*Buteo lineatus*)

Red Spruce (*Picea rubens*)

Red Squirrel (*Tamiasciurus hudsonicus*)

Red-Tailed Hawk (*Buteo jamaicensis*)

Red-Winged Blackbird (*Agelaius phoeniceus*)

Red Wolf (*Canis rufus*)

Ring-Necked Pheasant (introduced) (*Phasianus colchicus*)

Ruby-Throated Hummingbird (*Archilochus colubris*)

Ruffed Grouse (*Bonasa umbellus*)

Rufous Hummingbird (*Selasphorus rufus*)

Russian Olive (introduced) (*Elaeagnus angustifolia*)

S

Sailfish (*Istiophorus albicans*)

Sassafras (*Sassafras albidum*)

Sawtooth Oak (introduced) (*Quercus acutissima*)

Saw-Whet Owl (*Aegolius acadicus*)

Sea Oats (*Uniola paniculata*)

Sea Robin (*Prionotus carolinus*)

Shagbark Hickory (*Carya ovata*)

Sheep's Head (*Archosargus probatocephalus*)

Short-Faced Bear (*Arctodus simus*)

Shortia (*Shortia galacifolia*)

Silverthorn Olive (introduced) (*Elaeagnus pugens*)

Smallmouth Bass (*Micropterus dolomieu*)

Smooth Cordgrass (*Spartina alterniflora*)

Snapping Turtle (*Chelydra serpentina*)

Snow Geese (*Chen caerulescens*)

Solomon's Seal (*Polygonatum biflorum*)

Sourwood Tree (*Oxydendrum arboretum*)

Southern Appalachian Brook Trout (*Salvelinus fontinalis*)

Southern Magnolia (*Magnolia grandiflora*)

Southern Stingray (*Dasyatis Americana*)

Spanish Mackerel (*Scomberomorus maculates*)

Spicebush Swallowtail (*Papilio troilus*)

Spiny Softshell Turtle (*Apalone spinifera*)

Spot-Tailed Bass (*Sciaenops ocellatus*)

Spotted Jewelweed (a.k.a. Touch-Me-Not) (*Impatiens capensis*)

Spotted Weakfish (*Cynoscion nebulosus*)

Stiltgrass (a.k.a. Microstegium; introduced) (*Microstegium vimineum*)

Striped Bass (*Morone saxatilis*)

Striped Maple (*Acer pensylvanicum*)

Striped Mullet (*Mugil cephalus*)

Swamp White Oak (*Quercus bicolor*)

Sweet Birch (*Betula lenta*)

Sweet Gum (*Liquidambar styraciflua*)

Sweet Shrub (a.k.a. Sweet Betsy) (several species in genus *Calycanthus*)

Sycamore (*Platanus occidentalis*)

T

Tarpon (*Megalops atlanticus*)

Tautog (*Tautoga onitis*)

Tiger Salamander (*Ambystoma tigrinum*)

Tiger Swallowtail (*Papilio glaucas*)

Tree of Heaven (*Ailanthus altissima*)

Trumpet Vine (*Campsis radicans*)

Tulip Poplar (*Liriodendron tulipifera*)

Tulip Tree (*Liriodendron tulipifera*)

Tundra Swans (*Cygnus columbianus*)

Turkeybeard (*Xerophyllum asphodelioides*)

Turk's-Cap-Lily (*Lilium superbum*)

V

Venus Flytrap (*Dionaea muscipula*)

Viburnum (several species in genus *Viburnum*)

W

Walleyed Pike (*Sander vitreus*)

Water Tupelo (*Nyssa aquatica*)

White Ash (*Fraxinus Americana*)

White Oak (*Quercus alba*)

White Pine (*Pinus strobus*)

White Shad (*Alosa sapidissima*)

White-Tailed Deer (*Odocoileus virginianus*)

Wild Turkey (*Meleagris gallopavo*)

Winged Elm (*Ulmus alata*)

Witch Alder (*Fothergilla major*)

Wood Thrush (*Hylocichla mustelina*)

Woolly Mammoth (*Mammuthus primigenius*)

Woolly Mullein (a.k.a. Lamb's Ear; introduced) (*Verbascum thapsus*)

Woolly Worm (caterpillar of Isabella Tiger Moth) (*Pyrrharctia isabella*)

Y

Yaupon Holly (*Ilex vomitoria*)

Yellow-Billed Cuckoo (*Coccyzus americanus*)

Yellow Birch (*Betula alleghaniensis*)

Yellow Buckeye (*Aesculus flava*)

Yellow Rat Snake (*Rhynchophis boulengeri*)

Z

Zebra Swallowtail (*Eurytides Marcellus*)

Suggested Readings

No one book or set of writings will meet the needs of all wildlife lovers, birders, or wildflower enthusiasts—and certainly not the entire naturalist community. I offer this list of personal favorites not as a comprehensive bibliography of scholarly works, but as suggested readings from one naturalist to another. All have influenced my understanding of North Carolina as a hot spot of biodiversity and a crossroads of the natural world.

Game Changers
These are the vital books, both old and new, that helped shape my understanding of, and approach to, nature.

Carson, Rachel L. *Silent Spring*. New York: Houghton Mifflin Company, 1962. This book marked the starting line for the environmental movement in the second half of the twentieth century.

Lawson, John. *A New Voyage to Carolina*. Chapel Hill: University of North Carolina Press, 1967. The book is based in part on John Lawson's historic walk from Charleston to Bath in the winter of 1701. It is simply the best "baseline" description of the natural world that would become North and South Carolina.

Leopold, Aldo. *A Sand County Almanac*. Oxford, UK: Oxford University Press, 1949; reprint, New York: Ballantine Books, 1970. As much as any other book, this work provided the philosophical and ethical underpinnings for the environmental movement.

Louv, Richard. *Last Child in the Woods: Saving Our Children from Nature-Deficit Disorder*. Chapel Hill: Algonquin Books, 2006. This book explains why time in nature is important in the life of every child.

Tallamy, Douglas W. *Bringing Nature Home: How You Can Sustain Wildlife with Native Plants*. Portland, Ore.: Timber Press, 2007. This is the best work to date on why native plants should be part of every home-landscape plan.

Wells, B. W. *The Natural Gardens of North Carolina*. Chapel Hill: University of North Carolina Press, 1932; reprint, 2002. This 1932 classic by the legendary botany professor from N.C. State University contains wonderful descriptions of plant communities. It remains as relevant today as it was eighty years ago.

Wilson, Edward O. *Biophilia*. Cambridge, Mass.: Harvard University Press, 1984. Can an ant specialist and evolutionary biologist write for the general public? In reading this and his other books, you'll understand why Wilson has won two Pulitzer Prizes.

Geology, Archaeology, and Paleontology

This section also includes works about Pre-Columbian American Indians.

Barnard, Frank Kenan. *How to Find and Identify Arrowheads and Other Indian Artifacts (Southeastern United States)*. Graham, N.C.: self-published, 1983. This is a longtime favorite of collectors in North Carolina.

Justice, Noel D. *Stone Age Spear and Arrow Points of the Midcontinental and Eastern United States*. Bloomington: Indiana University Press, 1987.

Mann, Charles C. *1491: New Revelations of the Americas before Columbus*. New York: Alfred A. Knopf, 2005.

McPhee, John. *Annals of the Former World*. New York: Farrar, Straus and Giroux, 1981.

Perdue, Theda, and Michael D. Green. *North American Indians: A Very Short Introduction*. New York: Oxford University Press, 2010.

Stewart, Kevin G., and Mary-Russell Roberson. *Exploring the Geology of the Carolinas: A Field Guide to Favorite Places from Chimney Rock to Charleston*. Chapel Hill: University of North Carolina Press, 2007. This is the most comprehensive general-audience guide to North Carolina geology available today, and it is also the most readable.

Ward, Trawick H., and R. P. Stephen Davis Jr. *Time before History: The Archeology of North Carolina*. Chapel Hill: University of North Carolina Press, 1999. There is neither a more complete reference nor more captivating history of American Indians in North Carolina than this volume.

Historical Naturalists and Scientists

This section includes collected works containing important material on the North Carolina environment.

Catesby, Mark. *Catesby's Birds of Colonial America*. Edited by Alan Feduccia. Chapel Hill: University of North Carolina Press, 1985. Mark Catesby was one of the first to record in paint a large number of the birds of the New World, along with the plant life on which they depended—and he did it decades before John J. Audubon.

Claiborne, Jack C., and William Price, eds. *Discovering North Carolina*. Chapel Hill: University of North Carolina Press, 1991. On pages 3 through 99, you will find a valuable collection of historical writings relating to the North Carolina environment, including "The Poorest State in the Union" (25–31), in which Francis Ann Kemble finds nothing good to say about a land of pine forests and swamps.

Darwin, Charles. *On the Origin of Species*. London: John Murray, 1859; New York: Oxford University Press, 1996. If you haven't read this before now, you might wonder what all the fuss is about.

Lawson, John. *A New Voyage to Carolina*. Chapel Hill: University of North Carolina Press, 1967. This book is also listed under "Game Changers" above. With a little editing help from North Carolina historian Hugh Lefler, the Lawson *Voyage* is a must-read.

Rankin, Richard, ed. *North Carolina Nature Writing*. Winston-Salem: John F. Blair, Publisher, 1996. This collection is a wonderful sampler of works by important naturalists who have written about North Carolina for over 300 years—including John Lawson, William Bartram, John Muir, H. H. Brimley, Jan DeBlieu, and Bland Simpson.

Modern Naturalists and Natural Historians

Earley, Lawrence S. *Looking for Longleaf*. Chapel Hill: University of North Carolina Press, 2004. This is the most complete work ever written on the Longleaf Pine, its history, and its unique ecosystems. This is natural science writing at its best.

Frankenberg, Dirk. *The Nature of North Carolina's Southern Coast: An Eco-Tourist's Guide to the North Carolina Coast, from Portsmouth Island to Calabash*. Chapel Hill: University of North Carolina Press, 2000. Still the best guide I know to the hidden gems of our southeast coast.

———, ed. *Exploring North Carolina's Natural Areas*. Chapel Hill: University of North Carolina Press, 1997. A mountains-to-the-coast collection of ecotours of some of North Carolina's most unique natural places written by the naturalists who know them best.

Louv, Richard. *The Nature Principal*. Chapel Hill: Algonquin Books, 2012. Louv's insights into the benefits of time in nature will make you want to reconnect with the natural world.

Silver, Timothy. *Mount Mitchell and the Black Mountains: An Environmental History of the Highest Peaks in Eastern America*. Chapel Hill: University of North Carolina Press, 2003. Tim Silver proves that great history and natural history can share the same pages, and his writing is simply a joy to read. Silver chronicles the work of Elisha Mitchell and the politics of North Carolina in the second quarter of the nineteenth century.

Climate, Barrier Islands, and Sea-Level Rise

Barnes, Jay. *North Carolina's Hurricane History*. Chapel Hill: University of North Carolina Press, 2001. The photography is excellent, but Barnes's writing is even better as he describes the effects of important storms on people, property, and the land, even the storms that occurred before hurricanes were named.

Braasch, Gary. *Earth under Fire: How Global Warming Is Changing the World*. Berkeley: University of California Press, 2007.

Cumming, William P. *The Southeast in Early Maps*. Chapel Hill: University of North Carolina Press, 1998. This book provides a unique view of North Carolina's changing coastline and multiple inlets over the last 400 years as seen through the eyes of early navigators, explorers, and cartographers.

Frankenberg, Dirk. *The Nature of the Outer Banks: A Guide to the Dynamic Barrier Island Ecosystem from Corolla to Ocracoke*. Chapel Hill: University of North Carolina Press, 1995.

Hansen, James. *Storms of My Grandchildren*. New York: Bloomsbury Press, 2009. Hansen is the highly respected leader of NASA's Goddard Institute for Space Studies. Along with his early work on global warming and this book, he may well be regarded in the future as the Rachel Carson of climate change.

Pilkey, Orrin H., and Keith C. Pilkey. *Global Climate Change: A Primer*. Durham, N.C.: Duke University Press, 2011.

Pilkey, Orrin H., and Rob Young. *The Rising Sea*. Washington, D.C.: Island Press, 2009.

Riggs, Stanley R., Dorothea V. Ames, Stephen J. Culver, and David J. Mallinson. *The Battle for North Carolina's Coast: Evolutionary History, Present Crisis, and Vision for the Future*. Chapel Hill: University of North Carolina Press, 2011. If you only read one book to explain the dynamic nature of the Tar Heel coast, this should be it.

Robinson, Peter J. *North Carolina Weather and Climate*. Chapel Hill: University of North Carolina Press, 2005.

Stick, David, ed. *An Outer Banks Reader*. Chapel Hill: University of North Carolina Press, 1998. This anthology could also be placed under "Simply Great Writing," but I know of no better anthology spanning 400 years of writing on the Outer Banks.

Clay and Pottery in North Carolina's Triassic Basin

Crawford, Jean. *Jugtown Pottery: History and Design*. Winston-Salem: John F. Blair, Publisher, 1964. This is not really a book on geology or clay but one of the first great books on North Carolina potters, with an emphasis on master potter Ben Owen.

Hewitt, Mark, and Nancy Sweezy. *The Potter's Eye*. Chapel Hill: University of North Carolina Press for the North Carolina Museum of Art, 2005. This is a beautiful reference work on potters and the magic they perform with clay across North Carolina.

Lock, Robert. *The Traditional Potters of Seagrove, North Carolina, and Surrounding Areas from the 1800s to the Present.* Greensboro, N.C.: The Antiques and Collectibles Press, 1994. This is an important work about the men and women who turned pots from native clays in the Triassic basin.

Simply Great Writing about the Wild Side of North Carolina and the Southeast

DeBlieu, Jan. *Cape Hatteras Journal.* 1987; reprint, Winston-Salem: John F. Blair, Publisher, 1998. This is one of several wonderfully written natural history works by DeBlieu, who later won the John Burroughs Medal for Distinguished Natural History Writing for her book, *Wind.*

Lembke, Janet. *Skinny Dipping and Other Immersions in Water, Myth, and Being Human.* New York: Lyons and Burford Publishers, 1994. As with Bland Simpson, I could have just as easily listed several other books by Janet Lembke. Her writing about nature is as elegant as it is provocative.

Simpson, Bland. *The Inner Islands: A Carolinian's Sound Country Chronicle.* Chapel Hill: University of North Carolina Press, 2006. Simply read anything Bland Simpson has written about the North Carolina coast, starting with *Great Dismal: A Carolinian's Swamp Memoir* (1990). No one does it better.

Terres, John K. *From Laurel Hill to Siler's Bog: The Walking Adventures of a Naturalist.* Chapel Hill: University of North Carolina Press, 1969. If you want to know what a master naturalist can observe in a couple hundred acres of land near Chapel Hill, you will love this simple, elegant book, for which Terres won the John Burroughs Medal for Distinguished Natural History Writing.

Field Guides and References to Flowers, Plants, and Trees in the Southeast

These include works on plant communities.

Adkins, Leonard M. *Wildflowers of the Blue Ridge and Great Smoky Mountains.* Birmingham, Ala.: Mensha Ridge Press, 2005.

Blevins, David, and Michael P. Schafale. *Wild North Carolina: Discovering the Wonders of Our State's Natural Communities.* Chapel Hill: University of North Carolina Press, 2011.

Justice, William S., C. Ritchie Bell, and Anne H. Lindsey. *Wildflowers of North Carolina.* Chapel Hill: University of North Carolina Press, 2005. This is the updated edition of the most useful and complete reference to wildflowers from the mountains to the coast. My copy is ragged and dog-eared.

Kaufman, Sylvan Ramsey, and Wallace Kaufman. *Invasive Plants: A Guide to Identification and the Impacts and Control of Common North American Species.* Mechanicsburg, Pa.: Stackpole Books, 2007.

Kirkman, L. Katherine, Claud L. Brown, and Donald J. Leopold. *Native Trees of the Southeast: An Identification Guide*. Portland, Ore.: Timber Press, 2007.

Nelson, Gil. *Best Native Plants for Southern Gardens*. Gainesville: University Press of Florida, 2010.

Sorrie, Bruce A. *A Field Guide to Wildflowers of the Sandhills Region: North Carolina, South Carolina, Georgia*. Chapel Hill: University of North Carolina Press, 2011.

Spira, Timothy P. *Wildflowers and Plant Communities: A Naturalist's Guide to the Carolinas, Virginia, Tennessee, and Georgia*. Chapel Hill: University of North Carolina Press, 2011.

Valentine, James. *Southern Appalachian Celebration: In Praise of Ancient Mountains, Old-Growth Forests, and Wilderness*. Chapel Hill: University of North Carolina Press, 2011.

Field Guides and References to the Animal World in the Southeast

Beane, Jeffrey C., Alvin L. Braswell, Joseph C. Mitchell, Jack Dermid, and William M. Palmer. *Amphibians and Reptiles of the Carolinas and Virginia*. Chapel Hill: University of North Carolina Press, 2010.

Biggs, Walter, James F. Parnell, and Wm. David Webster. *Mammals of the Carolinas, Virginia, and Maryland*. Chapel Hill: University of North Carolina Press, 2004. This is a wonderful reference to mammals of this region and their habitat requirements.

Braswell, Alvin L., and William M. Palmer. *Reptiles of North Carolina*. Chapel Hill: University of North Carolina Press, 1995. This is the go-to book for teachers and naturalists on the reptiles of this state.

Daniels, Jaret C. *Butterflies of the Carolinas: Field Guide*. Cambridge, Minn.: Adventure Publications, Inc., 2003.

Gaddy, L. L. *Spiders of the Carolinas*. Duluth, Minn.: Kollath-Stensaas Publishing, 2009.

Gibbons, Whit, and Mike Dorcas. *Snakes of the Southeast*. Athens: University of Georgia Press, 2005.

Manoch, Charles S., and Duane Raver. *Fisherman's Guide: Fishes of the Southeastern United States*. Raleigh: North Carolina Museum of Natural History, 1984.

Potter, Eloise F., James F. Parnell, and Robert P. Teulings. *Birds of the Carolinas*. Chapel Hill: University of North Carolina Press, 1980.

Sibley, David Allen. *The Sibley Field Guide to Birds of Eastern North America*. New York: Alfred A. Knopf, 2003.

Skeate, Stewart. *A Nature Guide to Northwest North Carolina*. Boone: Parkway Publishers, Inc., 2004.

Tekiela, Stan. *Birds of the Carolinas: Field Guide*. Cambridge, Minn.: Adventure Publications, Inc., 2001.

Tilley, Stephen G., and James E. Huheey. *Reptiles and Amphibians of the Smokies*. Gatlinburg, Tenn.: Great Smoky Mountains Natural History Association, 2001.

Wagner, David L. *Caterpillars of Eastern North America*. Princeton, N.J.: Princeton University Press, 2005. If you've ever needed proof that caterpillars are more beautiful and interesting than the butterflies into which they morph, you'll find it in this work.

A Cookbook

Because every list of suggested readings needs one.

Harkers Island United Methodist Women. *Island Born and Bred*. Edited by Karen Willis Amspacher. Atlantic Beach, N.C.: Weathers Printing Co., 1987. This is a remarkable community effort recounting the history of Harkers Island and Core Sound, with the added bonus of dozens of Down East recipes.

Three Magazines for North Carolina Naturalists

Coastwatch. Published every other month by North Carolina Sea Grant at North Carolina State University. It is an indispensible publication on the ecology, climate, and geology of the Tar Heel coast.

North Carolina Naturalist. Published biannually by the North Carolina Museum of Natural Sciences, this magazine features excellent articles by some of this state's best naturalists. Perhaps more important, it also includes a listing of programs, trips, classes, and events for those who want know more about the natural world.

Wildlife in North Carolina. Published six times a year by the North Carolina Wildlife Resources Commission. If you are under the impression that this magazine is mostly about hunting and fishing, you are thinking of how it was more than a decade ago. It is an exciting publication for teenagers of all ages, with great articles and photography about the wild things of North Carolina.

Four Naturalist Websites That Never Disappoint

These feature regional fauna and flora information and superb photography.

www.carolinanature.com. You'll find yourself visiting this website by Will Cook (who works at Duke University) over and over again. Cook provides remarkable photographs and information for naturalists interested in birds, animals, and plants in North Carolina.

www.duke.edu/~jspippen/nature.htm. Another Duke naturalist, Jeffrey Pippin, has an equally exciting website about North Carolina fauna and flora—especially his work on butterflies and dragonflies. You and your children will return often to Pippin's and Cook's websites as go-to nature Web addresses.

www.naturalsciences.org. For the news of the day in the natural sciences, go to this
Web page of the North Carolina Museum of Natural Sciences. You'll find articles,
video presentations, and cutting-edge research from some of this state's and the
nation's best scientists and naturalists.

www.ncsu.edu/goingnative/. If you have questions about why native plants are
better for your land and its wildlife, this is the website for you. It not only gives you
the best native alternatives for your location; it also tells you where to find them.

Index